HOUR OF TRIAL

HOUR OF TRIAL

The Conservation Conflict in Colorado and the West 1891-1907

By G. MICHAEL McCARTHY

UNIVERSITY OF OKLAHOMA PRESS : Norman

Library of Congress Cataloging in Publication Data

McCarthy, George Michael, 1940–
Hour of trial.
Includes bibliographical references.
1. Conservation of natural resources—Colorado—History. 2. Conservation of natural resources—The West—History. I. Title.
S932.C6M3 333.7'2'09788 75-29410

DEDICATION

To Mom and Dad and Beth and Helen, with my love

Preface
All Honor to Them

On a July morning in the summer of 1955 I sat on the summit of Longs Peak in Rocky Mountain National Park and watched the sun rise. Though I did not know it then, that singular experience was to affect my attitude toward the environment for the rest of my life.

Perhaps because I was a native of Colorado—and because I was young and unappreciative of such things—I had never had any particular awareness of the beauty that surrounded me daily. I had literally grown up with Pikes Peak, with the Sangre de Cristos, with South Park and Wild Basin and the Wet Mountain Valley. Never had I had any real cognizance of their beauty; rather, I had taken them for granted. But something profound began to happen to me in the summer of 1955 when I was fifteen and sitting on the crest of Longs. To this day I can still feel the chill air and hear the wind and see the iridescent pink glow spreading over the Front Range. From Meeker and Pagoda north to the Never Summer Range, along half a dozen glaciers, across countless valleys, it was a scene beautiful beyond description. In a single morning, literally, I began to understand much of the meaning of wilderness. And I have not yet lost the feeling that I had that day.

In a sense I have been handicapped by my affection for the Colorado wilderness; it tends to make my writing of objective history difficult. Thinking back to a walk through an aspen grove on an autumn afternoon, it becomes virtually impossible for me to excuse—for *any* reason—those who would have destroyed it. It is more natural, instead, for me to identify with

Colorado conservationist Enos Mills, who once wrote that "it is doubtful if any other influence is so generally and lastingly beneficial as our primeval beauty" and that "our gardens of wild beauty are immortal and will give us their inspiration forever."[1] Recalling similar experiences of my own, I instinctively concur with novelist Hamlin Garland in his contention that man has not fully experienced life until he has "lain down beside his fire, in a land of pines and peaks and roaring ice-water," and absorbed the "splendid solace" of the wilderness.[2] Feeling so, it becomes difficult, and remains difficult, to deal with those who occupied and exploited the timber and grasslands of the Great West. Even knowing that much, perhaps most, of their action was carried out in innocence helps little. In other words, in writing a narrative of the conservation movement in Colorado, the historian's vision is blurred by the impulses of the outdoor romantic.

On the other hand, I have tried to avoid sounding like a conservation zealot. I think, as do others, that proconservation sentiment and action can be carried too far. I do not agree with one contemporary critic who claims that today "environmentalists are imposing their regulations [on the nation] with all the indiscriminate enthusiasm of Carrie Nation swinging a baseball bat in a saloon." But I must agree with his opinion, in reference to the neoconservation movement, that "it is so easy to move from the moral to the moralistic, from a concern for what is right to a passionate self-righteousness, from a desire to improve our social reality to a blind and mindless assault against the real world which so stubbornly fails to conform to our ideological preconceptions."[3] I would hope that this study is devoid of any moralistic judgments—specifically, of any finger pointing at Colorado insurgents. Unless it is, it fails as history. Worse, it fails in its fairness to the pioneer.

I should say, too, in case it is not apparent in later chapters, that I have a deep and abiding admiration for those who settled the land. Walking through the ruins of Ashcroft, standing at the summit of Boreas Pass, deciphering inscriptions on headstones in the cemetery at Rosita, I have marveled countless times at the courage and incredible persistence it must have taken for men to breach the wilderness. As one pioneer settler wrote to a friend in 1909, speaking of his life on the Colorado frontier, "no language could convey to one who sees this country now, with all its marvelous beauty and grandeur, how forbidding and desolate it was when you and I first looked upon it."[4] It was a cogent statement, one that should be taken to heart by weekend environmentalists today. We ought not allow the "beauty and grandeur" around us to obscure the fact that the pioneers *were* the architects of our own civilization. Looking about us we almost must agree with the old man when he said "We were building better than we knew."[5]

In the end my theme is that both sides—conservationists and insurgents alike—were right, and both sides were wrong, in their battle for the land. On one hand, the pioneer deserves his due. As an unknown poet has phrased it:

Come, you children of the pioneers,
And join me in their praise;
Let us shout three roaring cheers,
To awake the memories of their frays. . . .
Though unseen dangers hovered near,
On open plains or in mountains high,
They bravely pushed forward with a cheer,
Determined to conquer the West or die.[6]

It would be only just should "the brightest pages of history" be "those that contain the names and deeds of those who carved an empire out of this forbidden land."[7] In other words, their activities in opposition to conservation never should be allowed to detract from their constructive achievements.

On the other hand, conservationists should be praised for their actions in defense of what they construed as the common good. Hamlin Garland has graphically written of the Colorado they faced at the turn of the century:

Each year the flood of humdrum settlement rises a little higher in the Colorado valleys. Each spring growing herds of cattle crowd out the elk. Year by year the brazen clamors of the sawmills thicken. . . . In the canyons of the Crestones the thunder of the miner's bomb is heard. The mountain sheep are surrounded; they cannot escape. . . . The madness to kill, to destroy, is abroad, armed and ruthless, and a wave of plows, resistless as a glacier, grinds at the base of Shavano. Soon the mountains . . . will be silent, barren of life, with not even a soaring eagle to cast a shadow on their naked cliffs.[8]

The conservationists' response to the "madness" was eloquent. They operated on the simple premise that "he who feels the spell of the wild, the rhythmic melody of falling water, the echoes among the crags, the birdsongs, the wind in the pines . . . is in tune with the universe. He will know what human brotherhood means." In the name of "brotherhood," they conserved. And "by their acts," wrote Garland, "some little part of our splendid heritage is now secured for future generations, so that, when all the interior valley of the Mississippi is clipped and dusty with traffic, a breathing space will still exist on the mighty ranges of Colorado."[9]

The pioneer and the preserver: *both* left their legacies to Colorado and the West. Referring to Theodore Roosevelt and the conservationists, Garland once wrote: "All honor to them!"[10] But perhaps it would be appropriate to amend his line. Perhaps, for both the past and the future, it should be: "All honor to them *all*."

Denver, Colorado G. Michael McCarthy

Acknowledgments

I began my research for this book some fourteen years ago, in the summer of 1962. Because a good deal of time has passed since then, I find it almost impossible now to look back over the decade and remember the names of the many people who helped me along the way. I hope that they will understand if I generalize in my expressions of thanks.

I am grateful, first, to the staffs of the Western History and Conservation Libraries at the Denver Public Library and to those of the Colorado State Historical Society Library and the Colorado State Division of Archives and Records. They, along with my late mentor at the University of Denver, Professor Harold Dunham, helped me extensively in putting together at least a skeletal manuscript.

I am indebted even more to my valued friends Philip Vaughan and James Hansen for their painstaking readings of my manuscript and the scholarly help they provided me in my revising of it. As much as anything I can think of it was their personal and professional support that helped me to finish the book. Without their help the book never would have come to print.

Finally, to my wife, Helen, and my daughter, Beth, I express my gratitude for their endless patience. It was always difficult to explain to them why I spent days on end in archive vaults and library reading rooms and why I sat at my typewriter night after night, often oblivious of them, reconstructing little bits of the past. I am not sure that I could explain even now why I was so compelled to do what I did. I can only hope that they—as well as my friends and colleagues—will accept my book as a form of repayment for whatever sacrifices they might have made for me.

Contents

Illustrations

Map

HOUR OF TRIAL

I. Conservation and the Western Mind

In late nineteenth-century America no single issue more graphically illuminated the complex nature of the national "mind" than the question of natural-resource conservation. Just as national attitudes toward ecology and the environment today reflect, at least in part, the aspirations and values of the present generation in a mass society, so did the attitudes of men toward their environment two generations ago mirror their concepts of life then.

As historian Roderick Nash wrote, the state or condition of American society's environment at any point in history "reveals [its] culture and traditions as clearly as does a novel or a Fourth of July oration."[1] What society did to and about its environment at any given time, and what society thought about it as well, gives a clue to what kind of society it was. As Nash concluded, "inextricably involved" in how Americans have approached their land and environment have been ideas about their "national identity and purpose," as well as their "aesthetic, religious, and ethical convictions."[2] Historians in search of the late-nineteenth-century American mind have exhaustively culled the issues of tariff and imperialism, gold and silver, Darwinism and the social gospel, business, and politics. But no event, these issues included, has ever revealed more about its inner workings than the collision between the pioneer West and the "wilderness cult" at the turn of the century over the question of conserving the vanishing natural wealth of the nation.

Well into the late nineteenth century America's attitude toward its environment was unsophisticated and simplistic: the land existed to be exploited. The contention rested on several assumptions: that the rich bounty of the West was limitless, set aside by God for the use of man; that it was the duty of the pioneer to harness the bounty to constructive ends; and that the end result of the process should be civilization, governed by democracy and peopled with "a fearless, self-sacrificing, intelligent, hardy Christian race."[3] Imbued with these ideas and with a romantic sense of mission, entranced by the legends of Daniel Boone and the frontiersmen of James Fenimore Cooper, and beguiled by the myths of the yeoman farmer and the "Garden of the World," nineteenth-century pioneers carved farms and cities out of desolation. And in the process they illustrated, clearly, what traditions, symbols, images, and myths their civilization rested upon.

As the century waned and the vast wealth of the garden faded with it, many distressed Americans suddenly took stock of the nation's environmental philosophy and summarily rejected it. Stunned by Frederick Jackson Turner's dramatic announcement in 1893 that the frontier was closing and convinced that its disappearance would lead to the dissipation of most of the forces that had shaped the national character—what Theodore Roosevelt called its "virility and greatness"—they became determined to conserve what was left of the wilderness and its influence for as long as they could.[4] Joined by others interested in preserving both the economic and esthetic values of the wilderness, the new wilderness cult triggered a full-scale rebellion against American tradition. And in the process the rebellion afforded insight into new values—cultural, ethical, and esthetic—held by a rapidly growing sector of the nation.

The purpose of this study is to provide a look into the turn-of-the-century American mind by analyzing in microcosm the clash between the traditions of pioneer America and the land ethic of the wilderness cult. To a certain extent, of course, this territory has been covered before, but only in general works emphasizing the national dimensions of the problem. The intent here is to isolate a single pivotal state within the overall context of the controversy and to utilize its "experience" as a case study. To analyze in detail what happened to a particular people in a particular setting and time in United States history, to understand their moods, rhetoric, and reactions to one of the most bewildering problems of the century, is to take a step toward understanding the national mind as a whole.

Colorado has been selected as the case study because in relation to the conservation question it was typical of virtually every state in the American West. Both its pro and anticonservation forces were highly representative of similar factions throughout the region. Its insurgents were perhaps more militant than those of Utah and California and perhaps slightly less so than those of Washington, Wyoming, and Montana, but for the most part anticonservation rhetoric and action in Colorado matched and typified that elsewhere. As for the state's conservationists, they were almost identical to those throughout the West.

When Coloradans attacked forest reserves—the overriding issue of the conservation era—they reflected sentiment similar to that existing among anticonservationists everywhere. The rhetoric and actions of the state's miners, for example, typified those of their counterparts in Idaho, where the governor of the state complained that "with outside mining practically ceased" because of reserve restrictions, the state had been "to a considerable degree" thrown upon "its own resources." Like Colorado miners and their sympathizers, he concluded that "the pretext that our lands and forests are the just inheritance of posterity is not only hackneyed, but illogical and overdrawn."[5] Colorado homesteaders, so violently (and often rebelliously) opposed to reserves, found their actions standard procedure all over the mountain West in the conservation period. While they burned forests in the White River Reserve to protest its creation, others fired forests in Wyoming for the same reason. Their protest meetings, so prevalent up and down Colorado's Western Slope, were matched in size and content from Washington to New Mexico. Perhaps no meeting in Colorado in the entire period, however, equalled an 1897 demonstration in South Dakota where thirty thousand people massed to condemn a new reserve as "disastrous" to the economy of the Black Hills.[6]

Colorado cattlemen, the nucleus of the anticonservation movement in the state, clearly mirrored the militant feelings of their brethren elsewhere. In particular their outrage over grazing restrictions on the reserves and proposed federal lease laws on the open range was shared by insurgent cattlemen in virtually every corner of the Rocky Mountain West. When northwest Colorado stockmen refused to pay reserve grazing fees, they but followed a general pattern. In southwest Montana, decrying "this crackpot scheme of politicians in Washington" and declaring their rights as "free-born American citizens" to do as they pleased, cattlemen also refused to pay the fees, as they did in parts of Wyoming and Arizona. And in Nogales, Arizona, as in Gunnison and Craig in Colorado, ranchers suggested that federal "tree agents" be hanged from the trees they came to protect.[7] The feelings of stock growers everywhere were articulated by Senator Clarence Clark of Wyoming who damned the reserves as a "new-fangled way of dealing with the public domain." Such feelings could have been spoken just as easily by Colorado's Henry Teller.[8]

The state government of Colorado was clearly anticonservation, but no more or less than other state governments. When Governor Alva Adams stated in 1906 that "we have got enough forest protection and reservation at present to look after, without taking in the entire country,"[9] he was speaking for most governors in the West. Idaho's Frank Steunenberg, Wyoming's William Richards, New Mexico's Manuel Otero, Washington's Marion Hay, Montana's J. K. Toole, and most others concurred, and, like Colorado's Charles Thomas, almost all of them made pilgrimages to Washington at one time or other to protest various aspects of the federal conservation program. Their state legislatures, also like Colorado's, supported them with unswerving opposition to conservation doctrine.

Colorado's congressmen in Washington were highly characteristic of the representatives of other western states. In the House, for example, the utterances of John Bell and Herschel Hogg perfectly summed up the philosophies of Frank Mondell and Henry Coffeen of Wyoming, Binger Hermann of Oregon, and dozens of other men (and indirectly, of course, of their constituencies). In the Senate the vitriolic Henry Teller and Thomas Patterson enunciated perfectly the feelings of their fellow westerners. In their incessant—and often intemperate—attacks against conservation, the Coloradans spoke for William Borah and Weldon Heyburn of Idaho, Thomas Carter and Lee Mantle of Montana, Washington's John Wilson and George Turner, Jonathan Bourne and Charles Fulton of Oregon, William Stewart of Nevada, Francis Warren and Clarence Clark of Wyoming, and others. Teller's critical assessments of forest reserves, for example, were no more extreme than Carter's contention that the system "showed contemptuous disregard" for the peoples' interests and was designed exclusively to "harrass and annoy" them.[10] And Patterson's constant references to the "eastern conspiracy" to destroy western economy was no more unusual than Wilson's plaintive question, "Why should we be everlastingly and eternally harrassed and annoyed and bedevilled by these scientific gentlemen from Harvard College?"[11] Carter's angry cry at the 1907 Denver Public Lands Convention that "if the people of this country are to be held in terror, now is the time to resent it"[12] was the battle cry of the entire insurgent West.

Colorado's vociferous anticonservation press was representative of newspapers from Washington to Texas. Little difference existed between the *Portland Oregonian*'s denunciation of conservation "sentimentalists" and the *Glenwood Avalanche-Echo*'s persistent ridicule of eastern "dudes."[13] On the question of reserves, when the *Yampa* (Colorado) *Leader* editorialized that "it is perfectly right that all forest land be protected, but good farming land should always be open to entry,"[14] its statement bore a remarkable similarity to the proclamation of the *Seattle Telegraph* that "there is abundant room for pleasure without depriving the people of property of immense value in a commercial way."[15] And the warning of the *Seattle Post-Intelligencer* that unless the government altered its conservation policies it would trigger "bitter revolt" in the West[16] coincided with the blunt announcement of Denver's *Rocky Mountain News* that "a condition of revolt" already existed.[17]

A look at the conservationist strain in Colorado reveals that it, too, was similar to conservation feeling elsewhere in the West. While Colorado reservationists differed from their fellows in one sense, in that they stressed the economic necessity of conservation over its other aspects, their general ideals dovetailed with those of other groups and individuals. If the *Denver Republican*, for example, was proconservation, it was no more so than the *Great Falls* (Montana) *Leader*, the *Deseret News* of Salt Lake, the *San Francisco Argonaut*, or scores of similar papers; when it gloomily warned that if forest destruction continued unabated, "the children of the generation existing at this time will hardly ever see the ground covered with a growth of trees again,"[18] it spoke for them all. The Colorado State Forestry Association had a direct parallel in the Sierra Club. Edgar Ensign, the head of the association, spoke the same eloquent language as naturalist John Muir. And the battle for Yosemite was fought with no more passion in California than the conservationists fought for forest reserves in Colorado.

The Colorado experience, then, was the western experience; and, in a larger, sense, the western experience was the national experience. But even so, several major questions remain to be asked about the entire subject of the battle for the wilderness: What was its importance? Why study it today? What lessons can it teach a society a half century or so removed from it? The answer is relatively simple. By affording contemporary society the opportunity to understand what Americans held to be important in terms of their environment in another period of history, we—their legatees—have a chance to better understand ourselves and our environmental attitudes now.

To a remarkable degree nothing has changed through the years. Even a cursory examination of today's newspaper illustrates the fact that the same controversies that divided Colorado and other western states seventy-five years ago divides them still and that the same groups that fought then still fight now.

On one hand the opponents of conservation remain much in evidence, and both their rhetoric and their basic ideas borrow much from the past. In February, 1973, for example, a spokesman for Boise Cascade, one of the nation's largest lumber companies, stated that while America needs "some wilderness areas" today, excessive future forest conservation would be "detrimental to the general welfare." The conservation movement, he said, has gone to "extremes" by "locking away" the wilderness. His primary question, no less provocative now than it was in 1900, was whether or not America today "could afford an excess of such preservation."[19] Others voice the same fears. "Preservation is fine," says Frank Norris Jr., director of the Wyoming Travel Commission. "We're all for a good environment. But preservation for preservation's sake? . . . Ridiculous!"[20] The way to "environmental action" today, concludes Ian MacGregor, chairman of American Metal Climax (operator of the giant Climax molybdenum complex) is hardly to insist on continued land reservation, to "throw up our hands and say, 'stop all progress.'"[21]

If antireservationist forces remain strong in Colorado today, however, conservationist forces may be more powerful and vocal than ever before. If "time was . . . when an environmentalist was something you walked on" in the West, such is no longer the case.[22] Without a doubt large numbers of Coloradans agree with the contention of Environmental Protection Agency Director Russell Train that "those which oppose environmental progress" are "antigrowth forces" rather than advocates of social and economic advance.[23] "There's talk about not using [wilderness], but that's just economics," states conservationist Arthur Carhart. Those "in there resisting the wilderness" are the "fast buck artists."[24] From former Governor John Vanderhoof—who emphasized the need for "wise and prudent use of our natural resources"[25]—to countless others, such a view has taken root and has gained acceptance in Colorado. It may be, as Carhart has said, that today more than ever "we need to have some place for human beings to go and establish their proportion to nature . . . to have a thunderstorm hit 'em in the face."[26] And it may be that we now are beginning to recognize the urgency of that need. If so, one might readily understand the popularity of the view expressed by *Denver Post* columnist Joanne Ditmer: "The time for environmental control and preservation is right now; tomorrow may be too late."[27]

Despite continued polarity over the environmental issue, however, signs of rapproachment today are stronger than ever before. And here is where study of the past is important; here is where contemporary Coloradans apparently have been able to look at the past and learn some of its lessons. When the day comes that stockmen, miners, lumbermen, *and* conservationists unite in support of the creation of a wilderness area in the mountains of Colorado, one may be sure that at least some education has taken place.[28]

It may be, of course, that the spectacle of history repeating itself has small impact on many of those involved in the process. In that case any look into the past has little meaning. Presumably, however, westerners today are perceptive enough to look at the original conservation conflict, make the deduction that they have "been there before," and resolve that past mistakes will not be repeated again. If the current generation cannot analyze itself in light of past history, it faces a future of environmental chaos. But if it can, it should be able to confront its environmental problems with purpose, with honesty, and with confidence.

II. "Marching Through Georgia"

On the cool, early spring afternoon of March 4, 1891, the Congress of the United States adjourned in Washington after a long and bitter fifty-first meeting. In the House of Representatives, congressmen burst into song in a "remarkable and unprecedented" ending to the session. Republicans, gathered in a large, boisterous body near the front of the House chambers, sang out "Marching Through Georgia" and "made the hall ring" as it had not in years. From across the aisle a Democratic chorus replied with the "Doxology." Then, as quickly as it had begun, the singing stopped and the great hall emptied.[1]

In a meeting marred by unusually acrimonious political bickering, the Fifty-first Congress had passed an abundance of critical legislation. Public attention focused on two bills in particular—the McKinley Tariff and the Sherman Silver Purchase Act—both of which had caused extensive congressional and national controversy. Ironically, however, the nation ignored a third measure—the General Revision Act—passed alongside the tariff and silver bills in the waning moments of the session and destined to become more important than either. While the body of the act—a land revision law—was of no particular consequence to the nation, one of its riders was:

The President of the United States may, from time to time, set apart and reserve in any State or Territory . . . any part of the public lands wholly or in part covered by timber or undergrowth, whether of commercial value or not, as public reservations, and the President shall, by public proclamation, declare the establishment of such reservations and the limits thereof.[2]

The new law, passed undebated by Congress in the midst of its chaotic adjournment and unnoticed by the public afterward, nonetheless was a landmark in the history of American territorial expansion. As the culmination of a desperate crusade to save the nation's vanishing forests, it marked the end of a campaign that by 1891 had already spanned nearly two decades of American life.

As the westward movement accelerated in the United States during the last quarter of the nineteenth century and American pioneers scattered across the prairies and mountains to take up the land, the devastation of the West's natural resources inevitably accompanied the quest for civilization.[3] As the years passed and damage mounted, many Americans, particularly in the East, came to fear that if the exploitation and waste of western lands continued indefinitely, the day might come when their natural wealth would vanish entirely, to the permanent detriment of succeeding generations. Such thinking was a radical departure from the past. There had been a time in the nation's history when the possibility of the exhaustion of natural resources had seemed as remote as the mountain walls beyond the plains. Throughout nearly three centuries of territorial expansion, the dominant philosophy of the American nation—and especially its pioneers—had been that the soil, the metals, the timber, water, and natural grasses of the Great West were limitless, inexhaustible, God-given treasures to be conquered and employed in the process of creating civilization. By the 1870's and 1880's, however, except in the West, many Americans were increasingly convinced that the "pioneer ethic" no longer worked for the betterment of the nation. Assessing the ever-escalating devastation of the West, many concluded that if the price of progress and civilization was the permanent annihilation of the public domain, it was too high a price for the nation to pay.

Those concerned about the condition of western lands—*conservationists*, as they came to be called—had definite ideas of the importance of resource preservation. To a remarkable degree the conservationists shared a common vision; yet, in its particulars the matter of saving the West's natural wealth meant different things to different individuals.

To many Americans the conservation concept had distinctly esthetic overtones. One of the dominant themes in conservation rhetoric was the beauty of nature, particularly that of the primeval forest. The popular belief existed that natural beauty had the power to revitalize man when he became tired and disillusioned with life. Like Henry David Thoreau, conservationists held that nature, through its reflection of spiritual truth and moral law, possessed a "fertilizing capacity that civilized man needed for strength and creativity."[4] If American civilization rested on man's moral and emotional strength and if man, in turn, needed the forest retreat to sustain this strength, conservationists reasoned that the nation faced a dilemma: Walden had vanished, the forests of the East were gone. If the primeval forest were to be salvaged anywhere, it would have to be in the West. The objective of many conservationists, then, became the locking up and isolation of the western public domain, primarily its timberlands, for the esthetic enjoyment of both present and future generations.

Many advocates of the land-reservation idea also saw a direct correlation between conservation and the continued development of the American character. Adhering to ideas eventually popularized by historian Frederick Jackson Turner—that the unique character of America had been forged by the nation's three-hundred-year "frontier experience"[5]—they believed that if the developmental process were to continue, the experience would have to continue as well. Turner's famous pronouncement in 1893 that the American frontier was closing deeply distressed them. If, as he claimed, the frontier had been primarily responsible for the establishment of American civilization in the past, there existed good reason to worry about the future. Several basic questions were raised: Would civilization somehow continue to develop along democratic lines despite the absence of a frontier experience, or would it fall into decay? Would the "safety valve" continue to function? Would the unique traits of the American character disappear? Many Americans were skeptical, as was Turner himself. The Old West with its free land had offered "an exit into a free life and greater well-being," he wrote. But, he concluded, "never again" could "such an opportunity come to the sons of man."[6]

For those concerned about the quality of American life, there appeared to be a dual solution to the problem of a vanishing frontier: the preservation of what was left of it and the extension of both it and its abundance beyond the point at which they might otherwise have ended. Unlike others, their concern was not the preservation of nature's beauty for its own sake. Rather, theirs was an attempt to maintain the remaining abundance of the West that the frontier experience might continue. It remained their conviction that only the conservation of the wilderness environment could deny the chilling implications of Turner's pronouncement.

Yet another concern of conservationists was the maintenance of political democracy and economic equality in the West. They believed, as did other Americans, that an intimate connection existed between the nation's abundance—its land and the natural wealth contained in it—and the amount of economic equality and political independence attainable by man. As historian David Potter has written, if a man's access to America's material abundance was not blocked, if he was able to participate fully in the nation's "success promise," then he became, in effect, "equal"—free from any "system of status," free to establish his own place in society, and free to pursue further opportunity. Abundance, then, led directly to economic and political parity. For Americans, "a boundless continent enabled them to fulfill the promise of mobility [or equality]. Democracy made this promise, but the riches of North America fulfilled it; and our democratic system . . . survived because an economic surplus was available to pay democracy's promissory notes."[7]

If the abundance of the public domain was so important, the conservationists felt it imperative to cordon it off, that it might not be destroyed. It was their impression that "somehow the common heritage had started to pass into the hands of vested interests" which siphoned off its benefits into the hands of a few.[8] The process reduced the chances of the "little man" to make his way in the West and made difficult the attainment of either economic or political independence. To restore economic equilibrium—as well as for esthetic considerations and concern for the American character—conservationists hoped to impress their ideas upon the nation.

In retrospect, it is clear that the conservationists were guided by no single cohesive philosophy. But they all shared a common general idea. As Roderick Nash has written, conservation was, to them all, "the new frontier, keeping the nation young, vigorous, democratic, replete with opportunity for the individual, and, because of its relation to nature, wholesome and moral."[9]

In the mid-1870's the conservation movement began in the United States. Initially, American conservationists concentrated on establishing their policies and practices on the state level. Lobbying for the creation of state forestry commissions and societies, working for the revamping of state land laws, promoting naturalist organizations, conducting public-information campaigns, they slowly developed a foothold in the midst of laissez-faire America.[10] This done, they began to shift their emphasis from the preservation of state lands to the preservation of the nation's public domain. Their ultimate target was the anachronistic land policies of the federal government.

In approaching the problem of federal land policy, two main trends concerned conservationists: first, the engrossment of vast areas of the public domain—especially its timberlands—by large American business corporations, and second, the careless everyday destruction of forest lands and plains by small cattlemen, miners, and homesteaders who occupied the land, exhausted it, and moved on to repeat the process elsewhere. Conservationists realized that no amount of activity on the state level could alter such long-standing patterns. They reasoned that resource devastation was the result of inadequate land laws passed by Congress over the course of decades. Consequently, they believed that if the process was to be stopped, Congress would have to be influenced to do it, preferably by locking up the remainder of the public domain and parceling it out more carefully, more rationally in the future.

Congress in the 1870's and 1880's did not respond favorably to the complaints and requests of the conservationists. Congressmen, who considered themselves the elected guardians of laissez-faire capitalism, economic prosperity, and traditional American individualism, were by no means prepared to roll back decades of liberal land policy at the simple behest of what they considered to be a handful of "forest cranks." It was not surprising, therefore, that conservation made little headway on the national level prior to 1891. Nor was it surprising that the first conservationist land law passed by Congress in the history of the United States—the General Revision Act—was enacted entirely by accident.

The process began on February 19, 1890, when Congressman Lewis Payson of Illinois introduced into the House the General Revision Bill.[11] Its provisions were simple and uncontroversial. It called, primarily, for the repeal of the much-abused Timber Culture Act and pre-emption laws, and it provided for the amendment of the Homestead and Desert Land acts. Significantly, the measure made no mention of conservation in any sense. The bill, with minor amendments, passed the House in March and the Senate in September before being sent to committee for discussion of its proposed amendments. It was in committee that the bill was altered to make it one of the most significant measures of the conservation era.

Late one February evening in 1891, as the conference committee discussed the Payson bill, a rider was added to it at the urgent insistence of Secretary of the Interior John W. Noble, Special Land Office Agent Edwin Bowers, and lobbyists of the American Forestry Association. The amendment—section twenty-four—empowered the president to create forest reserves on the public domain of the United States. The committee, composed of midwesterners receptive to the conservationists' ideas, accepted the rider and reported out the bill in its entirety on March 2, 1891. Strangely, it was not printed after emerging from conference; it received only a single oral reading in each house of Congress on March 2, and because adjournment was near, all debate and discussion regarding it was suspended. In the Senate no questions were posed at all; in the House an attempt was made at debate, but potential amendments to the bill were declared out of order. And in the confusion apparently no one read section twenty-four.[12]

On the same day, March 2, Congress passed the Payson bill, and the next day it was signed into law by President Benjamin Harrison. The legislators apparently still failed to realize the significance of the conservation section; according to one authority, it was "highly doubtful if Congress knew what it had done."[13] What it had done, of course, was to pass a bill containing a provision which a majority of its members probably did not favor and would not have passed as an independent bill.[14] Only later would Congress realize its mistake: it had become responsible for one of the most "far-reaching conservation decisions ever made."[15]

The state of Colorado, like the rest of the West, paid scant attention to the General Revision Act. The reason, however, was more a case of poor (or imperceptive) press coverage than it was a lack of interest in the subject. For years prior to 1891, Colorado had witnessed a growing antagonism between the advocates of maximum land use and those who called for restraints. On one hand stood those who desired the fullest exploitation of the region—pioneer homesteaders, miners, cattlemen large and small, corporations, and spoilsmen. On the other hand stood the conservationists. In between them lay the ultimate prize: both Colorado's own undisposed lands and the unoccupied lands of the public domain lying within the state's borders.

In the years between the gold rush and the last decade of the century, the prize largely had fallen to the exploiters, and resource devastation had been the inevitable result. The primary victim was the forest; in a relatively short period of time miners, charcoal burners, lumbermen, and railroaders seeking ties for track had virtually decimated many of the prime forests of the state. They felt no particular compulsion to save the timberlands, for in Colorado, as elsewhere in the West,

the forest was nothing more than a lucky convenience to supply the meager wants of a few. Lumber as such had not the remotest export value. The forest could not be regarded, or treated, as a natural resource beyond the simple needs of the hour. If there was destruction, the matter was of no concern, for the forests of the Rockies seemed unlimited in extent and inexhaustable for all time.[16]

In 1886 the Colorado state forest commissioner warned that unless the remaining timberlands of the state were preserved and protected, the result to the state would be "desolation."[17] It was this fear that spurred the conservationists to action, and it was their action that brought about the tension that existed in 1891.

Conservationist forces began forming in Colorado as early as 1876, but at no time in the next fifteen years did they achieve more than a small degree of cohesion. Not until 1884 did they create a workable organization—the State Forestry Association—and even then its importance was minimal. The association, composed chiefly of civic-minded urban businessmen and a handful of teachers and scientists, worked diligently for forest preservation. Lobbying for state and national conservation laws, mapping blueprints for national parks, inundating newspapers with conservation material, and pressuring hostile congressmen for further land-law revision, the organization became a prototype for similar groups all across the West. For all the association's work, however, it did little immediate good. Similarly, little was accomplished by individual conservationists working independently. In the fifteen years prior to 1891, because they were fragmented, cautious, occasionally at odds with each other, and faced with almost insurmountable public apathy (if not outright hostility), early conservationists failed to establish any concrete forestry program in the state.[18] They did, however, begin to establish the soundness of their general beliefs through their eloquent appeal to the public:

If our forests are to be saved for the use of coming generations, the people must be compelled to realize the folly and danger of not saving them. Till they do, the robbers of the public domain will continue their work of destruction. . . . The tie contractor, the man who cuts the best trees for the poles that disfigure our city streets, the lumberman who moves his sawmill deep into the mountains, that he may more profitably follow a business that injures the state—not one of these men cares for the forest or the general good. Their homes are not among the hills they denude and disfigure. They are in their business of destruction for the money they can make. And their business subverts the general good.[19]

Significantly, the philosophy of most Colorado conservationists differed in many respects from that of many conservationists elsewhere—particularly in the East. Only rarely did Coloradans voice esthetic concerns. Their primary consideration was the economic welfare of the state, and they spoke of little else. Most importantly, they did not advocate the total withdrawal and locking up of land. Aware, unlike many (though not all) of their eastern counterparts, that such action was as potentially damaging to the state as unmanaged settlement, they urged the withdrawal of land, accompanied by a policy providing for its regulated use.

What concerned Colorado conservationists was the economic irrationality of forest destruction. The forests were critical in that they held back winter snows in the high country, allowing them to melt gradually throughout the spring and summer. That natural process, as every conservationist understood, stabilized the water flow in the streams that emanated from the hills, minimizing the possibility of floods during the dry season

A photo from the *Denver Republican*, March 12, 1909, of a rare gathering of conservationists and anticonservationists. Included are conservationists Clarence P. Dodge, W. G. M. Stone, Murdo MacKenzie, and Professor Ellsworth Bethel and anticonservationists J. A. Eddy, Dexter Sapp, and Alva Adams.

Courtesy Denver Public Library, Conservation Library Center

and guaranteeing ample water for the irrigation of the valleys and plains during the rest of the year. Ellsworth Bethel, renowned Colorado botanist, stated the scientific case for conservation: "The chief value of our forests is not in the lumber resources, but as great conservators of rain and snowfall necessary for the irrigation of more than three million acres of farm lands. The rich, deep humus of the forest cover holds water and allows it to run off gradually, thus serving the purpose of irrigation throughout the summer when it is needed most."[20] Without the forests, Colorado invited devastating spring floods and summer drought, and both jeopardized the economy of the state. Writing in 1885, State Forest Commissioner Edgar Ensign pointed out that

in all her material interests, Colorado is greatly dependent upon the preservation of the forests and the maintenance of her water supply. Her agriculture and system of irrigation would soon come to naught, should the streams fail in their life-giving offices; her pastoral regions would become parched and barren . . . and her mining enterprises, railroads, and manufacturers, would greatly suffer had they no forest stores upon which to draw.[21]

Conservationists also sought to halt the waste of timber in Colorado in order that it might remain accessible to the growing pioneer communities of the state. From small mountain settlements along the continental divide to growing plains cities like Denver and Colorado Springs, most of the towns in the state were heavily dependent on forests for fuel, fencing, housing, and mining materials. Conservationists realized that in future years nothing could cripple the economic productivity of a growing state more quickly than lack of timber. Doubtless this deepened their resolve to conserve what they could. As Ensign had said, the life of the state depended on it.

From the very beginning of the conservation crusade in Colorado, strong, occasionally violent opposition materialized against it throughout much of the state. Roderick Nash has written that "for a civilization that had begun to notice its first gray hairs, conservation was a welcome tonic."[22] But such was not always the case in Colorado, where anticonservation elements were among the most vociferous in the West.[23] In a state uncommonly rich in natural resources, in an atmosphere of plenty where, theoretically, extensive material wealth existed for all, conservation ideas often were considered ludicrous, if not dangerous. By the 1870's and 1880's too many thousands of miners, cattlemen, and homesteaders had become entrenched in the state to be influenced by small groups of "theorists" calling for the reservation of land.

A primary reason for the insurgents'[24] attitude was an obsession with the idea of their civilizing mission in the West. Like most other late-nineteenth-century Americans, they had long romanticized the West as the Garden of the World, a kind of American Eden where sturdy yeoman farmers settled, put in crops, built cities, and established republican civilization.[25] In a real sense the pioneers believed that progress was their chief mission in the West and that it was their special function to subject the wilderness to it:

Insofar as the westward expansion of civilization was thought good, wilderness was bad. It was construed as . . . a barrier to progress, prosperity, and power. . . . On every frontier intense enthusiasm greeted the transformation of the wild into the civilized. . . . This taming of the wilderness gave meaning and purpose to the frontiersman's life. In an age which idealized "progress," the pioneer considered himself its spearhead, performing a worthy cause in the interest of all mankind.[26]

Opposition to conservation stemmed, in part, from this attitude. If it was "progressive" to settle the land, reasoned the pioneers, then no justification existed for its reservation. If exploitation and building resulted in the betterment of society, then it was not only logical, but patriotic, to oppose any concept that threatened to restrict it. As a group of Western Slope stockmen said in a 1907 resolution, the "very objectives" of statehood were "to gain in population and wealth." If the objectives were to be attained, the "monstrous affliction" of conservation would have to be "successfully defeated."[27]

To a great degree it was the belief in mission that instilled in the pioneers the strong feelings of self-righteousness that so inured them to the arguments of conservationists. Jefferson's heroic yeoman, James Fenimore Cooper's plainsman, Daniel Boone—simple, independent, idealized by society for selflessness, the aversion to commercialism, and the ability to produce and enjoy simple abundance from the land—the pioneer class had long considered itself a special breed.[28] Because of his particular relationship with land and nature, because of his past role in building the nation, the "idealized farmer" with his "sacred plow" envisioned himself as the backbone of American society, more moral, more democratic, more noble than the rest.[29] As self-appointed custodians of the nation's future, pioneers believed—however wrong they may have been, however deceived they may have been by the myth of agrarian superiority—that their rights, particularly to the land, transcended those of others. In their self-righteousness they could not countenance the attempts of any group or government to take them away.

Emphasizing their moral claims to the land, Colorado pioneers also argued—often with justification—that they should not be denied the same access to abundance and equality that had been granted their forefathers in times past. By the same token, they added, their state should not be penalized for the "mistakes" of others. As one embittered insurgent declared, "when the state of Colorado was carved out of the nation, it came in as a state with all the powers and all the implied obligations on the part of the people that went to the people of every one of the older states."[30] "I think it is with considerable effrontry," concluded another, "that a man comes to a Western state and, after having gotten the benefit of the liberal policy of the government as to the public lands in the state of Ohio, to say that now since we have eaten our cake we want you people of Colorado to divide your cake with us."[31] It was on these grounds that insurgents rejected the conservationists' correlary to the Turner hypothesis that the restriction of frontier settlement would insure the continued development of the American character. As they reminded the conservationists, it had been their fathers, laboring on earlier frontiers in earlier states, who had forged the character to begin with. If Turner was correct, they concluded, if the frontier experience had made the nation strong in the past, the key to continued strength was the expansion of frontier settlement, not its restriction.

Finally, anticonservation pioneers had compelling economic reasons for their position. In a late-nineteenth-century world transformed by the industrial revolution and ruled by the American business apparatus, western pioneers saw in the open spaces of the frontier their last possible hope for economic survival.[32] It was for this reason, perhaps, that they rejected the finality of Turner's pronouncement that the frontier was closing. Their contention was that it was not: "A scarcity of natural resources? Absurd! Over the next ridge was a cornucopia of wood, water, soil, and game."[33] For the farmer engulfed by the machine age, the small prospector and cattleman fighting against the growing dominance of mining and cattle cartels, the frontier was, literally, the last stand. Any doctrine which advocated its reservation was a danger. As a Gunnison lawyer publicly complained toward the end of the conservation era, "Is it fair to the people who have come out here . . . to upbuild the country, to do something with it and their own lives, to have at this late date, after 150 years of earnest endeavor, someone take these resources from us?"[34] To a man, insurgents agreed that it was not. Conservation was the enemy.

In most cases, perhaps, anticonservation sentiment was genuine; but that did not alter the fact that often the rhetoric of indignation hid spoilsmen as well as honest settlers. It was a matter of fact that Colorado was overrun with spoilsmen—charcoal burners, tie cutters, smelters, fraudulent land speculators, and others—all intent on the fullest exploitation of the land and its resources regardless of the consequences. Like other pioneers, they exalted the idea of the garden, but in their case only as a rationale to justify the monopolization of the land. And, like others, they denounced conservation as immoral, illegal, and destructive of their freedom. But, again, their main intention was to divert attention from their questionable actions. It was one of the primary tragedies of the anticonservation movement that spoilsmen spoke the same language as other westerners. They obscured the fact that many, perhaps even most, of the insurgents were honest men who sincerely believed in the validity of their cause.

In the 1870's and 1880's, as the struggle began for control of Colorado's lands, the anticonservationists numbered among them the most powerful pioneer groups in the state. In the front rank stood the mining interests. From struggling hardscrabble prospectors to shoestring back-country corporations, they utterly rejected any concept which threatened to lock up the mountains and curtail the pursuit of mineral. As self-reliant and independent as any insurgent group, as virtual "owners" of the Colorado mountains since the gold-rush days of 1859, they firmly believed that their tenure had earned them the right to the land. Beyond this, they maintained that their activities were vital to the welfare of the state. Had conservation been "in effect in the early days" of statehood, said a prominent miner in 1908, "Colorado never would have been developed."[35] Because of that attitude, some of the most persistently anticonservation sentiment in Colorado came from the mining camps and diggings of the high country.

Colorado's powerful cattlemen were never united on the conservation question; while probably most of them opposed conservation, large numbers did not. Those who objected to it did so largely on the grounds that federal control of mountain and plains ranges which had been theirs for a quarter of a century would radically alter the western way of life, probably for the worst. As will be discussed in a later chapter, anticonservation opposition cut across class lines. Some of the large operators, the long-entrenched range barons, fought reservation, feeling that the hegemony they had enjoyed for years would be destroyed, while others supported the idea. At the same time, small-scale cattlemen were divided. A few advocated conservation, but the majority—in 1891, at least—fought it.[36] Conservation, said one of their spokesmen,

> *should have no rights that would retard the settlement of the country. . . . It may be right to reserve land for the future, but what about the fellow who wants it today? Give him his chance. If he finds a piece of ground upon which he thinks he can make a living, let him have it. Give him an opportunity to show what he is good for and give him the right . . . to work out his own destiny.*[37]

Conservationists may have worried about the passing of the frontier, but anticonservation Colorado stockmen, motivated in their actions by both pride and economics, considered only the opportunities of the moment.

In large numbers the farmers and homesteaders of Colorado, especially those living west of the continental divide, also supported the anticonservation coalition. On the plains half of the state farmers rarely took a public stand on the issue (an unexplainable phenomenon, given the importance of conservation to arid regions). But west of the divide, along the rim of the Rockies from Craig to Durango, backwoods farmers settled in the hills and watersheds of the mountains generally were foes of conservation. To some extent, perhaps, their attitude stemmed from ideological beliefs—infatuation with the concept of the Garden, the conviction of moral superiority, and the presumption that they had the inalienable right to settle where they pleased. But economic considerations were more influential than ideology in shaping their philosophy. More than any other pioneer group, the small homesteaders who scratched out their living on the hills were directly dependent on access to the land that surrounded them. Any policy which threatened to seal off the timber and water resources of the land also threatened their survival. As historian Richard Hofstadter has shown, the idealized yeoman farmer was, in reality, a grasping, ambitious entrepreneur, more interested in exploiting the land for his own needs than in creating a stable civilization.[38] Without land to exploit, he faced ruin. So it was, in Colorado at least, that many a homesteader who "moved into the mountains, took up a little patch of ground in some valley nestled among the hills, and builded for himself and his family a humble cabin home," considered conservation "as nefarious . . . a scheme as ever disgraced the state."[39]

The fourth, and least defensible, anticonservation element in Colorado was the spoilsmen—the timber barons and small-time timber cutters, the furtive sawmill operators, charcoal burners, railroad tie men, land speculators, corporations, and, of course, the particularly dishonest among the farmers, miners, and cattlemen. Fearful of the prospect that their empire would

Timber destruction from fire and unregulated cutting, Pikes Peak area, 1895.

Courtesy Denver Public Library, Western History Department

be taken from them by conservation, they fought the movement as resolutely as any other group. It was their activities, of course, as much as anything else, that triggered the conservation movement to begin with; but even when conservation came to Colorado, it failed to alter their behavior or attitudes.

The anticonservation movement in Colorado derived powerful support not only from the various interest groups involved, but from the state government as well. Neither the state legislature nor the state's governors supported conservation theory. Their philosophy, myopic in hindsight, fell squarely within the context of late-nineteenth-century western economic thought. In order to compete in national economic life on an equal footing with older, more established states, Colorado statesmen considered it imperative that they construct a prosperous economy of their own, and the key to prosperity was settlement—the proliferation of farms and ranches and urban businesses. They equated conservation with declining settlement, decreased tax revenue, the stunting of agricultural, industrial, and pastoral development, and the erosion of an already-struggling economy. It was their contention throughout the conservation fight that Colorado, young, undeveloped, and searching for economic parity with the rest of the nation, was in no position to carry the burden of conservation, especially at a time when its silver industry seemed to be in jeopardy.[40] Not until 1895 did a Colorado governor even mention forestry in a public speech, and even after that none actively sought constructive forestry legislation. State legislators, many of them pioneers themselves, some with interests to protect, others representing anticonservation constituencies, followed suit.

By 1891 lines were drawn on both sides of the conservation question. If extensive ill will existed, however, the controversy still had not caused an irreparable breach in Colorado society. Conservationists, after all, had no actual power to achieve their goals, and until they did, their doctrine remained academic. On March 3 it ceased to be so. The General Revision Act gave conservationists the power they had sought for years. And on a warm afternoon in October the conservation conflict began in earnest when the first forest reserve was created in Colorado.

III. "This Damnable Outrage"

In late March, 1891, a small team of special agents from the government's General Land Office slipped into Glenwood Springs, allegedly to conduct an investigation of illegal timber-cutting activities in northwestern Colorado. For two weeks they traversed the wild White River country north of Glenwood, plotting maps, taking surveys, noting and recording the nature of the land. By mid-April they were gone, and not until autumn did Colorado come to understand the full meaning of their mission. On the afternoon of October 8, Thomas H. Carter, commissioner of the General Land Office, cabled the Land Office register at Glenwood Springs, directing him to withdraw from entry 1,200,000 acres of public land at the headwaters of the White River. Eight days later, on October 16, in accordance with the General Revision Act, the White River Timber Land Reserve was created by Benjamin Harrison.[1] Colorado conservationists were jubilant: for the first time the full force of the American government had been committed to the task of preserving the state's wilderness. The opponents of conservation also clearly understood the implications of the president's action. In the past they had faced small, politically impotent bands of conservation "theorists" armed only with rhetoric; now they faced the federal government armed with a powerful law.

The White River Reserve had been a long time in coming. In April, 1889, a handful of homesteaders nesting in the Trapper's Lake region of northwestern Colorado had begun agitation for

Fire destruction in the White River Forest Reserve, mid-1890's.
Courtesy Denver Public Library, Western History Department

some form of state or federal protection of the timberlands of the White River Plateau. There, where decades of irresponsible timber cutting and cattle grazing coupled with fires set by unfriendly Ute Indians had destroyed millions of acres of forest lands, "many citizens were afraid that unless some action was taken to protect and administer" the land, the entire region "would eventually be ruined."[2] Their agitation took the form of a half-dozen memorials drafted by conservationist leader Edgar Ensign of Colorado Springs and sent to United States Senator Edward Wolcott of Colorado between April, 1889, and September, 1891. Wolcott, however, was no friend of conservation, and he ignored the petitions. Later, when he rejected a bill drafted by Ensign proposing the creation of a federal forest reserve in the region, conservationists determined to bypass him entirely.[3]

The White River group next took its case to Secretary of the Interior John Noble, and it was he—the man who had been chiefly responsible for the addition of section 24 to the General Revision Act—who dispatched the Land Office agents to Glenwood in the spring of 1891. Acting on their recommendations, Noble determined in July that a reserve was warranted. Through an intermediary he appealed to Colorado Governor John L. Routt for help. If Routt would promote the idea of a reservation on the White River, suggested the secretary, it would be to his everlasting credit: "If you should live years longer, you would look back on it [his action] with as much pride and satisfaction as for any part of your estimable public career."[4] Routt replied that, in his estimation, the people of the White River region did not favor the scheme, and he did nothing to support the conservationists' plan.[5]

In the early fall of 1891, rumors began to spread throughout the White River Plateau area that a reserve was being planned in Washington. Opposition to the idea quickly materialized, primarily around Meeker near the western boundary of the proposed reserve, where the *Meeker Herald* rallied Rio Blanco County to the defense of its "interests." Accurately, if irrationally, the *Herald* reflected the feelings of many local citizens:

> *This scheme has thus far been worked through quietly, but it is not too late to defeat it. Citizens of Rio Blanco County arise in your might and protest against this damnable outrage! Will you sit still and let that government outfit drive you from the homes that you have acquired by years of toil? . . . We think not. Then be up and doing!*[6]

At the southwest tip of the proposed reserve the dusty cattle town of Rifle was alive with similar angry talk. Expressing the attitude of powerful local cattlemen, the *Rifle Reveille* urged the counties involved in the scheme—Garfield, Eagle, and Rio

Blanco—to cry out against "the dude design for an outdoor museum and menagerie."[7]

At Glenwood Springs sentiment was divided. Because it was the fastest-growing community in the White River region, Glenwood stood to suffer serious economic injury if conservation were to succeed in shutting off the plateau country to future settlement. On the other hand, however, it also stood to suffer if the area's forest and mineral resources were destroyed. Understandably, the town reflected mixed emotions about the proposed reservation. A few citizens, such as W. B. Devereaux, president of the Colorado Land and Improvement Company, welcomed federal guardianship of the land. "As a protection for the many against the few," said Devereaux, "I am in favor of that land being turned into a national park." If it were not, "everyone's rights will be subservient to the man who wants to build a cabin and claim sixty acres of land."[8] Devereaux and others had the complete support of the *Glenwood Springs Republican* and the partial support of the *Glenwood Echo* (which favored a reserve, not because it would protect timber, but because it could be utilized as a game preserve).[9] Only the anticonservation *Glenwood Avalanche* opposed the idea. Decrying the fact that the proposed reserve threatened to embrace the best farming and grazing land in Rio Blanco County, the newspaper bristled at the idea. Contending that the county, only three years old and desperately in need of tax revenue from settlement, could not survive conservation, the *Avalanche* appealed to its readers: "Let everyone who can express himself speak out against this national park scheme . . . until the county is on more solid terra firma."[10]

Whatever resistance the northwestern counties mustered came to nothing; on October 16 the proclamation was issued. The new reserve sprawled across 1,198,080 acres of timberland along the Western Slope of the Rockies, encircling the White River Plateau and stretching sixty miles east to west across northwest Colorado from McCoy to Meeker and thirty miles north to south from Pagoda to Glenwood Springs. The northern

Glenwood Springs, Colorado, in the 1890's.
Courtesy Denver Public Library, Western History Department

half of the reservation contained the critical headwaters of the White River, which flowed westward through Meeker and Rangely into Utah, and the tributaries of the Williams and Yampa rivers, which flowed northward across the Colorado badlands into Wyoming. Countless streams emptied from the southern portion of the reserve, rushing off the plateau into the Colorado.[11] The plateau itself was bordered on almost all sides by giant granite cliffs, but where valleys penetrated the interior, pioneers had settled.

Tiny communities, many of them relics of gold-rush days, lay in every valley in the region. Most of them—stagnant little shantytowns like Marvine, Buford, Pyramid, and Pagoda—had long since fallen into decay. But in 1891 the area also contained booming young towns such as Meeker, Rio Blanco, Glenwood, and Rifle. In the past all of them had drawn most of their wealth from the region around them, and their future no less than their past depended on the continued availability of the same local land resources. It was from most of these settlements, not surprisingly, that the first rumblings of protest had come. And after the October withdrawal they came again. Admiring, from a distance, the beauty of the White River wilderness, Aspen's *Crystal River Current* editorialized that the reservation was "a grand thing for Colorado and, in fact, the entire Union."[12] But there were those in the White River area who did not agree. Incensed by the government's action, anticonservationists vowed to harrass Congress and the Harrison administration until the reserve was abolished. "We'll kick," warned the *Meeker Herald*, "and it will be felt."[13]

True to their word, for the next few months the insurgents kicked. Led by H. H. Eddy, speaker of the Colorado House of Representatives and a powerful Bear River cattleman, they attacked the reserve concept on every front. On November 11, Eddy led off the campaign with a blistering denunciation of the White River withdrawal before a packed house at the Denver Chamber of Commerce building. Speaking before the largest crowd ever to attend a chamber meeting in the city, Eddy angrily charged that Harrison's proclamation contained "infamous provisions which have not been equalled since the days of William the Conqueror." Colorado needed settlement, said Eddy, not federal encroachment on its rights: "Too many people in Colorado are pioneers, too many have struggled with adversity to permit such an outrage to be perpetrated as the establishment of this park."[14] At the end of his speech, Eddy received polite applause, but no support. Denver, a growing plains city heavily dependent on the mountains for all its needs (primarily water) was no place for an anticonservation harangue. In a clear affront to Eddy, the chamber passed a resolution which read: "Resolved, that we most heartily concur with the

President in this behalf and earnestly hope that other needed reservations of a similar character will be established. . . . And we pledge ourselves to sustain in all proper ways a movement fraught with such great and general benefit."[15] And the *Rocky Mountain News* dismissed the entire incident by concluding that

on the question of the value of such a park to Colorado there can be but one opinion. . . . It is a region set apart for men to go into and leave the world behind, rejoicing that so much loveliness has been preserved by wise legislation. Colorado is fortunate in holding such a trust for the race, and if the state fails in its duty, mankind will be so much the poorer.[16]

Undaunted by his reception at Denver, Eddy next took his case before the Western Colorado Congress, a prestigious commercial organization holding its second annual meeting in Aspen shortly before Christmas. There, speaking before farmers and cattlemen and small-town businessmen, he was accorded a warmer reception. When he appeared at the old brownstone Wheeler Grand Opera House on the snowy afternoon of December 16, the small auditorium was filled to capacity with those receptive to his contention that the White River Reserve was an "injustice."[17] After Eddy's speech, the congress passed a resolution demanding that the White River Reserve either be reduced in area or abolished entirely.[18]

The action of the congress was not a fluke. Rather, it reflected a feeling of disenchantment with the reserve that had settled over the area almost immediately after Harrison's action. The primary reason for dissatisfaction, even in areas such as Glenwood Springs where many citizens had favored the creation of a federal reservation, was the size of the withdrawal: its final boundaries were far larger than even local conservationists had anticipated. Because of this, the reserve idea steadily lost support throughout the winter of 1891 and the early months of 1892. Speaking of the reservation in November, 1891, the *Glenwood Avalanche* had gloomily conceded that most of "the

Charcoal kilns in the Pikes Peak Forest Reserve, mid-1890's.
Courtesy Denver Public Library, Western History Department

residents of Glenwood Springs and the settlers of the Grand Valley are decidedly in favor of it."[19] But such was not the case two months later when the *Meeker Herald* reported, not without a measure of satisfaction, that Glenwood's enthusiasm had faded: "A noticeable change has taken place inasmuch as hardly a person in the Grand Valley can be found but what opposes it."[20]

In February, 1892, seeking to capitalize on the settlers' increasingly restive mood, Eddy petitioned Land Office Commissioner Carter for a new investigation of the reserve boundaries. When the government failed to respond, a sense of frustration began to take root in the territory. Insurgents, who had been outraged from the beginning, were joined by many who previously had opposed them. And, most importantly, a feeling that had begun as irritation and annoyance slowly crystallized into deep resentment.

On February 11, 1892, in the midst of the White River controversy, President Harrison established the second of Colorado's reservations: the Pikes Peak Timber Land Reserve, 184,320 acres of forest land on the southern half of the Rampart Range in El Paso County.[21]

Since at least mid-century the need for a federal reservation had been great in the high country west of Colorado Springs. Over the course of several decades the area's forests had been devastated by one misfortune after another. First, in the late 1850's the Pikes Peak gold rush had brought waves of miners into the mountains, which they ransacked for mining timbers and wood for dwellings. In the 1870's railroads had penetrated the area, compounding the destruction. Roads like the Denver and Río Grande, which skirted the eastern border of the Rampart Range, and the Colorado Midland, which ran through its middle, ravaged virtually every forest in the region in search of timber for railroad ties.[22] The extent of the railroads in the Pike—some four hundred miles of track, more than in any other forest reserve in America—was an adequate indication of their adverse impact on the woodlands.[23] Beyond the gold boom and the railroads, hundreds of major fires had charred the forests of the region. By 1891 local settlers, facing possible timber famine and the impairment of their water supply, petitioned the government for a reservation. In February, 1892, the government responded.

Although strong objections to the reserve were voiced later by local cattlemen and a handful of dissident lumbermen, initial reaction to the proclamation was mild. None of the local communities mobilized against the reserve as some had done in the northwest. One reason was that because of the rocky composition of the soil in the Rampart region, relatively few settlers lived there. Another was that, with the possible exception of Colorado Springs, few of the local settlements stood to be seriously damaged by the withdrawal. Unlike the White River country where the prosperity of several important towns depended on the proximity to and availability of forest materials, the rundown little settlements that dotted the Pikes Peak Reserve had little growth potential to begin with. In Palmer Lake, Woodland Park, Cascade, Glen Cove, and Green Mountain Falls there was little apparent interest in Harrison's proclamation, let alone dissent against it. In Colorado Springs, a busy pioneer city long conditioned by the *Colorado Springs Gazette* to the necessity of conservation, the response to the government's action was positive.[24]

In the summer of 1892, President Harrison added the northern half of the Rampart Range to the federal forest reserve system. On June 23, acting on recommendations made both by Colorado conservation leaders and the influential American Forestry Association, Harrison proclaimed the Plum Creek Timber Land Reserve, 179,200 acres of mountain land in the Ramparts north of the Pikes Peak withdrawal.[25]

Like other forest areas in central Colorado, the Plum Creek region was eloquent testimony to the undesirable side of laissez-faire economics. By 1892, after decades of mutilation by fire and at the hands of pioneer homesteaders, graziers, and gold seekers, the rolling cedar hills west of Castle Rock and Sedalia had been damaged practically beyond saving. To the south of Larkspur and Palmer Lake, however, the forests remained relatively healthy. Conservationists insisted that the area was worth protecting, that unless the watersheds of Plum, Trout, and West creeks (all tributaries of the Platte) were conserved, the water supply of Denver might someday be jeopardized. Outwardly the majority of local residents agreed. In Given, Daffodil, Dunaway, and Nighthawk—the only actual settlements in the reserve—there was no dissent to Harrison's action.

As pleased as they might have been about the extensive land withdrawals around Colorado Springs, conservationists remained concerned about the deterioration of other vital forests in the area. Specifically they remained unconvinced that the permanent safety of Denver's water supply had been provided for. Consequently, even as the Pikes Peak and Plum Creek

Timber stands in the Plum Creek Forest Reserve before and after logging by lumbermen.

Courtesy Denver Public Library, Western History Department

reservations were being carved out of the Ramparts, conservation forces began lobbying for the establishment of a national park in the remote Lost Park sector of the Tarryall Mountains southwest of Denver. It was there where most of the tributaries of the South Platte—Denver's chief source of water—were formed.

In February, 1890, when Edgar Ensign led seventy residents of Park County in petitioning the federal government for a reservation in Lost Park, they were flatly denied. The government claimed, accurately, that it possessed no authority to take such action. A year later, however, after the passage of the General Revision Act, the government reconsidered the petition. In the summer of 1891, when the massive snowpack began to melt in the Tarryalls, teams of federal agents were dispatched from Washington to survey the region. In November, when results of the investigation were complete, the government began a systematic withdrawal of land from entry in the area that the *Rocky Mountain News* called "one of the most beautiful and romantic spots to be found in all the Rockies."[26] On December 9, President Harrison proclaimed the South Platte Forest Reserve.[27]

In its final form, the South Platte Reservation, 683,520 acres of forest and mountain meadowland in Park, Jefferson, Summit, and Chaffee counties, included considerably more than the Lost Park region of the Tarryall Mountains. From the Tarryalls it swept southward to take in the rugged Puma Hills, and instead of terminating at Kenosha Divide in the west (which had been the original plan), a long arm of the reserve stretched southwesterly from the Kenosha Divide, skirted South Park, took in most of the Park Range, and finally ended a few miles north of Buena Vista. The reserve contained numerous important watersheds—including those of both forks of the Platte River—several mountain chains, and two large natural parks (Lost and Craig). And although the region had been victimized by fire and timber cutters for years, it still possessed immense value. As the United States Geological Survey concluded several years later, as a "feeder of streams" the South Platte was the most important of the three reserves yet created in the mountains west of Denver and Colorado Springs.[28]

As on the neighboring Pike and Plum Creek reservations, the creation of the South Platte was met with no outward protest by those who lived on or near it. Most of the local settlements, clusters of shacks perched in the mountains—Alma, London Junction, Park City, Buffalo, Estabrook, Rocky, and others—contained too few settlers to raise a significant outcry. Most of the communities were virtual ghost towns, economically inert long before the proclamation, perhaps too close to extinction already for their citizens to worry about a federal reservation. The ramshackle mining camps—Puma City, Gold City, and Jasper—were too tiny and too isolated to raise a protest, had the mining interests been so inclined.

While Colorado conservation leaders concentrated most of their reservation efforts on the mountains along the Denver-Colorado Springs axis in 1891 and 1892, they also mapped out plans for the public domain further to the west. As early as 1890 they began blueprinting a reservation in west-central Colorado on the Grand and Battlement mesas. In mid-1891, when their plans were complete, they sent Edgar Ensign to the Western Slope in search of local support. Before the first annual meeting of the Western Colorado Congress at Grand Junction in October, Ensign presented the case for a forest reserve directly to the settlers involved. The idea was acclaimed; before its adjournment the congress adopted resolutions supporting the Ensign plan.

By the time the congress met in its second session, two months later, its mood had changed radically. By that time—December, 1891—the creation of the White River Reserve to the northeast had ignited controversy all across western Colorado. Before the event the congress apparently had entertained few doubts about the wisdom of a reserve system, but by December, possibly bewildered by federal "intransigence" on the White River and most certainly influenced by the virulent antireserve attacks of H. H. Eddy, the congress refused to issue another endorsement of the Battlement proposal. Finally, at a third

Leavick, Colorado, a typical forest-reserve settlement in the late 1890's.
Courtesy Denver Public Library, Western History Department

session at Ouray in June, 1892, the congress came full circle. There, where the Battlement plan was "bitterly opposed by a majority of the delegates," the congress passed resolutions condemning "the establishment by the government in Colorado of any reserve whatever."[29] Summing up the feelings of many of his fellows, Eddy charged that "the proposition to establish governmental reservations in Colorado is ill advised and resented by the people. . . . The aesthetic Eastern people [who] are not interested in the country will plaster the West with reservations that will retard and cripple the hardy pioneers."[30]

Ignoring the results of the Ouray meeting, President Harrison proclaimed the Battlement Mesa Forest Reserve on Christmas Eve, 1892.[31] The new withdrawal, the largest and most imposing of any of the state's 1892 reserves, encompassed 858,240 acres of public domain in Pitkin, Gunnison, Mesa,

Timber devastation on the Battlement Mesa Forest Reserve, mid-1890's.
Courtesy Denver Public Library, Western History Department

Delta, and Garfield counties. In general it encircled two giant mesas: Grand, which lay north of Delta and east of Grand Junction, and Battlement, which paralleled the Colorado River from Glenwood Springs to Rifle. The huge landmass, in 1892 more unspoiled than any reserve in the state, contained vast expanses of primitive forests. And, most importantly, it sealed off from entry the watersheds of numerous important creeks, particularly the North Fork of the Gunnison River.

Much like their neighbors in the White River country, settlers in the Battlement region were divided over the question of whether the reserve was beneficial or not. To the west of the withdrawal, in Grand Junction and the Uncompahgre River towns of Montrose and Delta, sentiment overwhelmingly favored the reserve. In a region where agriculture and horticulture formed the backbone of the regional economy, the only thing of consequence to local settlers was the assurance that the flow of water from the mesas to the valleys would never be impaired. The reserve gave them that assurance.

To the east of Grand Junction and the Uncompahgre Valley, in the reserve itself, settlers were more prone to criticize its creation. Particularly galling to many of them was the fact that no provisions had been made by the government for even the limited use of forest materials on the reserve. For as far back as most could remember they had been free to utilize the wealth of the local forests; lacking that freedom, many reasoned that they could no longer survive on the land.

If, with the exception of the White River affair, the creation of Colorado's five reserves in 1891 and 1892 was attended by relatively little protest, the case was largely the same elsewhere throughout the West. Although Harrison created ten reserves in other western states between the fall of 1891 and the spring of 1893, only slight opposition emanated from that region.[32] The reason for such limited opposition is unclear, but in all likelihood the West was waiting to see what the government's next steps would be. Conservationists and their pioneer converts, of course, posed no threat to the government's plans. But others, perhaps the majority of western settlers, who had accepted the reserves only tentatively to begin with, were of a different mind. As one observer reported after a visit to a reserve region later in the decade,

what might be termed provisional antagonism is expressed by settlers who are uncertain as to whether the administration of the reserves will deprive them of some necessary privileges in them. If the maintenance of the reserves means a restriction to them of domestic fuel, building timber, water rights, etc., they are opposed to reserve policy.[33]

Clearly, if and when it became apparent to local settlers that they were to be restricted, that some of their "rights" were to be abridged, the government could expect them to drop all pretext of co-operation. The result would be—and soon was—protest on a massive scale throughout both Colorado and the rest of the West.

IV. Defenders of the West

In the fall of 1892, when Grover Cleveland unseated Benjamin Harrison from the presidency, a new phase opened in the American conservation controversy. As an "uncompromising friend of forestry,"[1] Cleveland approved of forest reserves. But he disapproved of the way they had been administered since their creation. Because the General Revision Act had made no provision for the maintenance and protection of reserve timberlands, most federal forests had suffered just as grievously from fire and timber depredators after 1891 as before. Publicly deploring the "utter inadequacy of legislation" enacted since 1891 to protect the reserves, Cleveland quickly served notice on Congress that he wanted such legislation passed.[2] And his ultimatum immediately placed him on a collision course with its anticonservation sector.

On the question of conservation, few delegations in Congress were more resolutely opposed to it than that from Colorado. Its leader was Henry Moore Teller, "Defender of the West."[3] An outspoken proponent of maximum land use all his political life, especially as secretary of the interior under Chester Arthur, the brooding, Lincolnesque Teller opposed the concept of land reservation as much as any man in Congress. In part, political considerations may have helped shape his philosophy. A staunch silverite, it was not inconceivable that he used the conservation issue to gain support for the silver cause.[4] At the same time, however, he was the very embodiment of the pioneer, with over thirty years of life behind him in frontier Gilpin

United States Senator Henry Moore Teller of Colorado, an archenemy of conservation.

Courtesy Denver Public Library, Western History Department

County. Whatever his motivations, however, whether formed by political expediency or not, Teller was very possibly the most imposing obstacle Cleveland faced in his attempt to secure forestry legislation in the Senate.

Teller received support for his policies in the House of Representatives from John Bell, a combative Montrose Democrat. A transplanted Tennessean who had practiced law in some of Colorado's most important mining districts (Del Norte, Saguache, and Lake City), Bell was practically a replica of Teller—an irascible, determined enemy of conservation. His position on the issue was simple (and standard for the day): if implemented, conservation in Colorado stood to destroy the state's already fragile economy. Advocating the rights of miners in particular, Bell went so far as to introduce a bill during his freshman term in 1893 calling for the abolition of the White River and South Platte reserves entirely.[5] Although he failed, he stamped himself permanently as a friend of the insurgents.

Collectively, Colorado's delegation—Teller, Bell, and two others—aimed at no less than the total abolition of the forest reserve system in Colorado.[6] Clearly they were not in accord with Cleveland. And, coupled with other congressional insurgents, they comprised a formidable alliance.[7]

In the fall of 1893, a year after the election of Cleveland, United States Representative Thomas C. McRae of Arkansas introduced into the House the conservationists' master plan to save the reserves. The bill's important stipulation was that all merchantable timber on the national forest reserves be sold in the future to the highest bidder. That provision, conservationists maintained, would reduce the waste and theft that plagued the timberlands and at the same time provide the federal government with an income which could be plowed back into the reservations in the form of improved administration. Because of its attractiveness, the McRae bill gained the support of every important national official concerned with federal forest policy and every major conservation organization in America. The West, however, "arose as one to denounce the bill."[8]

Colorado's congressional insurgents opposed the McRae proposal from the beginning for two reasons. First, they feared the provision empowering the secretary of the interior to sell timber on the reserves to the highest bidder. It was their impression that an "unfriendly" secretary would sell primarily to timber combines and corporations rather than to local settlers with little money and less influence. The McRae brand of conservation, they concluded, would enrich spoilsmen and corporations and continue to harm the little man. As the *Rocky Mountain News* editorialized: "Now comes the average Eastern congressman full of ignorance regarding the means of protecting the [reserves], and seeing an opportunity to make a dollar or two by the sale of timber on the reserves proposes to do damage beyond estimate. . . . The proposed bill is a monstrous one and cannot be too bitterly opposed."[9]

Second, the anticonservationists realized that if they officially recognized the power of Congress to legislate for the reserves, then they implicitly recognized the legitimacy of the reserves themselves. And this, of course, they felt they could not do. Mindful of that danger and "overwhelmed with remonstrances from settlers and others" protesting against the reserves and further federal attempts to deal with them, Teller and Bell acted to halt the bill.[10]

When debate on the McRae plan began in the House in October, 1893, Bell was one of the first to attack it. In a sharp personal clash with McRae on October 12, the Montrose Democrat condemned both the bill and the system that spawned it:

In the state of Colorado these reservations . . . take in farms, take in settlers, and in one county in particular they do not leave a single stick of lumber outside the reservation line, so from the day that reservation was declared every settler in the county has had to steal every stick that has gone into his fireplace. . . . Not only that, but there have been declared in a state reservation over a quarter million acres of land that has not a stick of timber or brush on it. . . . These reservations ought to be knocked out of existence. . . . In Colorado they have done us no good whatever.[11]

Bell was not alone in his feeling. Throughout the House other angry westerners, as disgusted as the Coloradan with conservation, supported his contention that the reserves should have been "knocked out of existence." After days of intense debate over it, the bill was shelved.

The McRae plan was proposed again at the third session of the Fifty-third Congress, and when it was, House insurgents greeted it with a deluge of amendments that altered its character entirely. Concentrating on increasing settlers' access to reserve areas (something which neither Cleveland nor McRae had called for) rather than protecting the areas from destruction, the insurgents added proposals retaining the permit system of timber cutting, prohibiting the sale of timber (except for dead and mature trees) to outside concerns, and, most importantly, allowing virtually unrestricted mining in the reservations.[12] The McRae bill, which had begun as a conservation measure, was mutilated practically beyond recognition. The House passed it on December 17, 1894. Convinced that the reserves had been opened up to the extent that they were no longer burdensome to his state, Bell voted for it.[13]

The modified McRae bill was stopped dead in the Senate by Teller and other insurgents. Rather than accept the proposal (which Teller contemptuously called "half a loaf"), the Senate favored a more stringent substitute proposed by the Coloradan which "represented fairly well what Western men considered right and proper in dealing with forest reserves."[14] The Teller plan illustrated clearly how much at variance many westerners were with conservationists over the question of forest reserves and public access to them. The measure provided, first, that future reserves be created only to insure the continuous supply of timber for states *in which the reserves were established*; second, that no agricultural or mineral lands be included in subsequent reservations (and that such lands included in withdrawals already made be eliminated); and, finally, that any settler living on a federal reserve be granted the option either of claiming damages against the government or trading his lands to it for public lands of a corresponding size outside the reserve. Although the Teller bill passed the Senate without debate or record vote, it died in conference.[15]

The McRae measure was resurrected and reintroduced in the Fifty-fourth Congress. When it came up for debate in the House on June 10, 1896, it was John Bell—still more convinced than Teller that, as amended in 1894, the bill adequately protected the rights of reserve settlers—who championed it. At his request, House rules were suspended, and the bill was passed. Both Bell and Colorado's new representative, John Shafroth, voted for it.[16] Again, however, the Senate killed it, this time permanently.

The action of the Senate enraged Cleveland, who would have preferred the amended McRae plan to none at all. Furious not only at the repudiation of the bill, but at the contempt shown by Congress for forest problems in general, he reaffirmed his earlier demand that "adequate protection be provided for our forest reserves" and that "a comprehensive forestry system be inaugurated" for the nation.[17] When Congress still failed to comply, Cleveland took matters into his own hands. In the spring of 1896 he created a six-man national Forestry Commission[18] to tour the West and study its forest problems with a view toward recommending the "comprehensive forestry system" which he sought. For almost a year beginning in the summer of 1896 the commission explored western lands, scouting unreserved timberlands, assessing the condition of forest lands already withdrawn, and gathering general information and ideas on which the new system might be based. On February, 1, 1897, the commission made its recommendations to the president, emphasizing its conviction that the West needed more reserves. On Washington's birthday, February 22, acting directly on the recommendations, Cleveland created thirteen new forest reserves, spanning over 21 million acres of timberland from Washington to Wyoming.[19] The action was as stunning a blow as western insurgents had ever suffered.

Some historians have characterized western response to the Midnight Reserves (so named because they preceded the end of Cleveland's term in office by only ten days) as instantaneous and violent—"the most remarkable storm in the whole history of forestry in America."[20] One has written, for example, that virtually without exception the proclamations "set the West aflame."[21] In fact, however, while much, perhaps most, of the West was angry, large sectors of it were not; special-interest groups resentful of their eviction from the public domain and pioneers jealous of their rights doubtless were incensed, but other groups, for various reasons, supported Cleveland's action. In both particulars, the response of Colorado to the new reserves was typical of that of the rest of the West.

Despite the fact that none of the new reserves had been placed in their state, many Coloradans opposed them. Judging from their rhetoric, they did so for two basic reasons.[22]

First, they resented the fact that reserve territory had been withdrawn at the behest of what the *Rocky Mountain News* called "theorists, enthusiasts, and cranks."[23] Their chief contention was that the withdrawals, made "without any examination, without any care" by Cleveland on the recommendation of a handful of easterners who "had never seen the country" in question, were too inclusive of land vital to the welfare of local settlers. John Shafroth, long an opponent of reserves set off and locked up from public use, charged that "serious wrongs" had been inflicted upon "the people of these regions" by the orders. "Too much of the land," he said, "is already settled, and now people . . . become criminals if they preserve themselves from freezing by cutting and burning a stick of timber."[24]

Compounding the anger of Colorado insurgents was the fact that Cleveland's action had been almost arrogantly unilateral. He had not consulted western congressmen in advance of his action, nor did he advise them of it later.[25] Wrote the critical *Denver Republican*, western senators and congressmen expressing "indignation" over Cleveland's tactics were "undoubtedly right in condemning the precipitateness" of the action.[26]

Not all Coloradans agreed with the assessment of the insurgents that the new reserves were damaging. Aside from its criticism of the Forestry Commission, for example, the *Rocky Mountain News* maintained that "actually, all the publicity has been wholesome [because it has made people think about forestry]. For three hundred years we have been a forest-destroying people. The time is coming . . . when the policy must be reversed. The coming American must become a tree-planting, forest-preserving individual."[27] The *Denver Republican*, more irritated with Cleveland's tactics than the proclamation itself, admitted that "if the proper use of the land and timber reserved is provided for, there will be no seriously objectionable results from the establishment of the new reservations."[28] Certainly others in Colorado felt the same.

Whatever the sentiment back home, in the United States Senate western insurgents exploded in protest over the Cleveland withdrawals. After several days of heated talk of impeachment, they finally turned their attention to the reserves themselves. Virtually inviting a power struggle between themselves and the president, the insurgents succeeded in attaching an amendment to the Sundry Civil Appropriations Bill of 1896 providing for the immediate and unconditional restoration to entry of all forest lands withdrawn on February 22. When the bill passed Congress, with the amendment essentially intact, Cleveland vetoed it in a rage.[29] Then he turned the White House, the government, and the western "problem" over to his successor, William McKinley.

When Congress reconvened on March 4, 1897, Senate insurgents, led by Teller and Thomas Carter and Lee Mantle of Montana, prepared to amend the Sundry Civil Bill again and confront McKinley with it as they had Cleveland.[30] The amendment, offered on April 8 by Senator Richard Pettigrew of South Dakota, contained three major provisions. First, it called for the immediate suspension of Cleveland's February withdrawals until March 1, 1898, possibly in hopes that the suspension might then be made permanent. In the interim, reserve areas were to be thoroughly resurveyed and all land more suited to mining and farming than to forestry eliminated. Second, it stipulated that in the future "no public forest reserve" could be established in the West except to "improve and protect the forest within the reserve," to establish "favorable conditions of water flow," or to furnish a "continuous supply of timber for the use and necessities of the citizens of the United States." Third, it specified that the free use of timber be granted all "bona fide" settlers, miners, and prospectors living in the reserves in question. Finally, it authorized owners of reserve land to exchange it for land outside reserve territory if they desired. The only concession granted conservationists by the Pettigrew Amendment was the proviso that the power to sell dead and matured timber on the reserves and make reserve rules and regulations would remain vested in the secretary of the interior.[31]

In the heated Senate debate that followed the introduction of the amendment, a debate that broke sharply along East-West lines, westerners vigorously defended it. While Teller said little of substance during the contest, his place was adequately taken by others—Pettigrew, Joseph L. Rawlins of Utah, John Wilson and George Turner of Washington, Stephen White of California, and Clarence Clark and Francis Warren of Wyoming—all of whom believed and spoke as he did. From Turner's contention that Cleveland's order was an "outrage, improvidently made and ignorantly made," to Clark's larger statement that "the whole proposition" had "almost aroused the people of the West against the whole theory of forest reservation,"[32] they spoke just as eloquently for Colorado's insurgent element as for their own.

The Sundry Civil Appropriations Bill passed the Senate on May 5, 1897, and went to the House. There, among others, John Shafroth and John Bell assigned themselves the delicate task of saving the Pettigrew proposal. On May 10, when debate opened, Shafroth led off in defense of the amendment, attacking Cleveland's withdrawals, the "Eastern scientists" who had recommended them, and the idea behind the reservation system in general:

> *It is most brazen for [conservationists] to tell us that they desire to protect us against ourselves. This proffered guardianship over Western local interests we most earnestly protest against. You may have the power, but it is not right. The Western senators and representatives know full well what is for the permanent welfare of their states, and they are far more eager to advance the welfare of their states than other representatives can possibly be.*[33]

Bell echoed Shafroth's thoughts throughout the debate. In one particularly incisive expression of Colorado's frustration, he spoke of the Battlement Mesa Reserve and its problems:

> *In Routt County there was not left any valuable timber in that county outside the line of the reservation . . . the reserve took in agricultural lands, pastural lands, and mining lands that had no timber. . . . That is why these reservations are so unpopular; that is why this cry has come from the West. It is of this injustice and this indiscriminate setting aside of reservations that the people of my district complain.*

The solution, said Bell, was the dissolution of the reserves. Failing that, it was the responsibility of the federal government to open them up for useful purposes.[34] The answer to western problems, at least for the moment, was the Pettigrew Amendment.

Despite the efforts of Bell and Shafroth (and, with them, Marcus Smith of Arizona, Freeman Knowles of South Dakota, Charles Hartman of Montana, and Frank Cannon of Utah) to salvage the amendment intact, the House balked. Eastern congressmen like Thomas McRae, who proposed to "save the West" from the same kind of forest devastation that had "destroyed" the Old World, considered it too blatantly pro-West for serious consideration.[35] And, almost as if to reinforce their concept of western congressmen as radicals, during the debate Shafroth made an amendment of his own providing for the immediate and *permanent* suspension of the Cleveland withdrawals.[36] The

House rejected both the Pettigrew and Shafroth amendments, and the Sundry bill was sent to conference. The *Rocky Mountain News* hoped aloud that it would not be emasculated, that the Pettigrew Amendment would stand: "The House . . . should . . . take some steps to right the grievous blunder committed by the last administration. . . . It is not with the policy of President Cleveland that fault is found, but with the manner in which he attempted to carry it out. Instead of making these reservations a benefit and an assistance, he rendered them a positive bar to progress and development."[37]

After a lengthy debate, the Sundry bill was reported back to the House with the Pettigrew Amendment essentially intact. Both the House and Senate passed it, and on June 4, 1897, it was signed into law by William McKinley.[38] "Thus ended," writes Roy Robbins, "the most heated land controversy since the days when the homestead issue had divided the nation."[39] Colorado, for that matter, remained divided. Insurgents may have been satisfied with congressional action, but conservationists were not. Looking back on the affair, an angry speaker before the Colorado Horticultural Society castigated the settlers who had allowed it to happen:

> *The preservation of the forests is everybody's business; but if it is the business of any one class, it is the business of the cultivators of the soil. Their interests have been suffering, are suffering more every year, and will continue to suffer for many years. . . . Yet they do not complain. When the forest reserves were set aside by Cleveland, the timber thieves made such a protest that Congress temporarily set aside the order. Those who have benefitted by the enforcement of the order did nothing.*[40]

In late June, 1897, the first regulations for the national forest reserves were issued by the Interior Department, based on recommendations made to Cleveland by the Forestry Commission in the spring and provided for by the act of 1897. On the surface the new code appeared to be a radical departure from the past conservation policies of the federal government. On paper, at least, it unlocked the forest reserves for the first time in six years and opened them up to local settlers. Prospecting for, locating, and developing mineral resources was allowed, as was the use of water for domestic, mining, milling, and irrigation purposes. Rights-of-way were granted settlers across all forest reserves for wagon roads, irrigation canals, ditches, flumes, and reservoirs. The pasturage of livestock, with the exception of sheep, who were banned entirely, was permitted. Lieu land claims were allowed. And, most importantly, reserve timber was no longer restricted; it could be used for firewood, fencing, and other needs free of charge by legitimate settlers living on or near the reserves.[41] If the act appeared weighted in favor of settlers, however, the secretary of the interior still retained the all-important power to make rules and regulations at his discretion for the over-all administration of the reserves. If westerners abused the reservations, theoretically they could be stopped.

For several years after the establishment of Colorado's five reserves in 1891 and 1892, relative peace had pervaded the high country along the great divide. The primary reason was that throughout 1893 and 1894 the government made only a feeble attempt to cordon off the reserves from the public. Thus the average settler was free to pursue his life as he always had, taking timber from reserve forests, digging mineral, pasturing his cattle. As late as 1895 a detente of sorts existed in reserve territories between local settlers and special-interest groups, such as lumbermen, determined to continue acting as they always had, and a government unsure as to how to stop them. As the government increasingly asserted its authority and began enforcing many reserve regulations, however, the state of "amiable hostility" disappeared. By 1897 a mood of belligerence had taken root.

The primary complaint of Colorado pioneers was that, as in the past, the forest reserves still were locked up: timber still was inaccessible, prime rangelands still were outlawed to entry, vast mineral lands still were shut off. Speaking of western conditions before passage of the act of 1897, one national leader remarked that "the situation" existing in reserve regions was "nearly impossible. . . . Legally, at least, no man could even set foot on a single foot of [reserve] land. . . . The attitude of the public . . . was natural and inevitable. Without timber there could be no development."[42] After the passage of the 1897 law, the same figure—Gifford Pinchot—insisted that the problem had been remedied; the new act, he said, was "the most important Federal forest legislation ever enacted" because it provided for both the protection and sensible use of forest lands in the West.[43] A great deal of disparity existed, however, between the promise of the law and what it actually produced. If, in theory, it promised land use, in reality it did not allow it—at least according to Coloradans. Evaluating the miner's dilemma in particular, John Shafroth declared that "the people of Colorado never would have petitioned for these reservations if it had been understood that the miner would be excluded from making mining claims thereon. . . . About 400 people are now located on these reservations. They hold possession of their claims only by sufferance. . . . The result is that now they are in a state of chaotic condition."[44] He well might have spoken for other pioneer groups as well. Much of the entire western half of the state was in a "chaotic condition."

A second major complaint was that the Colorado reservations still were poorly administered by the government. The charge was made by two entirely different groups: "honest" settlers who apparently were sincere in what they said and "dishonest" settlers who used the issue to embarrass the government. Comprising the former group were anticonservation pioneers who had come to accept the reserves as a fait accompli. Recognizing, perhaps, the futility of resisting the reservation system, they, however grudgingly, had assented to it in hopes that it might provide them with some benefits. For example, they expected the government to protect the timberlands from fire. It had long been their contention that "the great danger to the forests" by the state lay "not in their consumption by the public, but in waste by fire,"[45] but when the government took virtually no steps to stem such waste, the pioneers' anger mounted. Similarly, they expected the government to collar spoilsmen on the reserves. They voiced a legitimate concern: that it was difficult for those who complied with federal regulations to stand by and watch the land profitably utilized by those who did not. Again, when the government failed to support them by diligently prosecuting reserve violators, many settlers had good reason to wonder precisely what good the reserves did do them.

As for the "dishonest" class of settlers, their cries of "poor administration" were suspect. Those who tolerated spoilsmen such as timber cutters in their midst obviously cared little about effective reserve administration. The same is true of those who violated reserve laws themselves. By exposing the government's shortcomings to their neighbors, however, they may have hoped to establish the untenability of its entire reserve program.

On the question of administration, the Department of Interior's General Land Office drew most of the settlers' wrath. Their primary complaint was that its officials knew little about the West.[46] It particularly annoyed pioneers that land policies which stood to affect the life of the state for years to come were made not in the state by skilled foresters or even westerners but in Washington by "distant dictators with only a theoretical knowledge of the problems of the West."[47] Colorado Senator Henry Teller spoke for much of his pioneer constituency when he scorned agents "who had absolutely no acquaintance with the subject, who were too indolent to go over the country and examine its geography and topography and the necessity for reserves, who would sit in their offices and make the reservations, including large communities, doing the utmost injustice to the people of those sections of the country."[48] Colorado insurgents were not alone in their views. Even conservationist Gifford Pinchot concurred that

the management of the reserves was awful. The General Land

Office knew nothing about the reserves or what ought to be done with them. At that time not one man had ever set foot on a forest reserve or had seen one forest tree, unless from a Pullman car window. The abysmal ignorance of the Washington office about conditions on the ground was outrageous, pathetic, or comic, whichever you like.[49]

Even more disliked than Land Office officials were the rangers who carried out departmental policies "on the ground." To some extent the rangers were scapegoats. But to some extent, too, they warranted the enmity of the pioneer class. As easterners, which most of them were, with little knowledge of the West, they symbolized ignorance. Also, as political appointees—watchmakers, bookkeepers, veterinarians, saloon operators, invalids, protegees of eastern party bosses—they symbolized political corruption to men who "were not violently opposed to timber poaching, but were adverse to graft."[50]

Nothing about the rangers so infuriated local settlers as their cavalier attitudes toward local problems. For example, when a particularly serious forest fire broke out one July afternoon in 1898 on the Pikes Peak Reserve, the ranger in charge of the reserve left it to attend a flower show in Colorado Springs. On another occasion a district ranger who disappeared during a raging fire on the South Platte was later found at his headquarters, "half-clothed, enjoying a bottle of wine."[51] Clearly such irresponsibility was objectionable to settlers who sought benefits from unwelcome reserves placed among them. As the *Rocky Mountain News* angrily editorialized, "while campers and careless settlers have been setting the forests afire, the timber inspectors have been doing political work. . . . We should like to hear from some quarter of the state of a timber inspector who has been putting in some time at his duties."[52]

In a speech to Congress, Colorado Senator Edward O. Wolcott summed up the frustrations of his constituency. Lashing out at the timber agents and federal rangers who patrolled western forest reserves, he charged that *they tumble all over each other in the Western states, broken-down politicians from the Eastern states, hunting for a man who has a mine which looks like it might produce, . . . who may cut a little timber for his mine, that they might compel him by blackmail into giving them a few hundred dollars to save himself from the indictment of the federal courts. These men are not fit to stay at home so they are unloaded on the Western states. Talk about timber thieves! These people are worse than any timber thieves that Eastern men can imagine. . . . We do not want them in Colorado.*[53]

During the last several years of the century, as they suffered from both real and imagined indignities, Colorado insurgents made various attempts to improve their lot. For one thing, they argued that the public domain which the government had withdrawn and reserved in Colorado should have been ceded to the state for it to administer. The question they raised about landownership in Colorado was provocative. Legally, of course, the public domain which lay within the state's borders was owned by the federal government. Legality aside, however, many insurgents believed—or said they believed—that the state had a kind of moral right to control any land contained within it. The attitude of Colorado governor Alva B. Adams (1896–98) was one widely shared in reserve regions:

The ceding of this domain to the state will relieve the general government of a . . . burden and place the land affairs . . . where they will be managed for the general good. Such a change of control will give the state home rule over its entire territory and exempt every citizen of Colorado . . . from the liability of being a trespasser when he sets foot upon any part [*of the forest reserves*]. *The forests, waters, and all resources will be better conserved, as the state will use the sagacity and wisdom that comes with ownership. . . . All in all, such a transfer will insure domestic tranquility, . . . promote the dignity of the state, and advance the welfare of the people.*[54]

However sincere the contention may have been, it was weak. There was no avoiding the possibility that the argument for state control was, in fact, an argument for no control at all. After all, Colorado already had lands of its own—most of which it had never attempted to protect.[55] The federal government had no reason to believe that the state could, or would, administer lands ceded to it. It was little wonder, under the circumstances, that the insurgents' suggestions were met with cynicism and suspicion. Speaking for his fellow conservationists, William N. Byers of the Colorado State Forestry Association stated that he had "no hope that forest protection could be secured" by the state. "I think," he said, "that the general government is the only authority that can protect the public forests."[56]

While they promoted the idea of land cession, the insurgents also attempted to gain concessions from the government through the state legislature. On many occasions the legislature attempted to dissuade the government from its course of action. During the meeting of the Ninth General Assembly of Colorado, for example, Senator Charles Graham of Steamboat Springs (which lay on the edge of the White River Reserve) introduced a joint resolution which expressed the feeling of much of the Western Slope. Deploring the government's alleged "no use" policy, it resolved that

in setting up in this state large tracts of wooded country for reserves, there should not, and need not be any burdensome restrictions placed on any legitimate industry; the necessary and proper use of forest products should clearly be provided for. . . . And be it further resolved that Congress be earnestly requested to make early provisions for the . . . use of timber and other natural resources on the reserves.[57]

Such appeals, however, were ignored by the government in the same way it ignored the state's representatives in Washington. The reserves remained padlocked, and settlers continued to protest.

Typical pioneer timber cutters on the South Platte Forest Reserve, mid-1890's.

Courtesy Denver Public Library, Western History Department

When all attempts to reason with the government failed, Colorado settlers, ignoring the law, moved into the reserves and took from them what they wanted. Their attitude was characteristically simplistic: the forest existed only for the moment, and it was important only in how long and how comfortably it could sustain a man and his family. Presidential proclamations, acts of Congress, and rules and regulations were all meaningless technicalities. The government could be damned; the forest reserves simply did not exist.

Over the last several years of the century the most persistent violators of the five reserves were timber cutters, sometimes

Homesteaders in the White River Forest Reserve.
Courtesy State Historical Society of Colorado

individuals, sometimes larger groups, often virtual companies. Despite the fact that their actions were flagrantly illegal (timber could be cut by individuals for fuel, fencing, and housing, but not by individuals or groups for commercial sale), they were impossible for the government to stop. Local settlers often refused to report them, not because they feared implication with criminals, but because they largely sympathized with their activities. In 1897, after extensive interviews with settlers on the White River Plateau, an investigator for the United States Geological Survey reported his impressions:

Nearly all illicit lumbering and timber depredations are looked upon by settlers as blameless ventures. Such operations furnish a limited amount of employment to the poorer classes, and . . . they are considered to be taking only what rightfully belongs to them and all other settlers. The depredator's good name is not thought to be sullied by the veritable theft of timber from the public domain. The spirit of some landless settlers is well illustrated by the following remark made to this writer by a party suspected of selling dead building logs: "This timber belongs to us settlers and we're going to get it! The government officials can't prevent us either, with an army. If they attempt to stop us, we'll burn the whole region up!"[58]

Whatever their rationale, the timber cutters devastated the forests. On the Pikes Peak Reservation their damage was so extensive that by 1898 a federal surveyor unhappily reported that "practically no forests deserving of the name" remained in the area.[59] On the South Platte, sawmill operators, railroad tie cutters, and mobile bands of settlers manufacturing charcoal for sale to local smelters decimated virtually every major stand of timber in the reserve before the end of the decade. What they failed to destroy, larger lumber concerns took. Extensive lumber mills worked round the clock at Grant, Puma City, near Signal Butte, Florissant, Hoosier Pass, and Mountain Dale without any interference from federal authorities. By 1898 the U.S. Geological Survey noted that from border to border the surface of the reserve had been "very largely deprived of its most valuable timber by the rapacity" of local settlers.[60] On the Battlement the situation was the same. Capitalizing on the booming timber market around the fringes of the reserve at Newcastle, Parachute, Rifle, Mesa, Hotchkiss, and even Delta, timber cutters settled into the heart of the best timberlands and turned out fresh lumber. As elsewhere, they were accepted by the pioneer community. On examining the region, an inspector for the U.S. Geological Survey reported that the Battlement's timber raiders "seemed to enjoy the entire sympathy of the settlers. . . . All mill operators were in good standing with the settlers; so much so that . . . several settlers took special pains to inform me that [there were no illegal mills on the reserve].

One said: 'They used ter be on the resarve, but we had the line shifted. But this 'ere ain't no forest anyhow.'"[61]

Extensive damage also was inflicted on the Colorado reserves by anticonservation cattlemen, despite the fact that in the spring of 1898, Secretary of the Interior Hoke Smith established a grazing permit system on every reservation in the state. Those stockmen who had helped lead the antireservation movement from the beginning—as in the Grand Valley, for example—were no more inclined than settlers to relinquish rights earned from years on the range. Consequently, they simply ignored the permit system, even though its primary intention was to preserve the range for the cattlemen themselves. They also ignored Smith's supplementary rules and regulations requiring cattlemen to give top range priority to settlers who actually lived on the range, to consent to certain governmental "range management" practices, to participate in the "cooperative improvement" of the mountain ranges, and to submit to penalties for range trespass.[62]

As in the past, large numbers of local cattlemen continued to overgraze their cattle in the forests. The damage caused by their herds was serious and widespread: year after year cattle stripped the ranges of vital herbage and new grass and killed millions of conifer seedlings. Conservationists argued vehemently against the practice, insisting that grazing be halted on Colorado reserves until damaged forests grew back.[63] But the government, short of occupying the reserves with military troops and controlling the ranchers by force, could do little. The inaction was disastrous. By 1899 ranges on all five Colorado reserves were in a state of deterioration. The U.S. Geological Survey reported that on the Pikes Peak Reserve "excessive pasturage" had "greatly reduced or destroyed" grass and herbage in once-prime pasturelands; on the Plum Creek Reserve pasturage had "deteriorated greatly," and ground conditions were "yearly becoming worse"; on the South Platte Reserve (victimized not only by local cattlemen but by "nomadic" cattlemen and sheepmen as well), there had been a "decided reduction of the grazing value of the land"; and on the White River Reserve the "trampling of thousands of range animals" had virtually destroyed the range.[64]

Even as they violated the permit law, anticonservation cattlemen worked diligently to have it repealed. Using annual association meetings as sounding boards for their arguments, they attempted to popularize their position throughout the West. In January, 1901, the Western Range Association, a new, militant Colorado cattlemen's organization created chiefly to combat the federal government's nascent leasing plans for the public domain,[65] passed a resolution condemning the "hardship and injustice" perpetrated by the reserves in western Colorado. At the same time it called for the abolition of permits and regulations.[66] A week later at the National Livestock Association convention in Fort Worth, Colorado delegates voted with the majority which adopted resolutions calling for the rigid limitation of forest reserves to "timber-producing areas" only, the elimination of nontimbered lands from existing reserves, and the investigation by the secretary of the interior of "the many forest reserve enthusiasts" whose "unwarranted reports and unwise and unnecessary recommendations" led to more reserves, more rules, and more regulations in the West each year.[67]

In July, 1901, in what they billed as the final "showdown" on the forest reserve issue, Colorado insurgents invited Gifford Pinchot, chief of the Department of Agriculture's Forestry Bureau, to appear before the Trans-Mississippi Commercial Congress at Cripple Creek to defend the government's reservation program. On the morning of July 17, Pinchot told a large, silent audience in the opera house that "the general prosperity of the country" was "ultimately bound up with the protection and preservation of the forests." In a very real sense, he said, "the end of civilization may be described as the founding of homes . . . and forestry is therefore the handmaid of civilization."[68] His message, however, was not well received. Cripple Creek, a mining boomtown on the southeast edge of one of Colorado's most agitated reserves—the Pikes Peak—was no place for an eastern conservationist to speak of forestry. In response to his plea for understanding, the assembly of miners, cattlemen, and small frontier businessmen—all of whom survived, literally, off the adjacent forests—passed resolutions condemning reserve permits as "unnecessary for the protection of the forests."[69] Insurgent cattlemen rested their efforts there, at least for the moment.

Despite the furor on the Colorado reserves in the late 1890's, by no means did the entire state abandon the idea of conservation. State conservation groups were as active as ever, attempting to neutralize the impact of the insurgents' dissent on the general public.

The most important group was composed of proconservation cattlemen. Mavericks—for the moment at least—and small in number, they nonetheless were able to make a persuasive case for land reservation. They argued, first, that unless the wanton overgrazing of the range was stopped, the cattle industry faced possible extinction. Grazing permits, therefore, were beneficial. Second, they maintained that federal permits, if properly and judiciously granted, might reduce the number of cattle barons on mountain ranges and allow the little man more access to prime pastureland. As one Coloradan said in 1899, he opposed a system where "one or two lords own the land and all the rest are his vassals."[70] They supported permits and regulations and the reserves themselves primarily, however, because the reservations were their last refuge against the growing encroachment of sheepmen. By the late 1890's sheepmen had made inroads into mountain ranges all over Colorado; in some counties, such as Huerfano, Las Animas, Montrose, El Paso, Weld, and Archuleta, they had taken it over almost entirely.[71] Cattlemen, who had always seen the range as theirs to begin with, were doubly distressed by the damage sheep inflicted on it—stripping the forests of seedlings, chewing grass to stubble, and tearing up the earth. They supported the Sundry Civil Appropriations Act of 1897 and its supplementary rules for the simple reason that it barred sheep from almost every range in the West and required permits for the few flocks that were exempted.

Like insurgent cattlemen, the conservationists used national meetings to popularize their position. In 1899, for example, they launched an all-out campaign in support of federal land policy. Led by Jared Brush of Greeley, E. H. Milleisen of Dillon, J. E. Law of New Windsor, and A. R. King of Delta, they introduced a resolution before the National Livestock Association Convention in Denver recommending that as long as the grazing of sheep on Colorado reserves was "destructive of the forests," Department of Interior regulations should "not be abrogated."[72] From the beginning the conservation coalition insisted that the idea of land preservation and all it entailed was favored by "every farmer, every agriculturist, every stockman, every merchant, every professional man, and men of every official capacity" in Colorado.[73] And yet, at no time were they completely convincing—especially to the insurgent majority. The truth probably was that, despite their rhetoric, they no more approved of the idea of grazing regulations than their anticonservation neighbors. It may have been that they accepted permits and regulations only, and perhaps realistically, because "they were of more immediate importance to their business than was their dislike of regulation."[74] The desire of men like Edgar Ensign was to protect resources for "future generations"; the cattlemen's idea was to protect themselves.

Along with the cattlemen, another active group was the State Board of Horticulture. Meeting annually in Denver, it kept constant pressure on anticonservation congressmen with petitions and resolutions condemning the "impunity" with which timberlands were violated in Colorado, protesting the lax federal enforcement of reserve laws, and demanding "effective relief from the dangers of extinction that threaten the forests that are part of the peoples' heritage."[75] Equally as active was the State Forestry Association, which promoted the idea that if Colorado could secure "legislation and police protection" for its reserves and "prevent the destruction of everything, young and old," it could secure "a growth of timber that [had] never been seen in this country."[76] At its annual meeting in 1898 the

conservationists could hardly take comfort in the 1898 pronouncement by the U.S. Geological Survey that central Colorado reservations had been so devastated by local settlers and cattlemen that in many areas they remained of "little or no value" as reserves any longer.[81] Nor could they find encouragement in statements like that of Gifford Pinchot that "in no part of the country" were "the rights of the government and its property more disregarded" than in the central Colorado Rockies.[82] The decade had begun with opposition to forest reserves, and it terminated the same way. A Meeker resident, writing fifty years after the creation of the White River Reserve and looking back on its early days, said:

Well indeed do I recall the bitterness with which the cattlemen and others in Colorado greeted the forest reserves. The words "Hitlerism" and "regimentation" had not been written into our language in those days, but they are characteristic of the reception which was accorded federal intervention . . . in the name of conservation. At that time I doubt if a hundred votes could have been secured for the federal control of forests in Colorado.[83]

Perhaps the most important aspect of the Colorado experience in the late 1890's was the fact that it typified the western experience as a whole. In Washington, for example, while commercial and mountaineering clubs in Seattle and Tacoma lobbied for more forest reserves, business and civic organizations in the western part of the state worked to have boundaries of existing reserves reduced.[84] And in Montana, while Governor Robert Smith supported the concept of grazing permits, insurgents such as Congressman Charles Hartman decried conservationists who "sat down in the quiet parlors of hotels in the various states and there from their inner consciousness . . . evolved the wonderful results" that the West had come to see.[85]

While the U.S. Geological Survey documented case after case of homesteaders and cattlemen violating western forest reserves, perhaps the most recurrent state-to-state clash was between conservationists and graziers. In California, for example, where much of the state (except for the Los Angeles region) opposed reserves,[86] only John Muir, the state forestry association, and the Sierra Club stood between land predators, such as sheepmen determined to graze their herds on reserves despite the law,[87] and the ruination not only of the forest-reserve network but of such areas as Yosemite Park. In Oregon, sheepmen backed by Governor William Lord were opposed by such institutions as the state forestry association and the Portland Chamber of Commerce.[88] Both Wyoming and New Mexico were dominated by grazing interests. In Wyoming, conservationists had to fight men like Governor William Richards, who openly considered the forest reserves a "farce," and Senator Clarence Clark, who deplored the "absolute ignorance of the whole [reserve] proposition."[89] In the New Mexico Territory, while Governor Manuel Otero worked personally against the establishment of certain reserves, sheepmen took their cause before national livestock conventions on several occasions.[90]

In the Arizona Territory sheepmen fought rangers and were opposed in turn by lowland settlers who desired federal protection of forest watersheds vital to their welfare, a situation similar to that existing on Colorado's Battlement Mesa Reserve. The graziers were extremely active in cattlemen's conventions between 1898 and 1901. In 1898, for instance, they pushed an amendment through the National Livestock Association meeting calling for the "unlocking" of reserves to sheep. Similarly, in 1901, E. S. Gosney, head of the Arizona Sheep Breeders and Wool Growers Association, promoted a resolution denouncing reserves that created "damaging public sentiment among the honest settlers" of the West.[91] Utah, too, was divided between conservationists and insurgent sheepmen. While Governor Heber Wells actively lobbied for forest reserves in his state, graziers like J. C. Mackay, head of the Uintah County Wool Growers Association, attacked those who "would like to establish a feudal system in America, have large tracts of land set apart as reserves, so some idealist or scientific expert . . . might view dame nature in its primitive state."[92]

In one final respect—its fear of the "East"—Colorado also reflected the sentiment of the larger West. Assessing the attitudes of eastern conservationists—particularly their desire to lock up the land for esthetic purposes—it became the impression of many Coloradans that a conspiracy of sorts existed against their state. One Western Slope settler voiced the opinion that any policy of land withdrawal and reservation would not "recommend itself to anyone but residents of Eastern states" who would have "no interests in the hardships caused by such a false policy."[93] Added a White River pioneer: "If that great public domain passes into the hands of the general government, we people of the West will not be considered. The capital of the East will make the laws and we will have to follow them."[94] Similar sentiment existed elsewhere in the West. When a Massachusetts newspaper accused Washingtonians of being "timber thieves" in 1897, the *Seattle Post-Intelligencer* bitterly defended them.[95] During the heated debate over the Pettigrew Amendment in the same year, when senators George Gray of Delaware and Joseph Hawley of Connecticut championed the reserve system, Senator Joseph Rawlins of Utah charged that the "gentlemen of the East" had "contempt for the intelligence, the sense of fairness, the foresight of the people of the West." And Stephen White of California spoke for most western insurgents when he declared that he wearied of "western affairs" dictated, for the worst, by "tribunes of the East" who had never seen the West.[96]

By the summer of 1901, however they might have expressed themselves, insurgents from all corners of the West made one point abundantly clear: if there had ever been a time when they might have accepted forest reserves—in the early 1890's, for example—the time was past. On Colorado's Battlement Reserve and California's Sierra, in statehouses and on the floors of Congress, the message of the laissez-faire pioneer to the conservationist was blunt and defiant: American development had been achieved by the "energy, perseverance, industry, the trials, the self-denials of the hardy pioneers" who had "blazed the pathway of civilization into . . . an empire" in the Rockies.[97] What they had built they would keep. They would not acquiesce to conservation.

V. Roosevelt and Pinchot

When an assassin's bullet took the life of William McKinley on the afternoon of September 6, 1901, it ushered in, swiftly and spectacularly, the era of Theodore Roosevelt. As imperceptible and unimportant as the fact might have seemed at the moment, the New Yorker's accession to the presidency marked the beginning of a dramatic new day in the history of the conservation movement in the United States.

In the wake of McKinley's tragic death the state of Colorado soberly assessed its new president. It approved of what it saw. Roosevelt appealed to virtually all segments of Colorado society, but to no group more than insurgent pioneers. Looking at him, they thought they caught a reflection of themselves. He loved the West and its traditions. Because of his western experiences, perhaps, he shared with them a particularly irrepressible individualism. He possessed an abiding faith in the concept of personal independence. And, consciously or not, he implied in much of what he wrote and said that the pioneer, particularly the cattleman, was part of a special breed, "first cousin to the backwoodsman of the southern Alleghanies" who had first begun the task of building American civilization.[1] Because of this, Colorado insurgents assumed that in Roosevelt they had found a man with whom they could communicate, someone who would protect their rights and understand their aspirations. "The people of Colorado feel kindly toward him," said Henry Teller. "He has lived in our country and he knows what our needs are."[2] If the insurgents believed, however, that the new president, because of his bond with the West, would reverse the national trend toward conservation, they were wrong. They failed to realize it in the tragic fall of 1901, but by winter they would know.

Like their opponents, Colorado conservationists also approved of Roosevelt. The *Denver Republican* maintained that their "interests should fare well" with him "at the head of the government."[3] If the conservationists saw the president as one of them, they assessed him with more shrewdness than did the insurgents, for he emerged almost as soon as he took office as the most powerful and persistent conservation champion that the nation had ever seen. If the Harrison and Cleveland years had been unhappy ones for the anticonservationists, the Roosevelt era was a catastrophe.

Before examining the conservation philosophy of Theodore Roosevelt, it is necessary to understand the milieu that helped shape it. When Roosevelt entered the White House in the fall of 1901, essentially two conservation movements existed in the United States. One, led by naturalist John Muir and supported by easterners who desired to halt the use of the western public domain entirely, sought perpetual land reservation, mainly for esthetic purposes. Their idea—so repugnant to westerners—remained that wilderness was a "necessity," that mountain parks and reservations were "fountains of life" to be preserved at all costs for the benefit of "tired, nerve-shaken, over-civilized people" at the moment and for future generations as well.[4] The other movement, led by Gifford Pinchot, differed in one key respect: it advocated, along with land reservation, the wise, regulated use of land resources. While Roosevelt incorporated parts of both philosophies into his own creed, because the latter group was more powerful, with men in virtually every key bureaucratic position in Washington in 1901, he adhered more closely to it.

Essentially, the Pinchot conservationists adhered to what historian Samuel P. Hays has called the "gospel of efficiency."[5] Influenced, perhaps, by the growing progressive impulse in

America, they believed first in the importance of human achievement and the fulfillment of human potential—perhaps what conservationist W. J. McGee called the "divinity of human rights."[6] They believed, further, that only in a healthy physical environment replete with free (or at least cheap) land, personal democracy, and the possibility of individual economic advancement, could such fulfillment take place. Assessing the devastation of land resources in the West, they concluded that there, at least, the little man had little chance to achieve; the particular kind of environment essential to his development was being destroyed by special interests and monopolists who overran the land, thwarted democracy, and virtually wiped out any possibility of individual economic success.

In the course of studying the problem, the conservationists came to advocate a twofold course of action: first, that the government maintain control of its remaining lands as long as possible in order to prevent further monopolization,[7] and second, that it pursue a policy of rational resource planning designed to promote the efficient development and use of the West's remaining natural wealth.[8] As scientists and technologists confident that their conception of the problem was sound and that they had mastered all knowledge essential to understanding it, the progressive conservationists never wavered in the belief that their ideas—"efficiency," "wise use," "highest use," "resource development"—were or would be beneficial.[9] They became and remained completely optimistic that the utilization of science and technology in the area of resource conservation would open up unlimited opportunities for human achievement.

No one embodied the spirit of the "wise use" conservationists more than their leader, Gifford Pinchot. Like other of the progressive planners, he saw conservation as a social necessity rather than a luxury. He believed that under existing conditions conservation could only enhance man's environment, stabilize him, and allow him to develop his fullest potential. As Pinchot's wife wrote years after he died,

Gifford Pinchot talking with local forest-reserve supervisors, Denver, 1908, a picture from the *Denver Times*, March 15, 1908.
Courtesy Denver Public Library, Conservation Library Center

Conservation to Gifford Pinchot was never a vague, fuzzy aspiration. It was concrete, exact, dynamic, the application of science and technology to our material economy for the purpose of enhancing and elevating the life of the individual. The conservation he preached . . . dealt . . . first, last, and all the time with human beings. . . . To Pinchot, you see, man himself was a natural resource, the basic and primary resource for whose material, moral, and spiritual welfare the conservation doctrine was invoked. . . . Believing as he did that the planned and orderly development of the earth and all it contains was indispensable to the permanent prosperity of the human race, conservation in its widest sense became to him a philosophy of guiding principles through which such prosperity might be achieved, a bold, creative affirmation in ethical and spiritual terms of our faith in the dignity of man as a child of God.[10]

Specifically Pinchot geared all of his efforts toward the protection of the little man at the expense of monopolists who had, in his words, "captured" the resources of the West. "We preferred the small man before the big man," he said many times, "because his need was greater. We preferred him in honor and in privilege, in principle and practice. . . . 'Better help a poor man make a living for his family than help a rich man get richer still.' That was our battle cry and our rule of life."[11] Always a utilitarian, Pinchot's philosophy was that the small settler and the small stockowner were not helped by the locking up of the forests. Thus he advocated the logging of forests on a sustained-yield basis rather than their reservation for esthetic purposes, and he sought careful control of grazing rather than its abolition.[12]

Because of his skills, his position as chief of the Forestry Bureau, his vast practical experience, and his immense energy, Pinchot quickly and profoundly influenced Roosevelt. Guided, like Roosevelt, by the emergent progressive impulse, prodded, similarly, by a patrician sense of noblesse oblige, he was the heart of the American conservation movement in 1901. With

> *the moral fervor of an evangelist and a politician's intuition . . . he had the lean look of a Moses and a familiar sense of mission. . . . Pinchot was one of the great teachers of his time: he taught frugality when waste was the accepted creed. . . . and if Gifford Pinchot was not, as he liked to believe, the fountainhead of the conservation movement, he was nevertheless one of its vital sources. He was key man of a key decade.*[13]

If Roosevelt became the titular head of the conservation movement, Pinchot remained its architect.

Theodore Roosevelt, like Pinchot, adhered to the dominant conservation ideas of his day. To some extent, for example, his philosophy was rooted in economic considerations. With others he shared the fear that despite forest reserves, grazing regulations, and patched-up land laws, the vital natural wealth of the

West continued to be monopolized and exploited by corporations and spoilsmen. And, like others, he realized that what was lost could not be replaced. Partly because of that fact—that the economic future of the nation depended on the continued availability of natural resources—Roosevelt turned to the doctrine of conservation.[14]

Roosevelt also was concerned about the political damage caused by resource monopoly. Professing a belief in the right of every citizen to pursue his happiness, especially on the public domain which belonged to all equally, Roosevelt was angered by the theft and illegal engrossment of land by those who damaged the rights of others in the course of their activities. As the peoples' steward he resolved to halt resource devastation in the West, feeling that such an action might "democratize the handling of the common heritage," restore a semblance of political equality on the frontier, and "show that civilized man could profit from mistakes of the past."[15] "In the past," he declared in a 1901 speech, "we have admitted the right of the individual to injure the future of the Republic for his present profit. The time has come for a change. As a people we have the right and the duty second to none other but the right and duty of obeying the moral law of requiring and doing justice, to protect ourselves and our children against the wasteful destruction of our natural resources."[16] To a certain extent, then, Roosevelt's crusade was "in its final phase, the fight . . . for what [he] called 'real democracy.'"[17]

Like most conservationists, especially eastern reservationists, Roosevelt believed that a correlation existed between the nation's natural wealth and its social welfare. Time and again he contended that the increasing "scarcity of natural resources" in America led and would continue to lead to "diminishing social returns to economic effort." For that reason he rejected

the doctrine of laissez-faire, at least regarding the exploitation of natural resources, in the belief that "the trend of social welfare over time could be influenced by the extent to which men conserved and managed resources with an eye to the welfare of future generations." Society, in Roosevelt's mind, could thrive and prosper only so long as natural resources remained available to provide it with material comforts which, in turn, led to social stability. When natural resources dwindled, he concluded, economic productivity, moral character, social stability, and ethical standards declined correspondingly.[18]

Roosevelt worried not only about the spiritual atrophy of the nation but about its physical decay as well. As an environmentalist he subscribed to the theories of scientist George Marsh, who had examined the interaction between society and environment. Marsh postulated that the waste of natural resources led directly to the physical decay of civilizations dependent on them; deforestation, in particular, resulted in floods, the fouling of climates, the pollution of air, and the spread of disease. Resource destruction led ultimately to the rotting of cities, the destruction of their inhabitants, and the disintegration of the civilizations themselves.[19] It had occurred before, said Marsh, and the possibility that it could happen again haunted Roosevelt. As much as any other factor, the vision of doomsday led Roosevelt toward conservation.

Finally, Roosevelt's personal experiences in the West affected the way he thought about it and its problems. Whereas insurgents expected that his days as a Dakota rancher and Colorado hunter would cause him to side with them, the result was the opposite. It was precisely because Roosevelt was (or at least saw himself as) a man of the West that he sided with those who sought to conserve the land. Because he had been a pioneer of sorts himself and because he valued the experience, he desired to find a way that others could enjoy and profit by the land. In 1888, for example, Roosevelt mourned the passing of various facets of frontier life: "We who have felt the charm of the [western] life," he wrote, "and have exulted in its abounding vigor and its bold, restless freedom, will not only regret its passing for our own sakes . . . but must also feel real sorrow that those who come after us are not to see, as we have seen, what is perhaps the pleasantest, healthiest, and most exciting phase of

American existence."[20] Although Roosevelt did not speak exactly in Turnerian terms, his message was clear: the preservation of the West in at least a semiprimitive condition would allow for the continued development of frontier virtues and national idealism.[21]

Whatever the origins of his philosophy, Roosevelt helped alter the course of the conservation movement in America. It was not so much that his brand of conservation was newer or better than that of others, what made him important was the fact that he translated his philosophy into action. Without Roosevelt the conservationists would have achieved relatively little; with him, however, they inaugurated a "world movement for staying terrestrial waste and saving for the human race the things upon which a great and peaceful and progressive and happy life" could be founded.[22] Assessing the Roosevelt crusade in retrospect, one historian has concluded that only after he lent his power to the movement

> *did it receive the vigor and publicity it needed. More than any other man, he was responsible for awakening in the American people the desire to make effective and continuing use of existing natural resources for the benefit of both present and future generations. . . . What Roosevelt himself did to bring his message into the homes of farmers and merchants, factory workers and professional men, was as important as anything else he did while President.*[23]

In the fall of 1901, before they knew of Roosevelt's inclinations, Colorado insurgents watched hopefully as he took the oath of office. Afterward they waited for him to come to their aid by abolishing forest reserves or at least by suspending grazing regulations, dissolving the ranger corps, or opening up the reservations to all local settlers. But when Roosevelt acted, it was not for them. Speaking before a meeting of the American Forestry Association in Denver in September, Gifford Pinchot laid the conservation policy of the Roosevelt administration squarely on the line, calling in unequivocal terms for the "extension of forest reserves in almost every locality in the West"—especially Colorado, which had "no more pressing need than the extension of the reserve system over her forest lands."[24] Then, in his first inaugural address in December, Roosevelt himself added that "the practical usefulness of the forest reserves to the mining, grazing and other interests" had led to a "widespread demand by the people of the West for their extension." His policy would be to add to the reserve system "whenever practicable."[25] The insurgents' worst fears were realized: Roosevelt was not one of them.

In the ensuing years Colorado anticonservationists transferred wholesale their animosity from Roosevelt's predecessors to him. Their attitude was based on several assumptions. First, whether commercial interests—railroad promoters, land speculators, and mining and timber corporations—dismayed by the loss of exploitable land or little men angered by the loss of both land and traditional rights, the insurgents believed that Roosevelt possessed a faulty understanding of them and their region. "While they give him credit for knowing the Western people," said the *Glenwood Avalanche-Echo*, "he does not understand them as clearly as he might."[26] More bluntly, Henry Teller declared that Roosevelt knew "no more about the conditions existing" in the West than did a "woodchuck."[27] Further, it was their opinion that Roosevelt was too pliable when it came to Pinchot, that he was unwilling or unable to resist the Forester's arguments even when they "damaged" the West. "Teddy is too easily captured," said a disgusted northern Coloradan.[28]

Beyond those points, however, anticonservationist hostility seemed to be founded on the fear of governmental paternalism. Assessing pioneer feelings in 1900, ex-Chief Forester Bernhard Fernow commented that "a decidedly paternalistic, if not socialistic attitude, has lately been taken by the federal government; and by skillful construction of the constitution as regards the right to regulate interstate relations, has led to an expansion of federal power in various directions." One of the directions was resource regulation—conservation. Maintaining that in the West "particularistic and individualistic tendencies of

An anti-Roosevelt cartoon from the *Denver Post*, January 27, 1907.
Courtesy Denver Public Library, Conservation Library Center

the true democrat" were "antagonistic" to anything which smacked of "paternalism," Fernow warned the government that it was "necessary to keep in mind" that the states were "autonomous" and that conservation alone—the reservation of lands without any apparent respect for those who lived on or near them—was foolish.[29] Colorado sentiment seemed to bear Fernow out. Time and again during the Roosevelt term the thought was expressed that the president and Pinchot had "taken charge of the West," whose people, rather than participating in the development of their resources and the "building of free and independent American citizenship," would forever remain "tenants" of the federal government.[30] The insurgent element felt, as Henry Teller said, that "we do not need the fostering and kindly hand of the National Government. We want it taken off."[31]

If Roosevelt was hated by Colorado's insurgent sector after 1901, so was his lieutenant, Pinchot. By the time Roosevelt became president, Pinchot already had behind him ten years of applying conservation to the West—first as a national conservation agitator, then as a member of Cleveland's controversial Forestry Commission, and finally as head of the Agriculture Department's Bureau of Forestry. The ten years had gained him substantial enmity. From the instant he had come into contact with Colorado forests and Colorado pioneers, he had been "thoroughly hated by free-born American citizens who did not see why they 'hadn't the right' to cut down just as many trees as they wanted."[32] While Pinchot visualized himself a progressive humanitarian, to anticonservation pioneers he was a despot responsible for an illegal empire of forest reserves, a "whipper-snapper" violating the rights of "stalwart, honest citizens" in the process of "hamstringing the 'development' of the country."[33] When Denver physician C. E. Sirois called Pinchot an "impractical dreamer," a "rapacious, venal, petty aristocrat maliciously bent on destroying everybody,"[34] he spoke for much of Colorado's mountain population.

Several themes ran through the opposition to "Pinchotism" in Colorado. First, like Roosevelt, Pinchot was accused of stunting western economic development. In the past, for example, even without any direct jurisdiction over forest reserves, Pinchot had been partly instrumental in having the system established. In 1896, while with Cleveland's Forestry Commission, he, in his own words, "rode to the top of Pikes Peak in a stage, . . . saw Cripple Creek in all its lurid glory, and made a partial acquaintance with the five Colorado reserves."[35] Then, on the basis of the "partial acquaintance," including time spent in areas already withdrawn from entry, he had advocated the inclusion of millions of additional acres of Colorado wilderness into forest reserves. Later, in 1898, he had gone before a congressional committee to urge that grazing be restricted on the five reserves, and in July, 1901, he had defended federal policy at Cripple Creek. In every sense, as far as insurgents were concerned, he had worked for land withdrawal and against

Typical anti-Pinchot cartoon, from the *Rocky Mountain News*, September 20, 1908.

Courtesy Denver Public Library, Conservation Library Center

settlement and economic development. Under Roosevelt, with more direct power and influence than ever before (especially after jurisdiction over the reserves was transferred from the Interior Department to the Agriculture Department in 1905), Pinchot became even more feared and hated. As one central Colorado newspaper complained, under Pinchot and the "forestry octopus," the public domain was slowly "passing from the hands of the people." As the advocates of forestry destroyed "every line of industry" in every reserve, the pioneer became a "trespasser" in his own domain.[36]

Insurgents also took offense at Pinchot's personality, particularly his theorizing and his occasional arrogance. To the suspicious western mind he was the "epitome of egotistical, theoretical Eastern bureaucracy,"[37] a man distrusted as a thinker and feared as a trained expert in a scientific field. More than that, however, he was feared for his tendency to domineer. Time and again after 1901 the idea of Pinchot as a tyrant was raised. Maintaining that Pinchot was a "real danger to our representative institutions" because of his promotion of reserves, the *Denver Post* accused him of fostering "landlordism" on the public domain, compared with which "that of Europe and Ireland" was "superlatively wise, just, and beneficient."[38] In an open letter to his neighbors, one Colorado settler declared that "if your ancestors had come to America with mine over 300 years ago; if as many of them had fought battles for freedom from King George; if you had been trained in patriotism at the Philadelphia public high school; if you had breathed the spirit of liberty for thirty years on Colorado mountain tops, you would understand and hate 'Pinchotism' as I do. It is diametrically opposed to all true Americanism."[39] And in Leadville, comparing Pinchot with a "Russian Czar or a Turkish Sultan," the anticonservation *Leadville Press* condemned his "visionary schemes" which had destroyed local settlers, leaving them "buncoed, robbed, mistreated, and treated like serfs of English landlords instead of like decent, law-abiding, God-fearing, industrious, honest and honorable citizens of free America and the great commonwealth of Colorado."[40]

Finally, to a great degree Pinchot was attacked in Colorado not so much for what he did as for what—or whom—he represented. For example, he most certainly served as a lightning rod for anti-Roosevelt sentiment. One Colorado politician campaigning against William Howard Taft and the continuation of Roosevelt policies in 1908 lashed out at Pinchot as the "Crown Prince" responsible for many of those policies.[41] In Congress, too, Pinchot was "sniped at" by congressmen hoping to "annoy, and perhaps even to thwart, the President whom so many of them hated."[42] In addition, while most insurgents had far less quarrel with Pinchot than with the Muir coalition, because the Forester was more visible and vulnerable than Muir, he drew fire that otherwise would have been directed at the reservationists.

The attitude of Coloradans toward Roosevelt and Pinchot clearly illustrated the divergence of opinion that existed in the state over the conservation issue. For while the two men were accorded widespread contempt in the Colorado backwoods, they also commanded a large following all across the state.

Roosevelt's support came primarily from urban centers, plains cities such as Denver, Colorado Springs, and Pueblo and Western Slope settlements like Delta and Montrose, areas dependent on the preservation of mountain watersheds for irrigation and water supplies. Statewide the president's staunchest champion was the partisan *Denver Republican* which maintained that "the man in the President's chair" was with all Coloradans "first, last, and all the time."[43] While the *Republican* constantly reminded the White House that "overconservation" could impede the development of the state, it contended that "nothing could be further from the truth" than the charge that Roosevelt had "tied up the state to miners and homesteaders and stockmen." Instead of allowing the "great coal barons and a few stock and sheepmen, railroads and their subsidiary lumber companies to denude the West," he had enhanced regional development by providing for the "preservation and proper use of the land."[44] The Roosevelt years, it declared, would be remembered in the future as "the beginning of the era in which conservation of the nation's resources took the place of national extravagance and the policy of 'sufficient unto the day is the evil thereof.'"[45]

More than once during his term urban Coloradans demonstrated their affection for the president. In the spring of 1903, for example, when Roosevelt visited Denver, he was presented a gold badge bearing the Colorado state crest while 175,000 people—almost the entire population of the city—massed along the streets to see him. A day later in Colorado Springs he rode through the city with the mayor while he was "constantly cheered" by large crowds.[46]

Roosevelt with anticonservation leader John F. Shafroth, in Denver, August 29, 1910.

Courtesy Denver Public Library, Western History Department

Away from the cities, Roosevelt was never cheered. Nevertheless, he had his defenders. Even in the northwest corner of the state, for example, where settlers had fought conservation since 1891, a local newspaper declared that "President Roosevelt should receive the support of every earnest and fair-minded person in his efforts to conserve the natural resources of the country. . . . Truly it is time the people of the country awoke to the realization of the true condition of affairs."[47]

In the vicinity of Montrose, settlers echoed the thought that whenever Roosevelt initiated regulations and rules for the reserves that would not "hamper agriculture or mining or stockraising," the reservations would be accepted. "The sentiment

Roosevelt at Rifle, Colorado, 1905.
Courtesy Denver Public Library, Western History Department

here is divided," said the *Montrose Enterprise*, "but strongly in favor of reservations which shall protect the timber and underbrush."[48] Cognizant of the fact that such sentiment, no matter how scattered, existed in the Colorado backwoods, Roosevelt worked diligently to cultivate and extend it. By enlisting allies such as J. B. Killian of Delta and Murdo MacKenzie of Trinidad, he was able to neutralize some of the cattlemen's dissent. By hunting in the White River region twice during his term and by coming into contact with local people in the process, he was able to convert occasional settlers to his cause, at least in that particular part of the state. Combining new followers with old, Roosevelt more than held his own in Colorado in the years after 1901.

The process was not as easy for Gifford Pinchot. Characterized universally by Colorado insurgents as a "fanatical zealot," a "wicked man," a "forest king"[49] carrying out the tyrannical Roosevelt policies "on the ground," Pinchot was not fully accepted in Colorado in his lifetime. Nonetheless, like Roosevelt he maintained enough support to dispel the idea that conservation was totally unpopular in the state. Many Coloradans must have agreed with the judgment of Thomas Walsh of Wolhurst that Pinchot was, in reality, a "sterling character" who "threw his heart and soul" into the business of saving the nation's natural heritage.[50] As the *Creede Candle* editorialized in 1908:

The consumption of timber is about four times as great [*in Colorado*] *as the supply or growth, and in view of this fact it is very apparent that Mr. Pinchot is acting wisely and with foresight. The impression that Mr. Pinchot is usurping too much authority is entirely wrong. . . . He is a capable, fearless, and able man carrying out the policy of the government. . . . and his name will be revered in years to come.*[51]

From the very beginning of the Roosevelt era, the central tragedy of the conservation conflict in Colorado and the rest of the West as well was the fact that the insurgents simply did not understand the motives or the methods of the progressive conservation planners. As Roderick Nash has written, even though planners and scientists may have had valid, sensible ideas for the conservation of the nation's natural wealth, it was difficult to explain them to western men born and raised on the concept of laissez-faire.[52] Actually, Colorado insurgents had little difficulty understanding the aims of John Muir and the wilderness cult. Their beliefs were clear and their goals articulated with eloquence. But the objectives of the Pinchot-Roosevelt group baffled them.

What retarded understanding most was the progressives' emphasis on "efficiency." Contrary to what some historians have written, the planners were more concerned about the question of resource use than resource ownership; they were more interested in the prevention of waste than the prevention of monopoly. Because small farmers, miners, and stockmen were primarily responsible for resource devastation, the planners often came to work against them; conversely, in that large corporations often were receptive to conservation ideas and were willing to help stabilize their fields (like lumber) in the name of efficiency, the planners often supported them.[53] The implication was clear to the pioneer class: conservation was but another instrument of big business. For this reason they saw it as hypocrisy. And no amount of assertions, such as that of Roosevelt that it was "better for the government to help a poor man make a living for his family than to help a rich man make more profit for his company,"[54] changed their minds.

In assessing the attitude of Colorado insurgents during the Roosevelt years, one final conclusion may be drawn: either the anticonservationists were bewildered and victimized by a system they did not understand, or they did understand it and shrewdly played on its weaknesses and inequities to gain sympathy for their position. As far as Colorado conservationists were concerned, opposition to their program began and ended with "land sharks and timber thieves."[55] On the other hand, however, it was true that *efficiency* was a concept totally unfamiliar to simplistic, impulsive, and often ignorant frontiersmen whose lives never had revolved and never would revolve around such abstractions. In their minds they perceived the immediate and the concrete: Pinchot and Roosevelt spoke of helping the little man, then locked up forest lands the little man needed to live on; they spoke of democracy, then took away pioneer rights; they emphasized the preservation of Turnerian principles, then isolated the land in which the principles had originated. Right or wrong, for those reasons they could not or would not accept conservation. "Why did the Almighty clothe the hills with timber," asked Henry Teller, "if it was not that they might be made beneficial to mankind? . . .

Are not homes better than forests?" His answer expressed the feelings of many: "I say . . . that the Almighty intended these forests to be used."[56]

VI. The Grass That God Has Given

The first administration of Theodore Roosevelt, from September, 1901 to March, 1905, was marked by a handful of sharp disputes between the president and western insurgents over the question of federal resource policy. In Colorado two issues predominated: federal leasing of the public domain and the continuation of grazing rules and regulations on forest reserve ranges. Both questions involved Roosevelt and dissident stockmen, and both underscored the development of two major trends on the Colorado frontier: first, the ever-increasing division between state and national conservationists and many cattlemen over federal land policy, and second, the increasing discord among the cattlemen themselves.

The leasing issue, one Roosevelt inherited, originated toward the end of the nineteenth century when conservationists, long attuned to the idea of forest preservation to the exclusion of preservation of other parts of the public domain, began to shift their attention to the Great Plains grasslands as well. Assessing the condition of the open range, they perceived several critical problems. The first was the monopolization of the range by cattle kings and large corporations who had usurped the best grasslands, triggered range wars in the process, and generally choked off the economic aspirations of others. A second problem was the widespread land fraud that accompanied monopolization. For decades spoilsmen, under the guise of seeking land for cattle grazing, had obtained millions of acres in waterpower

Cattle grazing on the open range in Colorado.
Courtesy Denver Public Library, Western History Department

sites, mineral lands, and unreserved timberlands from the federal government. The last, and most important, problem was the overgrazing of the range.

Conservationists were distressed by range conditions for several reasons. Monopoly, for example, made a mockery of the free enterprise system and damaged both the economic and democratic rights of little cattlemen. Land fraud resulted in widespread resource exploitation and waste. And overgrazing, which resulted in increasing damage to range forage each year, threatened the very existence of the cattle industry. Motivated, as in the area of forest protection, by their interest in (or obsession with) efficiency, conservationist-scientists arrived at the conclusion that only a comprehensive system of range management undertaken and overseen by the federal government could save the range from annihilation. In their opinion the inauguration of a federal leasing plan which would limit the number of animals on any given range at any time, coupled with range improvement programs and studies in the growth, care, reseeding, and management of pastures, would do for the open range what forest reserves had done for the timberlands.[1]

From the moment the leasing idea surfaced in Colorado, it became a bitterly debated issue. No doubt, of course, the state was ripe for reform. As historian Hubert H. Bancroft has written, "the most objectionable feature" of Colorado's cattle industry was "the absolute control of immense tracts" of its range by "companies and individuals," particularly in Weld, Arapaho, Bent, Las Animas, Elbert, and Pueblo counties.[2] By no means, however, did all state cattlemen agree that the remedy for such a condition was federal land rental. Just as they were divided over the issue of forest reserves, so were they at odds over the question of leasing.[3]

Throughout the West leasing was consistently supported by large cattlemen. In most cases they had multiple motives: they hoped that federal range regulation would stabilize range conditions, make cattle growing more profitable, and fence out both sheepmen and nesting farmers.[4] It was their assumption, of course, that through their considerable power and influence they would receive the best leases from the government. Thus they would get to keep what they had—the bulk of the range and the best lands—legally. The idea of federal guardianship of the land probably was repugnant to them, just as it was to those who opposed leasing. But leasing offered them a means of survival at a time when their long-private domain was beginning to slip out of their hands. As unlike the conservationists as they were, they still willingly joined them.

For the most part, Colorado's more affluent cattlemen followed the western pattern and supported leasing. A good example was Murdo MacKenzie of Trinidad. Though he consistently disclaimed any "personal financial interest in the public range,"[5] it was a well-known fact that he possessed both close ties to the Roosevelt administration and a massive section of the public domain in southern Colorado that could best be stabilized and maintained under a leasing plan. Whether or not the size of MacKenzie's range and his support for leasing were coincidental was speculative. Certainly, however, he and others like him—especially a dozen or so cattle kings in Park and Routt counties—were vulnerable to criticism.

Unlike the larger cattlemen, who enjoyed a great degree of unanimity on the leasing question, Colorado's small stockmen were deeply divided by it. The vast majority of them opposed leasing, at least in the beginning, but enough of them supported it from the start to cause considerable dissention in their ranks. Those few who advocated a leasehold system did so chiefly in the belief that it would both root out range monopoly and halt the overgrazing of the grasslands. Few aspects of plains life were of deeper concern to fringe operators than the decimation of the grasslands. As one distraught Colorado rancher said in 1900 after his evaluation of a local range, "for the past twenty years we have been destroying the grass on the range at an ever-increasing rate. We have been burning the candle at both ends. . . . Ten days ago I passed over miles of desert which only a few years ago I remember to be good grazing land. Today the grass is utterly swept away as if it had never been."[6] As for the question of monopoly, they hoped that a leasing system impartially administered by the government would allow them to assert their rights in those parts of the public domain where they always before had been treated as intruders. They had little patience with their opponents. As one of them concluded, only those

who are in peaceful possession of the range, who have no questions to solve, and who are not disturbed in the possession of their grazing lands, and not put to the trouble, annoyance, expense and loss that some others have, are in favor of letting things go. . . . It is hardly fair for those Colorado men who have no grievances . . . to insist that no remedy be provided for those who do.[7]

Significantly, the leasers among the small cattlemen largely misunderstood the nature of their opposition. Perhaps logically, they believed that the nucleus of antileasing sentiment in Colorado was composed of large cattlemen fearful of being thrown off their ranges by federal edict and therefore prepared to fight any concept that might undermine their power. In reality, however, most of the antileasing sentiment in the state was voiced by their own fellows—by small cattlemen fearful that leasing fostered by a government traditionally friendly to big business in any field would only further entrench cattle kings on the domain they occupied. Far from being in "peaceful possession of the range" and certainly not in favor of "letting things go," they simply believed that leasing was not the answer to range problems. Vocalizing what was a very prevalent fear, the *Rocky Mountain News* declared that leasing would lead directly to the "grabbing up of practically all the public domain by cattle syndicates" who had "pull with the officials." The result, to the detriment of all who had "small flocks and herds" and to farmers who utilized land next to their homesteads for grazing purposes, would be "monopolies of the most gigantic character" in Colorado and the rest of the West.[8] Asserting that "more than 90% of the people" of northern Colorado opposed leasing, the *Middle Park Times* added that the land, a "heritage of the people," would become the "heritage of cattle companies and corporations" under a leasing system, thus destroying in the process the "masses" which composed "the bone and sinew of this country."[9]

Assessing the leasing attitudes of Colorado cattlemen in the early 1900's, one is struck by the high degree of correlation between them and their attitudes regarding forest reserves. That is to say, stockmen tended, generally, to view the two issues the same way. Large cattlemen who supported leasing usually supported forest reserves—and for the same reasons. It was more than coincidental that the same men active in the leasing campaign—large operators like Murdo MacKenzie—also stood among the administration's staunchest supporters on the question of forest conservation. And, just as they were divided on leasing, small cattlemen remained at odds on the subject of reserves. Those in favor of both argued one point: that their implementation would "democratize" the use of the range. Those against both utilized a different theme: that federal regulation would achieve the opposite. Exceptions to the rule existed, of course; some cattlemen were antileasing, for example, and for forest reserves. But for the most part the pattern was constant. Most importantly, if the two issues of leasing and forest conservation had ever been separate, they began to intertwine during the first several years of the new century. It might be said, further, that in terms of shattering the cattlemen's ranks, leasing finished the job that the forest-reserve issue had begun.

Throughout the conservation era both pro- and antileasers tirelessly sought to establish both political and economic hegemony in the state. The leasers, led by MacKenzie, A. E. DeRicqles of Denver, J. B. Killian of Delta, Merle Vincent of Paonia, and J. A. Lockhart of Rocky Ford, maintained the position that, as one of them stated it, "in all grazing territories in the West" lay "graves of stockmen" serving as "monuments to the folly of permitting the free use of the public domain by private individuals without governmental supervision or control."[10] Antileasers, led by Elias Ammons of Castle Rock, Edward Taylor of Glenwood Springs, and Isaac Baer and B. F. Montgomery of Meeker, countered that federal control of the range not only would perpetuate monopoly but would grant a "very dangerous political power" to the federal government as well.[11] Had the small cattlemen found some way to remain in agreement on the issue, they might have survived the conservation period as a reasonably united body. But, divided on the lease question and on the forest-reserve issue as well, not only did they fail to establish a sensible, equitable policy for their industry, but they destroyed whatever cohesiveness they had ever had.

The leasing issue, on a more or less regional level, first emerged in the early months of 1898. During the course of the First Annual National Livestock Growers Association Convention in Denver, when the Texas delegation proposed the cession of unreserved public lands to the various states for leasing purposes, the Colorado delegation objected. In a long floor speech, C. H. Harris of Glenwood Springs denounced the resolution on the grounds that any leasing arrangement invariably would favor large cattlemen over small. As it was, said the Coloradan, the public domain was at least relatively accessible to small cattlemen. But leasing would drive them "absolutely from the range."[12] The resolution was defeated.

In January, 1899, at the convention of the newly formed National Livestock Association in Denver, the leasers struck back. Conrad Schaefer, a member of the Colorado delegation, introduced a resolution similar to the one killed in Denver the year before calling on the federal government to cede its arid lands to the states for the purpose of leasing them. Facing his own neighbors, Schaefer declared that he was "not afraid that the legislature of Colorado" would "injure its own people" by leasing indiscriminately to large cattle concerns. Other members of the Colorado delegation disagreed. Ignoring the contention of John Springer of Denver that federal land cessions would enable the government of Colorado to "deal with its citizens and pass just laws leasing these great tracts of land," preventing, in the process, their "acquisition by syndicates and corporations," Coloradans voted virtually as a bloc against the proposal. Most other delegations also opposed it, and, as in 1898, it was defeated.[13] Round two went to the insurgents.

By the time the National Livestock Association convened again in Fort Worth in January of 1900, the leasing issue had emerged, along with the forest-reserve question, as the dominant one of the day among western cattlemen. Man for man the Colorado delegation still continued to oppose leasing. And, as it left for Fort Worth, the delegation was exhorted by the *Rocky Mountain News* not to vacillate: "While corporate cattle interests are backing measures to lease the public domain, the great majority of stockmen are in favor of free range. . . . It is a fact that the great corporations are doing their best to drive small herd owners out of business, and . . . this attempt of cattle syndicates to acquire control of the public domain must be resisted to the utmost."[14]

On the opening day of the convention a major fight materialized over the leasing issue. After John Springer opened the proceedings with a plea to the "citizens of the country" to support the conservation of "the great tracts of wild grazing land" in the West, a resolution was introduced—as in 1898 and 1899—advocating the leasing of all unreserved western grasslands, that the federal government (and not state governments) might bring them to "a state of usefulness."[15] During debate over the resolution, most of the Coloradans amplified their old fear that leasing would lend itself to corporate control of the range. It was the "simple desire" of the small cattlemen, said E. A. Harris of Sterling, "that the public domain be left alone."[16] On the other hand, J. G. Northcutt of Trinidad, a close personal friend of Murdo MacKenzie, accused Harris and others of acting out of self-interest. Addressing the convention, Northcutt asked whether the convention was going to take positive action to conserve the range or "have it eaten from your door, from your lawn, and from your back door" by the herds of nomadic cattlemen.[17] Ultimately the resolution was defeated. Eight Colorado cattlemen's associations voted for it, and eleven voted against it. In the end it seemed that the majority agreed with George Patrick of Pueblo. "We simply desire," he said, "that the public domain be left alone."[18]

Fearful that the McKinley administration might take the convention's consideration of the leasing idea (even if it did defeat it) as a sign of increasing interest in leasing among cattlemen, Colorado stockmen embarked on a campaign in February and March to stir up antileasing sentiment throughout the state. Their objective was to make themselves heard in Washington, perhaps to discourage Pinchot and his coterie of planners from generating any sustained interest in the concept. Interestingly, most of the antileasing activity took place in a region already strongly against forest reserves. On February 14, at a mass rally on the perimeter of the White River Forest Reserve at Steamboat Springs, Colorado stockmen expressed their belief that leasing was nothing more than a "well-disguised scheme inaugurated by the big cattle and sheep syndicates to forever shut out the settler and small stock owner from any future interests" on the public domain.[19] A few days later, at a raucous meeting in Glenwood Springs called by the powerful Roaring Fork and Eagle River Stock Growers Association, insurgents gathered several hundred people together to denounce leasing. Among crowds of cattlemen from Garfield, Eagle, Rio Blanco, Gunnison, and Routt counties, a few leasers attempted to defend their position. But they were rudely shouted down.

Edward Taylor, the fiery state senator from Eagle and Garfield counties,[20] sounded the keynote of the meeting. "We must strain every nerve to preserve the present condition of affairs" on the public range, he said. "We hope to arouse the sentiment of Colorado, and we must demand that the government protect the small stock owner" from the incursions of the cattle kings.[21] W. L. Grubb of Carbondale followed with an attack on large cattlemen allegedly "planning and scheming" to take over the range under a leasing system. And George Yule of Divide Creek terminated the meeting with a ringing defense of small Colorado stockmen seeking protection "against the range syndicates and large corporations" that sought to "grab every range for their own selfish interests."[22] Stamping their feet and waving their hats in the air, the cattlemen adopted a resolution declaring themselves in permanent opposition to leasing. Applauding their action, the *Rocky Mountain News* sternly warned the government that "these resolutions may be accepted as expressive of the opinion of the whole range country outside the circle of large corporate combinations. Farmers, homesteaders, and small stockmen are bitterly opposed to the leasing system . . . and the wrath of the people is sure to follow those who . . . turn over the ranges to the big corporations."[23]

Lest the Colorado protest go unheard in national political circles, Governor Charles Thomas, together with several other western governors, journeyed to Washington late in February to present his state's antileasing case to the McKinley administration. When Thomas returned to Denver he found word circulating throughout Colorado that a leasing bill was about to be introduced in Congress. Colorado congressmen, convinced that leasing would be no less paternalistic than forest reserves, bristled in defense of the rights of their state. Senator Edward Wolcott vowed to contest any legislation which failed to protect the interests of small cattlemen. Henry Teller, condemning the leasing idea as an "insane notion," expressed opposition to it on the grounds that it would stunt Colorado's economic development, curtail the private ownership of land, and impede future settlement.[24] John Shafroth and John Bell, as always, sided with Teller. Said Bell: "I hope there will be no leasing passed. . . . I am opposed to any meddling with the present condition of the public domain. The moment the idea of leasing gets into the heads of the people, the whole object will be to derive a revenue . . . to the great detriment of the people."[25] Despite such opposition, a leasing bill was introduced into Congress in March, 1900, by Senator William Stevens of Texas. Warmly endorsed by the McKinley administration, it outraged Colorado insurgents.

The Stevens bill prompted a new round of protest in Colorado, especially on its Western Slope. From Craig to Gunnison, in rally after rally, insurgent cattlemen vented their anger and called for regional unity in fighting the leasing proposal. Encouraged by the popular response to their position, they finally called for the creation of a new cattlemen's organization to be composed exclusively of Coloradans and dedicated to combating the leasing idea. Spurred on by the *Rocky Mountain News*, which demanded "an emphatic protest against the consummation of any [leasing] wrong on the people of the public land states," the antileasers scheduled a convention for Denver on April 9.[26]

In the chill weather of early April, as bands of cattlemen drifted into the capital city from across the state, antileasing feeling ran high. On muddy street corners, over saloon bars, in the back rooms of the Brown Palace, most cattlemen echoed the feelings of W. J. Grubb of Carbondale that "anyone acquainted with conditions throughout Colorado knows that if leasing kills off the stock industry, great injury will be inflicted upon everybody."[27] From all sections of the state stockmen reported that leasing was under fire. Hugh Torrance of White River told a Denver newspaper that "half of the ranchers in my county will move out if this Stevens bill passes Congress. . . . You won't find many men on the Western Slope in favor of leasing." From the arid eastern plains (an area that favored conservation when it pertained to forests but opposed it when it applied to local grasslands), A. B. Foster of Emma concurred that "everyone in our country is opposed to the leasing of the public lands. We are opposed to meddling with the public domain."[28] The Stevens bill, it appeared, had few supporters in Denver in April.[29]

On the morning of April 9, five hundred cattlemen were gaveled to order at the old Tabor Opera House. Then, in a daylong tirade, dozens of antileasing addresses were made. Most followed the theme set forth by Thomas M. Patterson, editor of the *Rocky Mountain News*, who demanded that "until the public lands are purchased by actual settlers, they must be kept free and open to all." In the late afternoon, to a standing ovation, Governor Thomas ended the day's activities with a passionate appeal to the cattlemen to "resist the leasing policy—and resist it as stoutly as you can. . . . Your cause is one which appeals to the justice of man!"[30]

The speeches terminated, the cattlemen turned to other business. With little debate they passed a bluntly worded antileasing resolution by a unanimous vote. In an emphatic denunciation of all proposed lease laws as "unAmerican and contradictory to the interest and development of our state," they argued that free range was and had been part of their heritage since the beginning of the nation, and that its loss would constitute a serious "breach of faith on the part of the government." Leasing would cause the depreciation of property values, promote ruinous litigation over the range, and virtually paralyze western homesteading. Worst of all, they concluded, adhering to an old theme, leasing would allow small cattlemen to be "devoured" by large cattle interests acting in connivance with the secretary of the interior.[31] The cattlemen were happy with their action. W. M. Hammond of the North Fork Valley Stockgrowers Association summed up what seemed to be the general feeling of his fellows: "Cattlemen have had free range since time immemorial, and it is not their desire to surrender their right to the range of the public domain" without a fight.[32]

In their final action, taken just before adjournment, the delegates officially formed the Western Range Stock Growers Association and dedicated it to fighting the leasing idea for as long as it took to defeat it.

In the midst of Colorado's agitation, the Stevens bill was killed in congressional committee. Insurgent cattlemen, however, had little time or inclination to rejoice. The *Rocky Mountain News* grimly warned them that the leasing concept itself had "not been killed" but was only "sleeping on the tables of Congress," ready to "spring up again, and maybe succeed." Said the *News*, it could be beaten "only with constant vigilance."[33] The words were prophetic. Even as the cattlemen trooped out of Denver through late winter snows back to the range, Californian John Irish, a conservationist, an ardent leasing advocate, and a prominent leader of the National Livestock Association, angrily served notice upon them that "California has nine members in Congress to Colorado's four, and we are going to put our ideas into law and if necessary pass a leasing bill over your protests. I give you fair notice that I'll trip you up in Congress."[34] The executive committee of the association, headed by John Springer and Conrad Schaefer of Colorado, met immediately to draft a new leasing bill for presentation to Congress.

With the death of the Stevens bill, the leasing furor subsided in Colorado, but only momentarily. In the fall of 1900, during statewide and congressional elections, candidates from both political parties campaigned on antileasing platforms. Surprisingly—in that they ran counter to the position of their national party—more Colorado Republicans campaigned against leasing than did Democrats. The state Republican party inserted a strong antileasing plank in its general platform asserting "unalterable" opposition to "any legislation that would deprive the farmer or small stock-holder from the unrestricted use of the public domain."[35] A Republican assembly at Meeker in Routt County refused nomination or endorsement to any candidate for office who did not specifically oppose leasing. Incumbent Senator Edward O. Wolcott sought and received the endorsement of cattlemen on the basis of his well-known opposition to leasing, and Republican Robert Bonynge of Denver, a candidate for the House of Representatives, ran on a platform that sharply condemned the Stevens plan. Democrats swept the state on the coattails of William Jennings Bryan, and both Wolcott and Bonynge lost. But they and others succeeded in keeping the leasing issue alive and controversial.[36]

If at the beginning of 1901 it appeared to Colorado insurgents that they had finally turned back the leasing challenge of Washington conservationists and their cattleman allies, they were wrong. Even though no mention was made of the issue when the National Livestock Association met in Salt Lake City in January, when the new American Cattle Growers Association held its first annual meeting in Denver in March, leasing was the primary topic.[37] At the Tabor Opera House, crowded and sweltering on March 7, John Irish presented a stringent proleasing resolution to the assembly. Led by Frank Goudy, a prominent Denver lawyer and unsuccessful Republican candidate for governor in 1900, the antileasers protested vehemently. They achieved nothing. Despite the fact that the *Denver Republican* (paradoxically, proforest reserve but antileasing) insisted that "the majority of the cattlemen actually on the floor of the convention . . . were opposed to any leasehold system,"[38] the resolution passed. The opponents of leasing were beginning to learn, slowly, what was to become an increasingly painful fact of life: that while they dominated in Colorado, their influence in national cattlemen's circles was on the wane. They could dictate policy at home, but intermingled with growing numbers of proleasing delegations, largely from the southwest, in national conventions, they were fast becoming a small, impotent minority.

In the fall of 1901, Theodore Roosevelt inherited the leasing imbroglio. If insurgent stockmen expected him to side with them, they misjudged him, just as they had initially on the forest reserve question. As early as 1888, Roosevelt, like many of them, had lamented the monopolization and overstocking of range grasslands by individual cattlemen to the detriment of others.[39] But, unlike them, he saw leasing as a cure for range problems rather than a perpetuation of the status quo. Motivated by his own personal faith in applied science and influenced further by Gifford Pinchot and his group of conservation planners, Roosevelt believed that the adoption of a federal leasing system would lead to a sustained-yield range program that would save the grasslands. Although he realized that his advocacy of leasing would force him to depend chiefly on large cattlemen for support, alienating small farmers and cattlemen in the process, apparently he felt that he had little choice in the matter. "The necessity for range conservation,"

Samuel Hays has written, "tipped the scales in favor of the [large] cattlemen."[40] The president immediately came to the support of the leasers.

Insurgent Colorado stockmen no more understood or condoned Roosevelt's approval of leasing than they did his support for forest reserves. Again, to their minds, he spoke of helping little men, only to give his backing to stockowners like Murdo MacKenzie. While the president maintained that "there should be full participation by local people in the management of the range,"[41] insurgents felt that his actions belied his words. Disregarding the contention of such Roosevelt loyalists as John Springer, who argued that Roosevelt would give small stockmen a "square deal,"[42] antileasing cattlemen became and remained convinced that Roosevelt aimed at nothing less than an "absentee landlord system" that would make Coloradans "tenants of the Federal Government."[43]

With the approval of the administration, conservationists introduced three new leasing bills into Congress in late 1901 and early 1902. The most important of the three, a measure introduced by Senator Justin D. Bowersock of Kansas, provided for the leasing of all western public lands at a uniform rate of two cents an acre and gave leasing preference not only to owners of cultivated land bordering on the public domain but to "stockgrowers who were in actual use and occupancy of the public domain in 1900."[44] In that those in "actual use and occupancy" of most of the public domain in 1900 were large cattlemen, the insurgents sensed conspiracy. Criticizing the measure as "singularly high-handed and inept," holding it up as "proof" of collusion between cattle kings and federal government to drive them off the range, they mobilized to fight it.[45]

At its second annual meeting in Denver in March, 1902, the American Cattle Growers Association endorsed the Bowersock bill just as it had endorsed the leasing idea in the past. When Nebraska delegates offered a resolution advocating passage of the bill, only the Colorado contingent protested. In the "most spirited incident" of the convention, Frank Goudy took the floor to indict the proposal. His efforts to amend it, however, failed; his proposal—that the Bowersock bill place restrictions on the amount of land leasable by any one man—was rejected, and the original resolution passed unaltered.[46]

The association's action, arrogant and irresponsible in the eyes of anticonservation cattlemen, propelled their organizations into action throughout Colorado. In late February the Gunnison County Stockgrowers Association ignited statewide protest with the passage of resolutions demanding the absolute "discontinuance of the leasing of the public domain in any form."[47] A number of large rallies were held in the agitated cattle country around Craig, all resulting in the passage of similar resolutions. Analyzing local feeling, the *Routt County Courier* admitted that, while the free range faced serious damage by uncontrolled herds, leasing was not the remedy for the problem. "The final solution," said the *Courier*, was "the individual ownership of the land" by small cattlemen.[48] In neighboring Rifle, long a hotbed of antileasing feeling, the Grand River Stockgrowers went on record against the Bowersock bill as a "lever" for northwest Colorado cattle kings.[49] And so it went up and down the continental divide.

In the midst of the clamor the Colorado Cattle and Horse Growers Association gingerly approached the question at its annual meeting in Denver in March.[50] Much had happened to the association, originally conceived in antileasing militancy, in its two years of existence. Its character had been sharply altered by two factors: a gradual infiltration of the organization by numerous proleasing stockmen (mainly members of the American Cattle Growers Association) and the conversion of some original members to the leasing position. At the association's 1901 meeting, leasers had been strong enough to vote down an antileasing resolution; but in 1902 they failed. After a wild, name-calling two-day debate, insurgent cattlemen succeeded in formulating a condemnation of the Bowersock bill into a series of resolutions which then were passed. One newspaper reported that the leasers had "tried in every way to spike the guns of the anti-leasers, but . . . were lucky to get out with their scalps."[51] The *Saguache Crescent* gloated that

> *it was pitiable to see the few erstwhile big guns in the cattle business trying to hold their own. Their voices rose like the wail of a lost soul in purgatory. . . . The day of the extensive ranch has reached its twilight stage. The individual or corporation controlling millions of acres . . . must soon in the economy of things give way to the little man who looks after hundreds of fine cattle with care and puts the kibosh on the whole leasing propaganda.*[52]

In April, congressional committees opened hearings in Washington on the Bowersock bill. Henry Teller, irascible and in a fighting mood, bluntly declared that he was prepared to exhaust himself opposing the bill in the Senate Committee on Public Lands.[53] He was not given the opportunity to carry out his threat; the bill was killed in the House Committee on Public Lands after a bitter round of hearings pitting John Bell against John Irish of California. In several heated exchanges with Irish, Bell vehemently claimed that "barely a baker's dozen of stockmen in the state of Colorado would favor passage of the bill" and that countless small stockmen would suffer grave economic loss if it were enacted into law.[54] Irish, enraged at Bell's obstinacy, insisted that what the West most desperately needed was an airing of the "wrongdoings" of specific Colorado cattlemen—especially those who operated in Bell's district. A leasing law, said Irish, would bring more justice to the Colorado range than anywhere else in the West. Bell countered that Colorado stockmen were as honorable as any other western pioneers, and he insisted again that the result of any leasing law would be irreparable damage to small stockmen and homesteaders who would be barred from the range.[55]

When the Bowersock bill was killed in committee, picked apart by irreconcilables like Bell, the insurgents voiced approval. One happy Colorado newspaper summed up the feeling of many western Coloradans: "The stockman will now be left alone to pursue his chosen vocation without fear of being driven off the face of the earth by syndicates. . . . It has to be shown to Congress that land leasing and settlement under homestead laws are diametrically opposed to each other, and cannot be tolerated at the same time."[56] Jubilation, however, was short-lived. No sooner was the Bowersock bill buried than another was introduced into the House by John Lacey of Iowa, chairman of the House Committee on Public Lands and one of the most ardent conservationists in Congress.

Though somewhat similar to its predecessor in its general provisions, the Lacey bill was markedly less discriminatory toward small cattlemen. Its major provisions reduced the period of leasing from ten to five years to lessen the likelihood of monopoly; limited to 320 the number of acres that any one individual could lease; raised the rental fee from two to six cents an acre, again to discourage monopoly; and made it mandatory that leases be granted only to homesteaders and small stockmen—and under no circumstances to known syndicates or corporations. Because of its sensible provisions, many Colorado cattlemen, even some insurgents, were satisfied with the bill. M. J. McMillan of Carlton, writing to Lacey on behalf of the Bent and Prowers County Cattle and Horse Growers Association, stated the sentiment of many of his fellows: that drastic measures needed to be enacted to protect the range for small cattlemen before they were forced out of business by others. Lacey's bill, many thought, appeared to be the most workable solution to the problem.[57]

Most of the anticonservation cattlemen were unimpressed, however, and in Colorado they greeted the Lacey bill with a new round of protest meetings in the early spring of 1902. Their efforts were rewarded. In Washington the bill was pigeonholed by the House Committee on Public Lands, and again it was John Bell who helped lead the action. In the summer of 1902 a third bill also was shelved by the House, thus completing the destruction of all leasing measures introduced in the first

Roosevelt years. The president himself was disgusted and appalled. In early 1903, in his first public utterance on the subject of leasing, Roosevelt stated that "the general lack of control in the use of public grazing lands has resulted . . . in overgrazing and the ruin of millions of acres otherwise suitable for grazing. Some form of government control is necessary" on the range.[58] The implication was that leasing was the only way to achieve "governmental control."

The majority of western cattlemen continued to balk. In January, 1903, the National Livestock Association met in Kansas City and failed to support the president with a leasing resolution. Obstructionists, like most of those in the Colorado delegation, controlled the meeting. And even association president John Springer (who unaccountably vacillated on the leasing issue almost from year to year) lashed out at the leasers. In a statement apparently aimed at conservationist politicians, like Pinchot, who fought for leasing under the guise of "helping the people," Springer charged that "all these crocodile tears shed every election by politicians about the public lands being sacred; that they should be kept for our children; that they belong to the whole people, ad nauseum, is pure tommyrot. They want some office, hence the awful solicitude about the public lands."[59] Despite Roosevelt's words it appeared that the leasing idea was moribund, at least for the moment.

One reason why leasing provoked such extensive controversy in Colorado during the first Roosevelt term was that cattlemen remained divided on other issues as well, primarily that of forest reserves and the grazing restrictions on them. The situation, of course, was not peculiar to Colorado. In Wyoming, for example, cattlemen persuaded Senators Clarence Clark and Francis Warren to work in Congress for the abolition of grazing permits on reserve ranges. Allegedly speaking for stock interests in their states, senators from Montana, Idaho, and Utah concurred, but all to no avail.[60] During the same period, congressmen from Washington and Idaho worked, unsuccessfully, for the prohibition of any further reserves in any western state.[61] On the other hand, proreserve agitation continued in the same regions. In Arizona, sheepmen placated by the opening up of several key reserves to grazing began to give their support to federal land policy.[62] In southern Oregon, where sheep interests had long balked at federal law, the *Portland Oregonian* not only supported existing reserves, but constantly lobbied for more.[63] And even South Dakota Senator Richard Pettigrew, once an archenemy of federal reservations, now spoke in favor of them. "I believe the forest reserve law was a good one," he said, "and that it has been of great advantage to the West, and that we ought to keep these forests, keep down the fires, and renew the forests as trees are cut down."[64]

In Colorado pro- and antireserve cattlemen collided on numerous occasions between 1901 and 1905. Their major point of contention was the so-called transfer plan, a conservationist proposal sponsored by Pinchot and his group of planners to transfer jurisdiction of the forest-reserve system from the Department of Interior to the Department of Agriculture. From the viewpoint of the conservationists the plan was highly logical. For a full decade reserve lands had been under the control of the Interior Department, which did not contain a forestry bureau. Paradoxically, the Agriculture Department, which maintained a progressive Bureau of Forestry under Pinchot, had no authority whatever in conjunction with the system. Desirous of bringing the reserves under his control that he might apply enlightened forestry practices to them and halt their constant deterioration, Pinchot called for a change.

Colorado stockmen disagreed on the proposal, though not as sharply as on other questions. Conservationists, of course, happily ratified the plan, and they were joined by some who cared less about conservation than about the establishment of order by the federal government on ranges they still hoped to dominate. Surprisingly, many insurgents, such as Elias Ammons, also agreed to the transfer, but only in hopes that Pinchot would allow broader use of the reserves than that allowed by the Interior Department.[65] Irreconcilables, on the other hand, wanted no transfer, reasoning that over the years they had learned to coexist with the Interior Department and its policies (and its notably lax enforcement of many reserve laws). Their assumption was that under a zealot like Pinchot their lives would be made considerably less comfortable.

In early 1902 a transfer measure was introduced into Congress by Congressman John F. Lacey of Iowa. Sanctioned and supported by the Roosevelt administration and the American conservation establishment, the bill was reported favorably out of the House Public Lands Committee in late March. The committee's unanimity was destroyed, however, by a minority report filed by John Shafroth, Frank Mondell of Wyoming, and William Jones of Washington. Shafroth's point was one shared by most western insurgents: that dual jurisdiction on the reserves—the Interior Department still ruling on land-lieu selections and mining claims while the Agriculture Department maintained overall control—would create more red tape than ever for reserve settlers. Despite the westerners' obstructionism, however, the Lacey bill moved ahead.

In June, as time to vote on the transfer bill drew near, Shafroth and John Bell spearheaded renewed opposition to it. In an address to the House on June 2, Shafroth repeated his long-standing objections to the transfer, re-emphasizing his belief that dual control of the reserves would create immense problems for local settlers forced to deal with not one, but two, hostile departments. And in a bitter supplement to Shafroth's argument, Bell declared:

. . . we in the West are opposed generally to any change in this respect. . . . We have had this question of the timber reserves up for the last eight or nine years. We have, with great patience and endurance, found out what the theory of the Secretary of the Interior is. We have now come to the point where we can deal with him. . . . Must we now learn to conform to another

chief's way of running these reserves and be a shuttlecock between the two departments? . . . We want none of it in Colorado. . . . As it is, the settlers are so prejudiced against these reservations in Colorado that they are, as it were, up in arms for the repeal of every reservation in the state.[66]

On June 9, the day before the final House vote on the bill, Bell made another address, attacking the reserves in general and angrily warning the "friends of the reserves" that "those who are so anxious for these reserves, if they insist on these continued encroachments . . . will find every man from the western domain coming in here with one voice and asking to abolish every one of these reserves within the limits of these states."[67]

On June 10, 1902, the House voted on the Lacey bill. It was killed, at least temporarily, and the insurgents were satisfied. From Oregon, where the state legislature memorialized Congress to keep reserves out of the hands of those with only "theoretical learning" in regard to western land problems, to Colorado the consensus seemed to be, as the *Denver Republican* phrased it, that "a great deal of dissatisfaction" existed with the transfer idea.[68]

Anticonservation cattlemen, especially those operating on ranges in southern Colorado, had little inclination to celebrate their victory. In the midst of the transfer debate, almost as if to impress insurgents with the futility of their cause, Theodore Roosevelt created a large new reserve in the heart of some of the most spectacular mountain country in Colorado. On April 11, 1902, he proclaimed the San Isabel Forest Reserve—the first major land withdrawal in the state in ten years.

The San Isabel was an impressive conservationist prize. Embracing 77,980 acres of wild timberland in Fremont, Custer, Huerfano, and Saguache counties, it stretched nearly seventy miles north and south, taking in the mammoth Sangre de Cristo Range and its countless vital watersheds. Originating in the ragged foothills south of Salida, the reservation angled along the crest of the Sangre de Cristos southeasterly to a point near Moffat; then, curling sharply around the Great Sand Dunes, it abruptly ended north of Fort Garland on the slopes of Mount Blanca. Pocked with hundreds of alpine lakes, criss-crossed by streams which penetrated nearby valleys, the San Isabel quickly became as important as any reserve in the state. No regions in Colorado were any more critical to its agricultural economy than the Saguache, Wet Mountain, and San Luis valleys. And their permanent welfare was made secure by Roosevelt's action.

The San Isabel proclamation was incontrovertible proof that the alliance between professional conservationists (those operating out of the Colorado State Forestry Association) and proconservation cattlemen was having an effect on Colorado. The reserve was far less the work of outsiders and eastern theorists than that of local stockmen who desired their land protected from timber destruction.[69] As the *Saguache Crescent* explained, San Luis Valley cattlemen had badgered the government "for several months" for a reserve.[70] If any antireserve cattlemen resided in the region, they offered no opposition to the government's action. Only later did they react, agitated by charges of the *Salida Mail* that the Interior Department had been "misinformed about the condition of the country and the timber on it" when it made the withdrawal. There had been, said the *Mail*, "a nigger in the fence, and some parties have a scheme for graft in embroyo."[71]

If 1902 produced mixed results for anticonservation cattlemen, 1903 was a deeply disturbing year. The transfer idea, for example, was revived. At the annual National Livestock Association convention in Kansas City, the Arizona delegation proposed a resolution advocating the shift. The primary spokesman for the idea was Colorado's John Springer, who complained that at the Department of Interior stockmen could not "get in the front door" to have grievances heard.[72] To the anticonservationists' dismay, the resolution passed. A few weeks later the continuing erosion of the stockmen's solidarity was illustrated again at the annual Denver meeting of the Colorado Cattle and Horse Growers Association. In a keynote address delivered to an organization once dedicated to combating leasing, association President Lloyd Grubb demanded that Colorado cattlemen "invite all the people to join us in a crusade against forest abuse and thus cause the government to enact laws that will produce in the heart of every man the feeling of respect and sacredness for every tree in the forest."[73]

The next day the association passed resolutions endorsing grazing permits and regulations on forest reserves. While they failed to make their voices heard, insurgent cattlemen stubbornly refused to compromise their position. Most of them remained determined to keep up the fight against federal reservations "set aside on the petition of the National Forestry Association, with headquarters in some codfish district of Massachusetts or Maine, the members of which know no more about the Western conditions than a Filipino does about Latin."[74]

For all their bravado and confidence, insurgent cattlemen saw their fellows defecting everywhere they looked. In the fall of 1903, for example, settlers and proconservation cattlemen from all over the Plum Creek-South Platte Reserve areas met at Castle Rock with local rangers to "ratify" the existence of the two reserves and the employment of grazing permits and other regulations on them.[75] At the same time, the South Park Ranchmen's Protective Association of Fairplay sought the aid of local rangers in halting illegal timber cutting on the South Platte Reserve. Writing W. A. Richards, the commissioner of the General Land Office, the association secretary complained that even though local rangers did their best to "help us keep the timber on the reserve and preserve our water supply," more help was urgently needed. He concluded that, while "the people in the towns are complaining of the ranger for not letting them cut timber, nevertheless he is doing the best thing for the ranchers, which is the best thing for the country at large as they pay the taxes and are here to stay and not here today and gone tomorrow like those Tie Chopers [sic] and contractors and sawmill men."[76]

Such sentiment must have gratified the federal government, and certainly it led to the impression that there had been a "notable improvement in public sentiment in relation to forestry" in Colorado.[77] On the other hand, the increasing exodus of cattlemen to the ranks of the conservationists only further reinforced the anticonservation attitudes of those who remained behind, those who felt increasingly—as one of them stated it—"crowded to the wall" by federal land policies.[78] Speaking for them in Congress during the Fifty-eighth session, Henry Teller promised continued action against the government's "disposition to set apart land for parks or forest reserves or for any other purpose save that of settlement."[79]

In late 1903, increasingly dismayed and frustrated by the leasing stalemate and the continuation of opposition to western forest reserves, President Roosevelt resolved to settle both questions. In an attempt to determine precisely where the West stood, regionally and collectively, on the two major conservation issues of the day, he appointed a Public Lands Commission to travel through the territory, hold public hearings on the question of federal land policy, and report findings and recommendations back to him. Specifically, the commission's assignment was to investigate the "conditions, operations, and effect" of existing national land laws, to suggest changes in them, and to propose ways in which the government could "secure in permanence the fullest and most effective use of the resources of the public lands."[80]

Because of the tension over reserves and leasing in the West, the activities of the commission augured trouble. The commission scheduled two meetings in Colorado, in January and August of 1904. And news of its coming "stirred up a hornets' nest," setting conservationists against insurgents and cattlemen against cattlemen and opening up wounds that would never be closed again.[81]

On the bitterly cold morning of January 22, 1904, two members of the commission—Gifford Pinchot and Frederick Newell of the Reclamation Service—opened hearings in Denver. Several hundred cattlemen from all over Colorado crowded into the Denver Chamber of Commerce Building, eager to carry their ideas for or against conservation to the president's emissaries. The anticonservationists were better organized, their singular objective being to "protest against the reserves and public land conditions. . . . To impress upon Pinchot and Newell . . . the belief among landowners and stockmen that repeal of present land laws would be disastrous to the development of the West, and that forest reserves in their present form were injurious."[82] There were those, of course, who did not come to dissent. But either they were few in number or so poorly organized that their collective voice was not heard.

Pinchot took the floor first to present the government's case for conservation, but after him the day belonged to the insurgents. Behind volatile Plum Creek cattleman Elias Ammons[83] and state Senator Edward Taylor, the dissidents eloquently pleaded their case against the Roosevelt program. While Colorado pioneers had "no objection to the forest reserves" per se, said Ammons in an address to the commission, they resolutely opposed "the destruction of the people who have gone and built up homes" in the mountain country. No federal policy, added Taylor, superseded the right of men to own their own land and to "establish" their own lives in the wilderness. "My own idea," said the senator, "is that what is everybody's is nobody's; there is no incentive to improve the land; there is no incentive even to keep it as good as you find it. For any permanent business . . . you have got to have some form of possessory right."[84] Virtually every other cowman who took the floor throughout the day concurred with Taylor that "what was everybody's was nobody's."

When the anticonservationists turned to leasing, their primary argument was a familiar one: the martyrdom of a generation of pioneers had earned them a right to the open range which no government could legally or morally take away. Leasing, argued cattleman George Downing of Glenwood, was "against the man who has worked and built up this great empire in the West." Added Taylor, "A leasing system . . . would drive

Cattleman Elias M. Ammons, a staunch anticonservationist.
Courtesy Denver Public Library, Western History Department

out . . . the ranchman and the small stockgrower, the man who has built up the country." He had earned his place on the land. "The streams and the mountains are his," said Taylor. "Uncle Sam has been paid a thousand fold already for the land by the blood and bones of these people."[85]

Throughout the hearings the conservationists desperately attempted to present their views to the commission. For three days, amidst catcalls and laughter, they defended forest reserves and leasing. In talks laced with references to God and "God-given" abundance, they spoke of leaving behind them a heritage for "future generations." Summing up the views of his fellows, Conrad Schaefer of Deuel said, simply, that "what we want is the best for the people, not the individual . . . and every word we have uttered in favor of this subject [conservation] has been for the boys and girls growing up. . . . And I would like to see some protection of the grass that God has given for this Union and this people."[86]

When the commission terminated the hearings and left Denver for Salt Lake City on January 25, conservationists hoped to regroup in time for the August session. They achieved little at the meeting of the National Livestock Association in Portland where one of their erstwhile leaders, John Springer, spoke out against the Roosevelt program. In a major address, Springer declared that "stockmen have no objection to honest reserves, where there are forests to protect, but where millions of acres are set apart by the Secretary of the Interior, when you could not locate a tree with a telescope, . . . this is the state where the American stockman insists on demurring."[87] At the annual meeting of the Colorado Cattle and Horse Growers Association, however, they achieved a victory of sorts. When the cattlemen convened in March, the insurgents secured passage of an anti-leasing resolution declaring that "the question of a lease law no longer need be considered by Western stockmen. . . . If ever there was a time when such a law could have been made, the time is past." On the other hand, conservationists pushed through a resolution endorsing the general idea of federal forest reservations on western public lands.[88] The general results of the convention were inconclusive. But the meeting indicated that the insurgents might not dominate the second session of the commission's hearings as they had the first.

On August 4, 1904, several hundred Colorado cattlemen crowded into the stifling ballroom of Denver's Brown Palace Hotel for the second round of hearings before the Roosevelt commission. Instantly the insurgents went to the attack.

The first day's proceedings were dominated by Elias Ammons and a large group of supporters bent on the elimination of "control by bureau" in the West with "a federal officer as the final court of appeal."[89] With a scorching Denver sun turning the ballroom into an oven, Ammons, sweating and coatless, launched into an assault against conservation that lasted most of the morning. His primary target was the forest-reserve system, which he called an example of bureaucratic uselessness administered by underlings who "never saw the west side of the Mississippi River." Drawing on his own experiences on the South Platte and Plum Creek reservations, Ammons lashed out both at the "absurd" rules of the reserves and at the continued inclusion, by Washington bureaucrats, of nontimbered lands on them. The Plum Creek Reserve, said Ammons:

comes out about three miles on the prairie. . . . Nobody can touch it or anything, and it has been an everlasting nuisance to every man in the neighborhood. . . . I recollect that one officer went out from that reserve and reported that every man there was satisfied except Ammons, and yet at that very time there was a petition on file at Washington, signed by every single man [*in the reserve*] *saying that they were not satisfied with those rules.*

Angrily, pounding his fist on the table where Pinchot sat, Ammons declared that the network of forest reservations spreading across Colorado was, however slowly, "destroying" the homes and lives of pioneers who had built up the country. The reservation movement, he concluded, was patently "oppressive." And in alienating the cattlemen as it was, the government was "punishing the best friends it ever had."[90]

Throughout the afternoon of August 3, others in the Ammons group followed him in his attacks on the conservation system. Major addresses by T. W. Gray of Gunnison, E. H. Grubb of Carbondale, Robert Grant of Pueblo, and Edward Taylor, all shored up his position. The next day, August 4, insurgents completed their presentation. This time Ammons stood in the wings; his place was taken by J. H. Halley of Delta, one of the leaders of the antireserve movement in the region. In a furious afternoon-long attack on conservation, Halley touched on virtually every argument used by anticonservationists in a decade of protesting to the government. Criticizing in particular the government's creation of the Battlement Mesa Reserve—which bordered on his land—Halley complained directly to Pinchot that in outlining its boundaries "the government agent in charge forgot his spectacles, and in going on the land mistook sagebrush for giant trees and generally mucked the thing up. The consequence was that I was beaten out of my range."[91] Pinchot's reply was that "we give you the best in the shop."[92]

Late in the afternoon of August fifth, conservationists thrust aside insurgent speakers long enough to put their own case before the commission. After a handful of speeches, Frank Goudy (who until recently had helped lead Colorado's fight against leasing) introduced a resolution calling in unequivocal terms for federal control of the public grazing lands of the West. And, supported by a large contingent of cattlemen from eastern Colorado who had arrived in Denver halfway through the hearings, the conservationists were confident that it would be adopted. "The anti-leasers have had to fight against great odds" to defeat the cattle barons and "conservationists from eastern Colorado," complained one state newspaper.[93] The insurgents' only hope seemed to be blockage of the resolution.

On August 6, the final day of the hearings, the leasing resolution was passed, but it was amended so heavily in the process by Halley and Ammons and their followers—who struck the provision for "federal control" from it—that it was rendered virtually meaningless. Then, to enhance their "victory," the Ammons group passed a resolution of their own calling for the radical revision of all existing forest-reserve laws.[94] So the matter rested—for the time being. The commissioners boarded a train for Washington on August 7, and the cattlemen went back to the range. For a brief moment the Colorado back country was calm.

In the fall of 1904 the focus of the state turned from the ballroom of the Brown Palace to the regional and national political arena. In a presidential election year, with their power at stake all over the West in local and state campaigns, Colorado conservationists and anticonservationists both viewed the elections with acute concern. Of particular interest to both groups were the congressional elections; in state offices their spokesmen were relatively useless, but in Congress, where they either stood with or against the president and his conservation policies, they were of great importance.

For the most part congressional candidates in 1904 showed respect for the voting power of the insurgent bloc.[95] Franklin Brooks of Colorado Springs was a case in point. Elected to the House in the fall of 1902 on a state platform stressing the importance of local forest conservation, the young Republican loyalist had quickly converted to the insurgent cause. In 1904, Brooks, who had migrated to Colorado from Massachusetts in 1891, incessantly reminded his constituency that he had worked during his freshman term to have most of the Battlement Mesa Reserve restored to public entry; for his efforts he was given editorial support even by the *Denver Republican*.[96] Robert Bonynge of Denver had followed the same path. A New Yorker who had moved to Colorado in 1888 and unseated John Shafroth in 1902, Bonynge had surpassed even Shafroth's record as an anticonservationist. And, like Brooks, he campaigned against the Roosevelt program in 1904, despite the fact that he was a Republican running—like Brooks—on a modified conservation platform. In terms of anticonservation intensity, however, neither man matched the state's third representative, Herschel Hogg, an Iowa-born Republican residing in Telluride. Elected with Brooks and Bonynge in the Republican landslide of 1902 and defeating powerful incumbent John Bell in the process,

Hogg since had bitterly disappointed conservationists by defecting to the insurgent cause.[97] For two years he had opposed every facet of the Roosevelt conservation program, but during the fall campaign of 1904 he outdid himself.

In March, 1904, the *Denver Republican* reported that Hogg was gathering data on Colorado forest reserves for inclusion in a major anticonservation address to be made to the House. Colorado conservationists, fearful of subsequent damage to their movement, immediately attempted to dissuade him. W. G. M. Stone, president of the Colorado State Forestry Association, urgently wrote Hogg that the American people were "killing the goose that has daily been laying a golden egg" and were "manifesting a most ruthless disregard not only of their own children's welfare, but of their own." Any man, Stone concluded, who abetted such attitudes did a grave disservice to society, especially in a state where forests stood to be extinct in thirty years.[98] Hogg was not impressed by Stone's arguments. In an intemperate reply to him, the congressman blasted the "goggle-eyed, bandy-legged dudes from the East and sad-eyed, absent-minded professors and bugologists" who had foisted conservation off on Colorado and its people. "The trouble with you gentlemen," said Hogg, referring to the Forestry Association, "is that you see but one phase of the [conservation] subject and do not consider the many and varied interests that are dependent on lumber and the supply of timber [in Colorado]. . . . So far there has been a reckless withdrawal of lands [in Colorado]. . . . I do not think in any area of government there has been such a reckless exercise of power" as in the area of conservation.[99]

On April 25, Hogg made his long-awaited address to the House. In a scathing attack on the forest-reserve system in Colorado, he angrily contended that the framers of the General Revision Act of 1891 had never "dreamed that the President or his Secretary of Interior would seek to practically overturn the public land laws of the mountain states" by virtue of the power vested in them by the act. The real tragedy, said Hogg, was that neither the president nor his chief administrators knew—or cared to know—about the West when dealing with its public-land problems:

Can it be expected that the Secretary of Interior, or even some subordinate sitting in his office at Washington, can be correctly informed of the character of lands contained within a reservation situated two or three thousand miles away? . . . They look at their maps and they see a mountain range marked thereon and know beyond any question that that country is just the kind of country to put in a forest reserve. . . . No difference to them if men have undertaken to reclaim portions of the public domain, are constructing systems of irrigation, building sawmills for the manufacture of timber so much needed in the development of our country; that men have embarked on the cattle or sheep business and have invested hundreds of thousands of dollars supposing that the public range would be open to them as it had been for years. All these enterprises involving so much . . . must come to a standstill

because of bureaucratic incompetence exercised by "ignorant high officials" and their Washington "underlings."[100]

Turning from forest reserves and federal bureaucracy, Hogg also attacked the East. In particular he scorned the popular eastern notion that, as he put it, westerners who did not subscribe to the theory of conservation were enemies of the government. "Is it true," Hogg questioned,

that the men of the West, whose enterprise and courage and daring have made possible that great empire, are nothing but thieves and rogues? Is it true that all of honesty and patriotism and virtue is to be found only in the departments at Washington, and because a citizen seeks to avail himself of his rights and seeks to better his condition by making entry of public lands he must be treated as though he was doing some act that made him an object of suspicion?[101]

Finally, with a bitter parting shot at the "forest crank" and the "dreamer" who had imposed the "crackpot" conservation scheme on Colorado and the West, Hogg appealed for understanding:

> *Colorado, blessed as she is with all that goes to make a splendid and glorious commonwealth, with her wealth of gold . . . and with an abundance of iron and steel, with agriculture exceeding in value even that of her mines, with her great herds of cattle and sheep, with a people brave, just, courageous, and patriotic, has a right to ask that you lay no further burdens on her industry nor destroy the possibilities of her glorious future.*[102]

Hogg's rhetoric served him well. In the fall, repeating over and over the theme of his April address, he was re-elected to Congress. And returning by his side were Franklin Brooks and Robert Bonynge. Colorado's insurgent bloc remained intact—the young Republicans in the House and Teller and Patterson in the Senate. All five men remained intent on a single primary objective: the ridding of their state of what Hogg called the "menace" of conservation.[103]

The major irony of the 1904 elections was the fact that while Hogg, Brooks, and Bonynge won their campaigns at least partly because of opposition to conservation, the chief architect of national conservation policy—Theodore Roosevelt—overwhelmingly carried Colorado in the presidential election. Several possible explanations existed for the seeming paradox.

First, in both a state and national context the Democratic party still had not recovered fully from the humiliating defeats of William Jennings Bryan in 1896 and 1900.[104] Colorado, attracted to "Bryan democracy" because of its identification with silver, had followed the Commoner both times. In 1904, however, with the silver issue dead and the national party disorganized, the Democrats may have had little appeal in Colorado. Roosevelt, then, might have won by default. On the other hand, it might be argued that Roosevelt won because of his progressivism, or, as some historians have suggested, his "enlightened conservatism." Certainly in Colorado such was a possibility. By 1904, Progressives were active in the state, and presumably the public had begun to respond to them.[105] The election of Hogg, Brooks, and Bonynge was, in fact, a reflection of Progressive popularity; except for one area—conservation—all three men adhered to the Progressive "center" themselves and "approved of Roosevelt's philosophies" in every respect.[106] As for conservation, one thing was certain: its advocacy by Roosevelt had not appreciably damaged him in Colorado. Either the state voted for him because he *did* promote conservation; or it voted for him *despite* the fact and because it approved of other facets of his political creed. Local conservationists, at least, believed the Roosevelt vote was a mandate for their cause. As the *Denver Republican* editorialized:

> *If there ever existed any doubt in President Roosevelt's mind as to his standing with the people of Colorado, his magnificent vote in this state . . . must have caused that doubt to flee like the mist before the morning sun. . . . And if there is anything that will keep this state in the Republican column where it belongs, it is* [*conservation*], *with the welfare of the people constantly in mind, instead of the wishes of the powerful few.*[107]

Disappointed insurgents, of course, did not agree. And the presence of their spokesmen on the land, in cattlemen's associations, and in Congress assured them of the fact that their long-held position would not be abandoned or compromised. The public domain, said one, had been "free" for "the settler, from the days of the Pilgrim to the last weary immigrant seeking a location on the Uintah. So let it remain."[108]

The battle for the wilderness, then, would go on.

VII. Encroachment on the Garden

Not long before his inauguration on March 4, 1905, Theodore Roosevelt remarked to an aide, "Tomorrow I shall come into office in my own right. Then watch out for me."[1] To those who knew the president, the statement was significant. And to his enemies it was ominous.

To a great extent Roosevelt's first administration had been a disappointment, especially to impatient American progressives who had expected more positive results from it and from the president himself. Harnessed by an often hostile Congress and by the contentious Old Guard that dominated his party, absorbed at all times by the fear of defeat in the 1904 campaign, Roosevelt had been uncharacteristically cautious during his first term on a number of critical national issues. Conservation, strongly opposed by much of the West and the Congress, was one of them. While Roosevelt had championed the cause, he had done so with little of his vast energy.

The annihilation of Alton B. Parker in the autumn of 1904 changed Roosevelt's posture overnight. In the spring of 1905, as president in his own right, free to become, as he put it, the "people's steward," he began to abandon caution and to alter the whole course of his presidency. Wielding his mandate on inauguration day, he served notice on the vested interests of the nation that the day of unrestricted laissez-faire was over. The warning was directed, in great part, at western insurgents.

In the area of conservation, Roosevelt's attitude was shaped by two important factors: first, the passage of the Transfer Act, marking the final step in Gifford Pinchot's rise to political prominence, and second, an upsurge in proconservation agitation in the West itself.

The Transfer Act, apparently killed by insurgents in 1902, was revived in 1903 and enacted into law in 1905 after two years of bitter debate. Over the increasingly angry objections of western anticonservationists, it passed Congress on February 1, 1905—one month before Roosevelt's inauguration. The reaction to it of Colorado insurgents was predictable. Henry Teller, speaking for most of them, disgustedly dismissed the idea as one with "neither law nor sense behind it."[2] On the other hand, however, it was praised in the same region as "just exactly what ought to be done."[3]

The Transfer Act was important, of course, in that Pinchot became the sole administrator of America's forest-reserve system. More important, however, was the fact that Pinchot's new position and enlarged status gave him a more direct access to the president than he had enjoyed before, and he used it to lobby for his programs. In Roosevelt he struck a responsive chord. Speaking of the immediate "ideological and political symbiosis" that existed between the two men, Elmo Richardson has written that the president "readily identified his own interests as a naturalist and his faith in dynamic executive power with the forester's personal crusade for planned conservation and use of reserves."[4] The result of the "symbiosis" was that when Pinchot suggested, Roosevelt listened; "Pinchot's ideas became Roosevelt's ideas," and all were quickly and effectively translated into conservation action.[5] If the president had vacillated on public-land questions before 1905, after that time he did not.

A second factor which prompted Roosevelt to take action early in his term was the increasingly proconservation attitude of various parts of the West. In 1905, for example, while Idaho delegates to the National Livestock Association Convention in Denver agitated for a stronger forest-reserve system, powerful Idaho Senator Fred DuBois supported the same idea in Congress. The final conversion of anticonservation Governor Frank Gooding to conservation, in fact, prompted Pinchot to remark to Roosevelt that "organized opposition" to his "forest policy in the West" was "completely at an end."[6] Several prominent Utahans, including Governor Heber Wells and Senator Reed Smoot, helped marshal new proreserve sentiment in their state.[7] T. J. Grier, president of South Dakota's Homestake Mining Company; Francis Warren of Wyoming, president of the National Woolgrowers Association; Governor George Pardee of California; and Senator Francis Newlands of Nevada may have been strange bedfellows; nonetheless, all of them were symbolic of the mood of much of their states.[8] Roosevelt could hardly ignore the fact.

Colorado, by and large, followed the trend. The Colorado State Forestry Association was primarily responsible for forest-reserve agitation in Colorado. As early as 1893 the association had called for the incorporation of "all public lands along the crests of the mountain ranges and spurs [in Colorado], and upon either side thereof for a distance of six miles" into forest reserves.[9] In December, 1903, dissatisfied with the fact that the government had created only one new reserve in Colorado (the San Isabel) since 1891, the association renewed its plea, requesting the secretary of the interior to establish reserves in watersheds "covering all streams proceeding from the Rocky Mountain range [in Colorado] at and above 8500 feet."[10] In early 1905 such requests became more insistent. Again the Forestry Association called for an increase in reservations, that Colorado might "break the wave of [forest] waste" that plagued it.[11] Supported by frequent editorials in the *Denver Republican*, by the militant Colorado Horticultural Society (which deplored "lawmakers" who had "not done their duty" to see that the reserve system was expanded),[12] and by growing numbers of settlers and cattlemen living in the areas in question, the association finally made its point.

Whether or not such proconservation sentiment reflected the feeling of the majority in the states involved, the government could not say. Nonetheless, encouraged by the strength of conservationist agitation and spurred on by Pinchot and other federal planners, Roosevelt acted in their behalf. Beginning in the spring of 1905 and continuing through the spring of 1907, he added millions of acres of timberlands to the forest-reserve system. He established fourteen new reservations in Colorado and in so doing triggered furious anticonservation activity in virtually every area of the state for the next decade.

On May 12, 1905, two months after his inauguration, Roosevelt created the Gunnison Forest Reserve, Colorado's seventh, 901,270 acres of prime timberland in Gunnison County in west-central Colorado.[13] Physically, in that it included some of the highest mountain areas in the state, the Gunnison was one of the most imposing reserves in the West. Running east to west from La Plata Peak at the northern end of the Collegiate Range to the small mining village of Marble, the reserve's northern boundary ran southwesterly from Marble to Paonia, then angled south to Cimarron on the Gunnison River. From there it ran due east to Gunnison and through Garfield before following the crest of the continental divide north along the Collegiate chain back to La Plata Peak. From the West Elk Mountains, which dominated the western half of the reserve, dozens of streams emptied into the Gunnison River, making its valley one of the most beautiful and most productive in the state. From the central part of the reserve the East, Taylor, and Slate rivers rushed into the Gunnison, and from along the rim of the Collegiate peaks, hundreds of streams flowed east into the vital Arkansas River. It was the importance of the Gunnison-Arkansas watersheds that led to the creation of the reserve.

The Gunnison Reservation had been in the planning stages since the spring of 1903 when the State Forestry Association launched its "statewide campaign of forest agitation for the purpose of interesting the citizens of Colorado in forestry and forest preservation."[14] Inaugurating the campaign, State Forestry Association President W. G. M. Stone called for the saturation of the entire central Colorado area with reserves: "For forty-five years our forests have been wasting away. All this tends toward the one great disaster which overtook Palestine and other important portions of the old world now lying in ruin on account of the total destruction of their forests. We must stop forest waste sometime. Has not the time come?"[15] Supported, paradoxically, by a resolution passed by Colorado's normally anticonservation legislature calling for the creation of a reserve in the Arkansas River watershed, the association petitioned the government for such action.[16]

In February, 1904, word began to circulate through the Gunnison country that federal surveyors in the area were preparing reports favorable to the idea of a reserve along the Arkansas River. Overnight, opposition to the reserve plan crystallized around Gunnison, anchored by militant local cattlemen who had run their stock in Gunnison Valley and Taylor Park for years, untouched and unhindered by federal rules and regulations. Ignoring late winter snows that virtually buried the valley, irate cattlemen held a string of protest meetings in Gunnison, Almont, and Crested Butte throughout February, climaxed by a giant rally at the Gunnison City Hall on February 25. There they agreed almost unanimously to fight the reservation. Speaking for what appeared to be a majority of local cattlemen, D. A. McConnell of Doyle on Tomichi Creek, declared them unstintingly opposed to the reserve idea. The preservation of timber, he suggested with some accuracy, could be better served by the stricter enforcement of existing land laws than by the creation of more reserves. There were dissenters—a half-dozen stockmen from Paonia and Crested Butte endorsed the reserve idea—but they were largely muzzled. Over their protests the insurgents passed a resolution declaring permanent opposition to any federal action in violation of the rights which had "become vested in the residents [of the Gunnison Valley] in the way of grazing, mining, and agricultural pursuits" over the years.[17]

The mood of the Gunnison country turned progressively uglier throughout March. During the early part of the month homesteaders and miners began to augment the protests of the cattlemen, and at another Gunnison rally they vocalized their feelings. "I am very much afraid of the disastrous effect upon mining," worried John McCormick of Gunnison, "if the reserve is saddled on us."[18] Lawrence Winsheimer from Tin Cup, perched on the rocky west slope of Mount Princeton, agreed emphatically that miners in the high country were "afraid of the reserve" because of mining restrictions that might accompany it.[19] Valentine Ehret of Iola on Tomichi Creek concurred that no man in his "neighborhood" desired the reserve. The cattlemen, as always, agreed: "None of us want it," said J. C. Leonard of Doyle. "The cattle business is poor enough as it is."[20] Antireserve resolutions were passed, and the cattlemen dispersed for a time.

Fifty-six miles west of Gunnison, in and around Montrose and Delta, the prospect of a forest reserve was met with unrestrained enthusiasm. East of the Delta-Montrose axis, where the Gunnison River coursed through miles of farmland, the conservation of faraway watersheds was considered imperative to survival. In the neighboring Uncompahgre River Valley the case was the same. There the massive Uncompahgre Valley irrigation project, one of the largest of its kind in the West, depended entirely on the steady flow of water from the Elk Mountains to the east. Nearly half of the farms on the Western Slope depended on the project for their existence. Valley settlers, therefore, had little sympathy for their neighbors up river. Said the *Montrose Enterprise:* "The people of Gunnison County are having a hot time over forest reserves. . . . But as the Interior Department makes rules that will not hamper mining or agriculture or stock raising, they will settle down. . . . Care in such matters can be arranged without injuring the legitimate businesses of Gunnison County."[21] Gunnison insurgents were irritated by what a local newspaper indignantly called "meddling" by one area in the affairs of another. Accusing Montrose citizens of acting "on the sly" to saddle Gunnison residents with a reserve for "purely selfish considerations," it branded the idea a "menace to our industries and a mortgage upon our future."[22]

Throughout March, April, and the early part of May, Gunnison anticonservationists attempted to enlist congressional support in their fight against the reserve. They found willing allies in Henry Teller and Herschel Hogg. "As for myself," said Hogg in a speech to the House, "I am opposed to forest reserves where they interfere with the securing of title to good agricultural land." And, he said, such would be the case in Gunnison County. Teller cynically declared that "a few cranks in Colorado and elsewhere" had "more influence in these matters than the representatives from the state." The solution, said the senator, was for local settlers to "get up and protest."[23] The insurgent bloc heeded his words and protested. But it did no good. On May 12 the reserve was proclaimed.

The anticonservationists reacted instantly and angrily. Under a banner headline that read "Immense Forest Reserve; Half of County Set Aside; Theorists in League with Railroad Attorneys and Sheepmen Continue to Withdraw From Settlement Over A Million Acres in Gunnison County!" the *News-Champion* launched a scorching attack on the reserve. In an indignant editorial on June 2 it set the tone of its campaign:

> *To those who had hoped the unanimous protest against the proposed reserve . . . a year ago by our citizens would have some effect in preventing the establishment, the blow is a severe one. . . . No one objects to the preservation of our forests. What we of Gunnison County object to is the idiocy of withdrawing from settlement a million acres of land, not one-fourth of which ever saw a stick of timber or ever will see one. A few theorists who learned their forestry by reading of European forests have decided that Rocky Mountain forests need preserving . . . and our good friends in Delta and Montrose have assisted under the mistaken notion that it was needed to preserve snow banks. . . . A large reward is waiting for the man who can point out a thousand acres of this reserve that has any snow in the forests. . . . It looks like a case of graft married to stupidity.*[24]

There was no explanation of the complicity of "railroad attorneys" in the affair, and for sheepmen to have agitated for a reserve from which they would have been barred would have been pointless. As for the slur against the "theorists," by 1905 it was instinctive.

In the aftermath of Roosevelt's proclamation, organized protest in the Gunnison region gradually diminished; shock and anger gave way, in time, to gloomy resignation. At a June 9 meeting of the Gunnison County Stockgrowers Association, area cattlemen fired one final salvo at the reserve, but the action appeared almost perfunctory. The *Gunnison News-Champion* reported that "the idea of a range governed by red tape officials in Washington" did not "appeal" to stockmen, and yet they made no more overt protest.[25] Meanwhile, down river on the Gunnison, Delta and Montrose rejoiced. Soberly—and accurately—the *Delta Independent* editorialized on the importance of saving local watersheds. "The mountain ranges of this region have been denuded long enough by lumbering," it said, "and the importance of reforestation is apparent."[26] Certainly, however, it was not apparent to all. Later trouble on the reserve attested to that.

On May 12, 1905, the same day he established the Gunnison Reservation, Roosevelt also proclaimed the Leadville Forest Reserve to the east of it. A massive withdrawal of some 1,129,947 acres in a half-dozen Colorado counties, it was the largest reserve yet created in the state.[27]

The Leadville Reserve had two large natural divisions, each of them critical to the preservation of some of the central Rockies' most important watersheds. Its upper section reached from the bustling mining enclave of Leadville as far north as Hot Sulphur Springs on the Colorado River. Originating at Leadville, the western border of the reserve ran due north through Red Cliff to a point south of Kremmling, embracing the Gore Range and the headwaters of the Eagle River; from Kremmling the boundary looped north to Hot Sulphur Springs, then east to the continental divide. Moving southward, skirting Central City, Idaho Springs, and Georgetown, it finally joined the northern boundary of the old South Platte Reserve (consolidated with the Pikes Peak and Plum Creek reservations in 1905 and renamed the Pike Forest Reserve) and curved southwesterly along the summits of Torreys and Grays peaks and Mount Lincoln and Mount Democrat back to Leadville. In this vast circle the reserve included the watersheds of Clear Creek, the Fraser and Blue rivers, and most importantly, the headwaters of the Arkansas itself.

The lower section of the Leadville consisted of two thin prongs which stretched south from Leadville along the Arkansas River, blanketing its entire watershed. The western prong, which took in Mount Massive and Mount Elbert, Colorado's highest peak, and the eastern slope of the Collegiate Range, ran as far south as Buena Vista, protecting the western flank of the river. The eastern prong, which also terminated near Buena Vista, ran down the east bank of the river, protecting that flank from the incursions of unwelcome pioneers.

Blueprints for the Leadville Reservation had been on the conservationists' drawing boards for years. As early as 1893, State Forest Commissioner Edgar Ensign had initiated a movement for federal withdrawals in the mountain country west of Denver for the protection of its water supply (and that of Golden, Georgetown, and Idaho Springs as well). The idea was never actively pursued by either state or national officials, primarily because of the determined opposition of long-intrenched local miners. Not until 1902 was the idea revived. At the annual meeting of the Colorado State Horticultural Society, Henry Michelsen, vice president of the State Forestry Association, broached the subject in a speech condemning the insurgent "mentality" which had "ruined" the West. Maintaining that a reserve in the mountains west of Denver was a "necessity" to which there could be "little objection" from concerned Coloradans, he concluded that the state of Colorado could not—or would not—protect the region's forests. By default, he concluded, the duty of conservation had to "devolve upon the owner of the soil—the national government."[28] Over a period of two years governmental officials became interested in the Michelsen proposal, and in 1905 they finally acted on it.

Despite the immensity of the reserve and despite the area's history of violence—especially among mining interests which had dominated the region since the gold boom of 1859—the creation of the Leadville elicited little immediate reaction from local settlers.[29] Only one newspaper complained: the *Summit County Journal* of Breckenridge reported that it had been deluged with inquiries from puzzled settlers seeking further information on the reserve. Such bewilderment was understandable, it said, in that "every stick of unoccupied timber and forest in Summit County" had been included in the reserve.[30] On the other hand, however, Central City's *Gilpin Observer* praised the withdrawal, reasoning that "the industry of farming and also that of stock raising throughout the widespread regions watered by streams heading in this section" would greatly benefit from it.[31]

Inevitably, resentment against the reserve began to materialize when local pioneers became familiar with restrictions placed on their activities in the timberlands. Mining interests, for example, were distressed by the prospect of federal restraints on reserve prospecting. Already suffering economic problems caused by a mining slump (despite a zinc boomlet in 1901), the area felt it could ill afford further impediments to prospecting.[32] Lumbermen, too, were unhappy with the new reserve. In November, shortly after local rangers began strict enforcement of timber-cutting restrictions, a handful of marginal sawmills at Leadville and Red Cliff were shut down due to the unavailability of timber. The economic significance of the closings was clear to local settlers, especially coming, as they did, at the beginning of winter. Reflecting a sharp wave of public indignation, the *Leadville Herald-Democrat* took the lead in denouncing the government's action, insisting that reserve restrictions would irreparably cripple the local economy and perhaps destroy the city itself. The problem, it said, was that "there is so much red tape connected with the cutting of timber on forest reserves that woodsmen are slow to take contracts. . . . Forming forest reserves will then increase the cost of manufacturing timber by one-third. And it will be some time before there is sufficient timber on hand to keep the mills going at full blast."[33] The government, however, paid no heed to any protests. The result was an escalation in anticonservation feeling and activity from late 1905 through 1907.

On May 17, 1905, five days after the creation of the Gunnison and Leadville reserves, President Roosevelt proclaimed the Medicine Bow Forest Reserve, 1,574,663 acres of timberland in the north-central Colorado Rockies between North Park and the Great Plains. From the Wyoming border to Hot Sulphur Springs, eastward to Ward, north through Estes Park back to the Wyoming line, the Medicine Bow boundaries encompassed some of the most primitive mountain territory in Colorado.[34] The landmass contained two mountain chains of significance—the Medicine Bow Range, which sliced diagonally through the reservation, and the Front Range which ran adjacent to the Great Plains. Together they held the headwaters of dozens of critical streams running west into North Park, north into Wyoming, and east to the plains cities of Fort Collins, Loveland, Greeley, and Boulder. It was chiefly to protect these streams—the Laramie, Poudre, Thompson, and St. Vrain rivers and the North Fork of the Colorado—that the reserve was established. But of added importance to conservationists (or, more precisely, to the extreme proconservationist element among them) was the pristine, almost primeval beauty of the region which they sought to safeguard for esthetic purposes.[35]

As in other areas, serious agitation for a federal reservation in the Medicine Bow area had begun in 1893 when the State Forestry Association petitioned President Cleveland to take action to save the Cache la Poudre, Thompson, and St. Vrain watersheds from the intrusions of timber cutters. The request went unheeded, and not until 1898 was the idea revived in a series of proreserve public meetings in Fort Collins. In 1899 tireless State Forestry Commissioner Edgar Ensign commissioned a formal survey of the Medicine Bow country and sent a personal report to Washington outlining the need for federal action there. A presidential proclamation was drafted by the McKinley administration, segregating the lands in question from public entry; but in October, 1899, when the White House was assailed by antireserve petitions from the area, the proclamation was scrapped.[36]

In 1900, again at the insistence of Fort Collins conservationists, the Interior Department reconsidered the Ensign proposal. The secretary concluded that timber cutting and fires had "wrought sad havoc" in the region and that "all of the evidence with the case" indicated "a public opinion favorable to the establishment of the reserve." But, while he advised that "early action" be taken, it was not.[37] Encouraged by federal vacillation, local anticonservationists mounted a campaign to kill the reserve idea for good. Led by H. J. M. Mattis, a sawmill operator in the foothills west of Fort Collins, and abetted by senators Teller and Patterson, insurgents succeeded in destroying much of the progress made by reserve advocates to that point. Teller made it clear that he "fully endorsed the protest" movement and would see to it that "the proposed reserve would not be made." And Patterson wrote a Fort Collins friend that under no circumstances would he permit a withdrawal to be made in the Medicine Bow country.[38]

From April, 1901, through the spring of 1902, the State Forestry Association and the State Horticultural Society allied with groups of citizens in Fort Collins, Longmont, and Eaton to breathe new life into the reserve idea. Conducting rallies and promoting letter-writing campaigns to Washington congressmen, all the while attempting to convince local dissidents that a reserve would—as W. G. M. Stone phrased it—"build this state up," they responded vigorously to Mattis and his followers.[39] But the lumberman, like others, refused to yield. In a bellicose August letter, Mattis protested directly to Roosevelt himself:

If a private citizen whose ancestors, like yours, have been in this country for centuries, can have the attention of its highest official, I would like to ask you to veto the Medicine Bow proposition. My home is on the reserve and I earn my bread with a little tenhorsepower sawmill, running the saw myself. If you wonder why I object to the reserve, it is because I love liberty, hate red tape, and believe in progress. I like self-government, but to be placed under a bureau and in a reservation is too much like going back to the kind of government you impose upon your Indians. And my neighbors share my sentiments. The mountains ever have been the preserves of human liberties. Do not blight ours.[40]

For two more years the insurgents held the line, even introducing partisan politics into the issue: Senator Patterson told one crowd that if the reserve were created by a Republican administration, it should be "sufficient reason for every Republican who uses timber to vote the Democratic ticket" in every future election.[41] But in the end Roosevelt decided in favor of the conservationists. On May 17 he created the reserve.

Widespread praise greeted the president's action. Said the *Fort Collins Express*: "The preservation of the forests is of more importance than the fanciful objections of the owners of a few little sawmills and of a few cattlemen who don't know what's best for them. After an extended acquaintance with the workings of the reserve system . . . [they] will be wholly unable to see anything but good in them."[42] Even the *Fort Collins Courier*, which in the past had branded the conservation impulse a conspiracy by "theorists and sportsmen" to take over the West, now agreed that the reserve would benefit the area and its people and that it would most likely be administered to protect "the conditions and needs of all concerned."[43] Not all local citizens agreed, however, and a substantial reservoir of ill will persisted and promised future trouble on the Medicine Bow.

On June 3, Roosevelt imposed a tenth reservation on Colorado: the San Juan Forest Reserve, a 1,437,406-acre withdrawal in the rugged southwest Colorado Rockies.[44]

Bounded by Silverton on the west, Pagosa Springs to the south, Durango to the southwest, Del Norte to the east, and Creede to the north, the new reserve encompassed the spiny San Juan Mountains as well as the smaller La Plata, Needle, Silverton, and Grenadier groups. And it blanketed the headwaters of dozens of major streams and rivers that flowed onto the nearby lowlands. On the west slope of the continental divide the beautiful Animas, Navajo, Blanco, and La Plata rivers merged into the San Juan, a primary tributary of the Colorado; and in the eastern sector of the reserve the headwaters of the Río Grande formed. Collectively these rivers—the lifeblood of the rich San Luis Valley—were among the most important in Colorado. To conservationists the maintenance of their watersheds was essential to the economic survival of the entire south-central part of the state.

The San Juan withdrawal was met with virtually no opposition at all. Where insurgent opposition had greeted several reserves, the San Juan was welcomed by editorials like that of Del Norte's *San Juan Prospector*: "Preservation of the forest cover" at the heads of local streams, said the newspaper, was "a matter of vital importance . . . to an increasing civilization."[45] Lack of response is difficult to account for, especially in that mining activity still was relatively heavy in some parts of the region. In 1901 and 1902, for example, large veins and pockets of gold and silver tellurium had been opened at Platoro and Stunner in the northeastern part of the reserve. At approximately the same time, the Premier and Tobasco mining companies opened up large mines and a mill near Sherman in the western part of the withdrawal. And at Spar City, 150 Kansans took over the entire settlement in 1905 to build summer homes and to mine.[46] At the same time, however, while little pockets of mining activity were apparent, the industry was in decline elsewhere, driving scores of miners away from the reserve region. Certainly, especially on such a large reservation, no cohesive protest was possible. For whatever reasons, the San Juan remained, in subsequent years, one of Colorado's more peaceful reserves.

During the second week of June, 1905, the president returned his attention to the troubled forest and rangelands of northwestern Colorado. On June 12 he established the Park Range Forest Reserve, 757,116 acres of land in Routt County between the Medicine Bow and old White River reservations. Though small when compared with other reserves, it encircled two immensely important mountain chains—the Park and Elkhead ranges—and included the sources of several major rivers.[47] In the northern reaches of the reserve the Snake, Yampa, and North Platte wound out of the hills, augmented by dozens of tributaries. And in the southern part of the reserve hundreds of smaller streams rushed off the crest of the mountains to the Colorado.

To the possible puzzlement of both government officials and local conservationists who had instigated federal action, the establishment of the new reservation failed to provoke a challenge in an area that had shown unsurpassed hostility toward conservation in the past. The reason, however, was not a mellowing of the insurgent mood. The reason was a crisis on the White River Reservation to the southwest which developed in the fall of 1905, drew insurgent fire away from the Park Range, and concentrated it on the White River instead.

On August 18, the reliable *Denver Republican* reported that American agrarian novelist Hamlin Garland and a small group of professional eastern conservationists had recently presented to President Roosevelt a plan to establish a "great national park" on the land occupied by the White River Reserve.[48] The plan, it reported, had the support not only of Colorado Governor Jesse F. McDonald, but of Roosevelt himself. The president, who had hunted and roamed the White River Plateau often in his adult years, told Garland that he was "performing a valuable service" for western Colorado and the nation as well.

Further, Roosevelt promised to give the project whatever support he could.[49] White River pioneers, many of them opposed to conservation to begin with, were skeptical about the plan.

The primary fear of many local settlers was that a national park, which they assumed would be larger and more strictly patrolled than the existing reserve, would restrict the grazing of their cattle even more than the reserve did. And there, where the underpinnings of the entire economy, especially in Rio Blanco County, rested on the prosperity of the cattle industry, such a possibility was not pleasant. Said the *Yampa Leader:* "If, in making a national park of the White River Reserve, the grazing of cattle and horses is to be prohibited within said park, we unhesitatingly say it will be an injury to this part of the state, will work a hardship on the cattlemen, and the benefits to be derived therefrom will in no wise offset the damage it will do to this community."[50] At one especially large protest meeting in September, several hundred Routt County stockmen complained in resolutions forwarded to Roosevelt that a park would "spell absolute ruin" for them and all other "citizens whose businesses" depended on the prosperity of the local cattle industry.[51] They waited one month for word of relief from the administration. When it failed to come, the controversy flared anew in October.

During the first week of October, Craig's *Routt County Courier*, in the past an opponent of the forest-reserve idea, launched an intensive campaign to promote the national-park idea among balky local cattlemen. Maintaining that a federal park would be a good "advertisement" for the area and possibly stimulate tourism, the *Courier* editorialized that the entire territory from Steamboat Springs to the Utah border

would be vastly benefitted by being made into a national park, would become a drawing card to this country that could bring many benefits to us. No better advertisement could be found. . . . When this matter is considered in its true light, it loses the phase of first appearances and becomes not only the feasible but the practical thing to do. Give us a national park![52]

Fear of grazing restrictions, said the newspaper, was a smoke-screen thrown up by the opponents of the park idea to alarm and "soft-soap" cattlemen whose support was necessary to destroy the Garland plan. The cattlemen, said the *Courier*, should have been able to "see through the artifice."[53]

The *Courier* drew blood. In a classic example of the kind of intrastate bickering the conservation movement provoked in Colorado, the volatile *Yampa Leader* scoffed at the "drawing card" idea: "Yes, if an Eastern philanthropist came out here and offered to erect a beautiful and enormous monument over your body, Mr. Courier, it would be a splendid advertisement, but would you jump at the chance? Most of our cattlemen would rather raise cattle than be famous."[54] The *Red Cliff Blade*, among other concurring area newspapers, disgustedly dismissed the *Courier*'s argument. Forest reserves multiplying every year in Colorado were reprehensible enough it said; but

about the last straw is the White River scheme. If this policy of "reservation" and "preservation" is carried out, the settlers of the West will begin to ask themselves why they became pioneers and settled up and opened up and made inhabitable the wilderness. . . . Along comes a poet [Garland] *and suggests a national park in an area that ought to teem with inhabitants. Away with him!*[55]

Insurgent cattlemen wasted little time in enlisting the support of their congressmen. On October 21, the *Yampa Leader* happily announced that Thomas Patterson and Franklin Brooks had "personally pledged their assistance in killing the project" and that Henry Teller had assured insurgents that an act of Congress establishing a national park would "not likely pass" while he was a member of the Senate.[56] Recoiling, perhaps, from the mushrooming protest movement and hostility in Congress, the government discarded the idea. Mourning its death, the *Denver Republican* conceded that pioneer resistance had been responsible for the government's action. And it hoped aloud that the land and the natural beauty of the region could be safeguarded better in the future than in the past under the existing forest reserve arrangement.[57]

Even as northwest Colorado debated the White River question, Roosevelt acted on another front. On June 12, at the same time he proclaimed the Park Range Reserve, he also created the 239,251-acre Wet Mountains Forest Reserve in south central Colorado.[58]

Conservationists had long coveted the Wet Mountains and the vast, mist-covered valley that swept westward from them to the Sangre de Cristos and the San Isabel Forest Reserve. As in other areas of the state, they sought to protect key watersheds, in this case those of Newlin and Hardscrabble creeks and the St. Charles and Greenhorn rivers. All four streams either fed the Arkansas on its way to the plains or watered the fertile Wet Mountain Valley, and all provided the water supply for the plains communities of Florence and Pueblo. The Wet Mountains tract was small as Colorado reserves went. But conservationists did not measure its importance by its size.

Roosevelt's action came as no surprise to settlers in the Wet Mountains. As early as 1900, urged on by the Custer County Republican Committee and "many of the leading citizens" of Pueblo and Custer counties, the government contemplated the creation of a reserve at the headwaters of Newlin Creek.[59] And when the reserve was proclaimed, except for a smattering of protest at Florence, no adverse reaction materialized; ranching was not extensive, and while the Westcliffe-Silver Cliff-Rosita area had once been alive with miners, the only activity in 1905 was confined to a tiny enclave around Querida.[60] Encouraged by the peaceful climate, the *Denver Republican* assured all potential protesters that the reservation would be "managed in the interests of the people."[61] And the *Canon City Leader*—which had opposed the San Isabel Reserve—added that the Wet

Mountains withdrawal would be "of great service to this portion of the state."[62] Perhaps because it was away from the mainstream of insurgent activity and was relatively unpopulated by both miners and cattlemen, the Wet Mountains Reserve never fostered major trouble for the government.

The Cochetopah Forest Reserve, a 1,333,330-acre withdrawal in Saguache County, was added to Colorado's growing reserve network on June 13, 1905.[63] Originating west of Salida near Monarch Pass, the Cochetopah's border angled south to Saguache, southwest to South Fork, northwest to Creede and Lake City, then followed the rim of the continental divide northeast to Ohio, where it connected with the southern boundaries of the Leadville and Gunnison reservations. Spanning the great divide from Monarch Pass to Lake City, the Cochetopah comprised both spectacular peaks and waves of broad, timbered mesas and rolling foothills. Streams abounded, rushing off alpine meadows to the Arkansas River in the north, winding down through the rich farmlands of the Saguache Valley in the east, and emptying into the Río Grande in the south shortly before it reached the San Luis Valley.

Beginning in 1900, responding to petitions from the Cochetopah region for a reserve to protect its vanishing timberlands, the government had planned a withdrawal there.[64] The overriding consideration, as always, was the protection of important watersheds. As of 1900 fully twenty-one streams heading in the region irrigated twenty-eight thousand acres of farmland in the Saguache and San Luis valleys, contributing to the production of crops valued at three hundred thousand dollars a year by 1905.[65] Another consideration, too, was the eradication of lawlessness and the establishment of economic and political stability on what had been one of the more unsettled ranges in the state.

Predictably, opposition to the reserve quickly developed among local cattlemen, especially among those who controlled the range. As early as 1903, even before the reserve was created, they had hounded federal agents attempting to survey the land. Goaded by the *Saguache Crescent*, which complained bitterly about the rules and "red tape" that would damage the region's economy, defiant stockmen had come close, in fact, to physical violence.[66] The final creation of the reserve did little to alter their feelings. Among miners, however, there was little grumbling. At Lake City on the western fringe of the reserve, the *Lake City Phonograph* expressed its belief that the reservation would benefit the local mining industry.[67] And at Creede, one of the West's last great gold camps (though a community in decline in 1905), the *Creede Candle* added that "the country is at last aroused to the peril of forest annihilation" and that the new reserve could only benefit the area and its crippled economy.[68] Still, however, the cattlemen demurred. "The strong protests that went up from every section in the county for two years," fumed the *Crescent*, "were ignored. All we can do now is make the best of it."[69] To the cattlemen, that might have meant continuing to act precisely as they had in the past.

To the southwest of the Cochetopah, President Roosevelt carved the Montezuma Forest Reserve out of the primitive Four Corners area on June 13.[70] The borders of the new withdrawal, from Lizard Head Pass near Telluride in the northwest, south to Hermosa, west to Dolores, north to the headwaters of Disappointment Creek, then east to Telluride again, encircled 567,719 acres of mountain territory. From the alpine tundra of Mount Wilson, Mount Dolores, and Hesperus Peak scores of streams rushed down both sides of the divide. From the west slope the San Miguel and Dolores rivers flowed into Utah, and from the east slope the Animas and Mancos rivers wound down toward New Mexico. The conservationists' case for a reserve here was persuasive: few forest lands in the state had been attacked more relentlessly by lumbermen through the years than those in the back country of Dolores and San Miguel counties. As early as the 1880's timber cutters had denuded the region in search of lumber for mines. Because of the importance of mining, the devastation of the timberlands had largely been ignored, but by the end of the century some citizens had begun to see the unwise nature of their attitude.[71]

At Mancos, a tiny mining-ranching settlement on the banks of Bear Creek in the far southwestern reaches of Colorado, local citizens instituted a movement to protect their local watersheds in the summer of 1901. Throughout 1902 and 1903, behind Mancos rancher Louis Paquin and a handful of proconservation cattlemen and local farmers, valley pioneers swamped the Bureau of Forestry with petitions requesting a reservation that might salvage what few good timber stands still existed in the region.[72] Belatedly, the government complied with the requests. On June 13 it created the reserve.

Given the nature of the reserved area, the Roosevelt administration might have expected opposition to the proclamation. Mile for mile the Montezuma covered one of the richest mineral-producing regions in the United States. While Telluride, Ouray, and Silverton had seen better days, their big mines—the American Nettie, Camp Bird, Revenue-Virginius, Smuggler-Union, and others—still were highly productive.[73] Conservationists might logically have anticipated an outcry against the locking up of an area of such value. At the same time, the area's miners had a history of impetuosity and violence. In both 1901 and 1903, Telluride mines had been hit by strikes, one severe enough to prompt the governor to request federal troops from Roosevelt.[74] For various reasons, however, no protest developed. The *Durango Herald*, apparently voicing the feelings of many, reported that "practically the entire population favored the establishment of the reserve."[75] Such a report was overoptimistic, as time was to show, but for the moment the Montezuma was calm.

Due north of the Montezuma, Roosevelt established, on June 14, the Uncompahgre Forest Reserve, 758,111 acres of land on the giant Uncompahgre Plateau in Mesa, Montrose, and San Miguel counties.[76] The new reservation, smaller than most and totally devoid of mountains, was nonetheless important to conservationists. Wrapped in broad stands of Engelmann spruce, yellow pine, and aspen, the plateau protected the headwaters of as many streams as any reserve in Colorado. From its west

Timber destruction around the Gold King Mill, Telluride, Colorado.
Courtesy Denver Public Library, Western History Department

slope hundreds of creeks flowed into the San Miguel River on its way into Utah; from its east flank more streams poured into the Uncompahgre and Gunnison rivers on their way north to join the Colorado. In both the San Miguel and Uncompahgre valleys water from plateau streams irrigated miles of productive farmland.

Conservationists had worked for the Uncompahgre withdrawal for two decades. As early as 1884, aroused by the destruction caused by local timber cutters, they had protested, but they had not been heard. Timber was so vital in Montrose, in Escalante, Ridgway, Naturita, and across the San Miguel Mountains in Ouray's flourishing mines, that pioneers paid little heed to critics. In the summer of 1900 small groups of worried

Mining destruction at the Gold Queen placers near Montrose, Colorado.

Courtesy Denver Public Library, Western History Department

valley farmers regrouped and sent petitions to the secretary of the interior and the president asking that "a portion of the Uncompahgre Plateau and the slopes thereto be set apart as a forest reserve."[77] After twenty years of vacillation, the government finally acted. Its action was widely applauded. The Grand Junction-Delta-Montrose triangle formed the core of proconservation sentiment in western Colorado, and Roosevelt found only loyalists to his program there.

On August 25, 1905, Roosevelt issued a proclamation creating the last reserve in Colorado's central Rockies—the Holy Cross Forest Reserve, 99,720 acres of timberland strewn over Eagle,

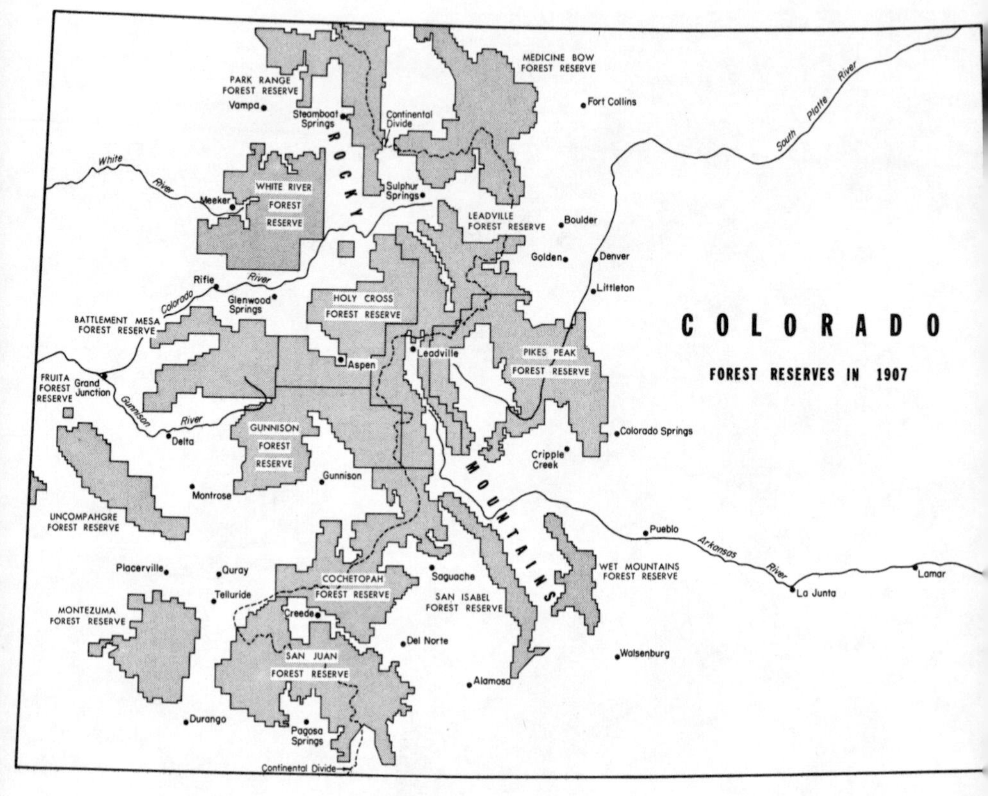

Forest reserves in Colorado, 1907

Pitkin, Lake, and Gunnison counties.[78] Bordered roughly by the Gore Range to the north, the Leadville and Gunnison reserves to the east and south, and the Battlement Mesa Reserve, Redstone, Aspen, Carbondale, and Glenwood Springs to the west, the Holy Cross embraced one of the highest sections of the continental divide—a towering thirty-mile chain of mountains from Tennessee Pass to Aspen. Out of the Mount of the Holy Cross, Castle, Pyramid, Snowmass, Capitol, and Sopris peaks and the Maroon Bells ran the Eagle, Crystal, Fryingpan, and Roaring Fork rivers, all of which irrigated lowlands for hundreds of miles around on their journey to the Colorado.

Compelling reasons existed for the government's action, primary among them, as usual, the desire to curtail rampant timber destruction and preserve existing watersheds. Large-scale timber cutting had existed along the fringes of the Holy Cross territory as early as the late 1880's, originating in the vicinity of Tennessee Pass and spreading, through the years, into the interior. Fueled by extensive demands from the nearby mining communities of Leadville and Red Cliff, as well as by the Colorado Midland Railroad which penetrated the area in 1880, the lumber industry flourished. Conversely, the timberlands suffered; near the mining hamlets of Mitchell and Pando, along the Roaring Fork near Independence, and elsewhere, the forests simply disappeared.[79] Not until the turn of the century, however, did the government take steps to halt the annihilation.

In 1900 small teams of federal agents entered the Leadville-Aspen-Red Cliff region, prepared reports on the land for government analysis, and enlisted the support of local conservationists to help work for a reserve. In 1905 a final report was submitted by the agents to the government showing that "in order to supply the timber needs of the miners in the region it was necessary to create a reserve and get it under supervision as soon as possible."[80] When the reserve at last came into being, James H. Clark, supervisor of all Colorado reserves, explained the reason to the *Denver Republican*:

> *There has been too much mining and prospecting in that part of the state and much of the large timber has been cut down and hauled away by people who had no right to it whatsoever. For years this stealing timber has been going on, but there has been no way to put a stop to it. . . . Now it is a very good thing to put aside this land for the purpose of saving the timber, for if it were not done there would be very little timber in a few years. The depredations have been outrageous.*

Henceforth, said Clark, the miners of the region would be rigidly controlled. From that time they would have to "show that they have the mineral or they will have to get off. There will be no more of this dog in the manger attitude, that is, a man gets a claim, doesn't work it and won't permit anyone else to work. This will help the government save the forests for the use of future generations."[81] Clark's attitude could not have endeared insurgents to the federal government. Though they raised no protest against conservation in 1905, peace on the Holy Cross did not last long.

The Holy Cross was the last of Roosevelt's 1905 withdrawals. Through August of the year he had blanketed the state with eleven new reserves spanning 8,876,523 acres of public domain from Wyoming to New Mexico and Grand Junction to the Great Plains. Colorado conservationists should have been gratified; their decade-old plan to bring watersheds "covering all streams proceeding from the Rocky Mountain Range" into the forest-reserve system had been almost fully implemented in their state. If they still believed as they had in the past that "whoever makes war on these forests, makes war upon our civilization, our prosperity, our happiness," then they should have been satisfied that it was over.[82] And yet, among them, a vague sense of unease seemed to parallel expressions of satisfaction. The extensiveness of the proclamations seemed to overwhelm even those who had targeted the territory for federal action. "The old adage that it never rains but what it pours," mused the *Denver Republican*, "seems to be particularly pertinent to Colorado."[83]

VIII. A Condition of Revolt

If Colorado forest reserves were comparatively calm in the wake of Roosevelt's action, they did not remain so for long. The reason was an announcement made by the government in mid-June, 1905, that, effective January 1, 1906, grazing fees would be instituted on all reserves in the state. Albert Potter, grazing chief of the Bureau of Forestry, quickly assured cattlemen that no damage would be done them by any regulatory changes made on the reservations. But all across Colorado insurgent stockmen, already angered by grazing permits, reserve regulations, the proliferation of the reserves themselves, and the transfer issue, were in no mood to listen to assurances. In the summer and fall of 1905 they exploded in protest.

Essentially their protest was based on several timeworn themes. Despite the fact that federal action was designed only to stabilize the range, an objective which was not new, insurgents treated it as an act of oppression.[1] They claimed, first, that only the Congress could levy a tax; establishment of a fee by presidential fiat was both illegal and suppressive. Second, they maintained that a tax, no matter how small, would drive small operators off the range and allow large owners, who could afford the tax, to control it.[2] As a disconsolate Glenwood Springs cattleman explained, "the cattle business is not a great profit-getter. . . . The men who have cattle on the range [will be] taxed just as high as their property can stand and if you go to put any more taxes on them there will be only one result, and that will be to drive them out of business."[3] Others agreed. Most of the best cattle-producing areas in the region had already been "cut to pieces by reserves," said the *Yampa Leader*, and "the recommendation by Forester Pinchot that a fee be exacted . . . is an injustice the cattlemen will not submit to without a fight. . . . The stockmen are willing that reserves be created . . . but contend that the hardship of paying a fee is contrary to the spirit and custom of the country."[4]

In actuality, the "spirit and custom of the country" was—as it always had been—the central point. Insurgent cattlemen, unconsciously or not, always returned to the fundamental idea that the land was "theirs"—by "spirit" and "custom." As Coloradan Fred Johnson, secretary of the National Livestock Association, explained to the 1905 American Forest Congress Convention in Washington:

> *From my knowledge of the West, I can assert that there is no class of men more vitally interested in sane and reasonable protection of the forest than the stockmen. . . . But the Western stockman is of a peculiar disposition . . . restless and impatient under any attempt to bind him to ironclad rules and regulations. . . . It has been the failure of governmental departments to understand this phase of his character. . . . As the pioneer, who braved the dangers and hardships of the frontier to open the way to civilization, he has felt that he acquired some moral rights which even the government should respect, and to have a stranger* [*ranger*] *ride up and tell him things he may or may not do . . . is galling to his pride and that feeling of absolute freedom which has been bred into his nature.*[5]

Perhaps because of this, they reacted to Potter's announcement with a certain arrogance. One northwest Colorado cattleman's association passed resolutions which summed up the feelings of many: "Resolved, that none of us know, or care to know, anything about grasses . . . outside of the fact for the present there are lots of them . . . and we are after getting the most of them while they last."[6]

When the insurgents began fighting back in the late summer of 1905, they attacked the tax proposal on two fronts: through extensive, often vitriolic newspaper campaigns throughout the state and through a seemingly endless chain of local protest meetings. The newspaper campaign was anchored in Denver by the *Record-Stockman*, the voice of Colorado's anticonservation cattlemen. While the newspaper stubbornly contended that stockmen did not object to reserves in themselves, it held that the proposed fees were "obnoxious" in all respects and that a "general protest against them" was taking root in the mountain country.[7] Surprisingly, on the tax issue even the *Denver Republican* agreed with its intracity rival: "There seems to be no adequate reason for imposing a per capita tax or other charge on cattle allowed to graze within the limits of a reserve. Let the sale of timber cover the expense of maintaining the forest, but let grazing privileges be as free as they are on the treeless plains."[8]

Elsewhere in Colorado other newspapers fell in line. In the northwest quarter of the state, always the scene of agitation, the *Glenwood Avalanche-Echo* quickly took up the insurgents' cause. Claiming that the newspaper had "received letters from all the people in the county" regarding the subject of taxes, it said flatly that "none of the cattlemen in Routt County are in favor of the grazing fees."[9] Further west, at Craig, cattlemen rallied around the *Routt County Courier*. Speaking for stock interests again (after having supported the White River national-park idea), it insisted that "in a country as wealthy as the United States, the government could find some other means of raising funds for paying the expenses of the reserves."[10] At Meeker the consistently abusive *Meeker Herald* openly derided the new federal policy and called for one "grand and vigorous protest from the Western Slope."[11] Significantly, however, protest was not confined to the Western Slope. At Sugar City, for example, a dusty, windblown plains community two hundred miles from the nearest mountains, the *Sugar City*

Gazette mounted a blistering attack on the fee plan. Supported by local cattlemen who were "up in arms" over the tax and "ready to fight it hard," the *Gazette* vowed to carry protest against it "up to Theodore Roosevelt himself."[12] Dissent even sprang up in areas long loyal to conservation. In Delta even the strongly proconservation *Delta Independent* attacked the plan: "Forest reserves in the state are . . . about to crowd out the livestock men . . . so a vigorous protest must be made against the rules of the forestry department, and justice demanded. . . . The restrictions are such that all stockmen in Colorado . . . are called on to make a protest that will be understood in Washington. . . . Turn out now or forever hold your peace."[13]

Buoyed up by such support all over the state, dozens of cattlemen's associations, allied in some cases with mining and farm groups, mobilized for a long series of protest meetings throughout the fall and winter.

At Gunnison, where opposition to the new Gunnison Forest Reserve undoubtedly intensified antitax feelings, the Gunnison County Stockgrowers' Association became the first major cattlemen's group in Colorado to officially condemn the government's plan. At tiny Basalt on the periphery of the Holy Cross Reserve, where, according to the *Glenwood Avalanche-Echo*, "indignation was at a fever heat," a large group of area cattlemen denounced federal "Redeemers" and their tax proposal. And at Rifle on the Colorado River a mass meeting of "very indignant" stockmen condemned the tax as "the biggest piece of machinery for graft ever introduced into any form of government."[14] From Hayden on the southern fringe of the Park Range Reserve came word that "the people . . . were very much in earnest in protesting the proposed grazing fees" and that absolutely "none of the resident cattlemen . . . were in favor of the grazing fees or rules of any kind."[15] At Florissant cattlemen from all over central Colorado passed resolutions branding the governmental proposal a "death net" for themselves and their industry.[16] Lending their support to the cattlemen (and drawing cries of demagoguery from conservationists), Herschel Hogg and Franklin Brooks stumped western Colorado exhorting insurgents to "get together and take united action against the government" so that they would have strong and united support behind them when they returned to Washington to fight the tax in Congress.[17]

Dissatisfied with the relative aimlessness of the protest movement, the militant Roaring Fork and Eagle River Stockgrowers Association from the Aspen-Glenwood-Eagle area called for a massive rally to be held in Glenwood in December. A local newspaper solemnly noted that the stockmen there intended to settle the grazing-tax question for good. "Confident that President Roosevelt" would not "allow this thing to go on" after he had "heard the evidence from both sides," the dissidents issued an invitation to Pinchot to participate in the meeting with them.[18] Apparently they believed that the Forester's "evidence" would be less convincing to the president than their own.

Most Western Slope newspapers eagerly supported the idea of a summit meeting. Even the *Montrose Enterprise*, which had championed federal conservation policies for a decade, hoped that the proposed meeting would lead to the end of the tax idea—"an injustice to the stock-raisers who have blazed the trail of this once wilderness."[19] In throwing its support behind the conference, the irrepressible *Glenwood Avalanche-Echo* called for a "rising up" of the "hardy pioneers of the forest," those who had been "treated as outlaws" in their own land.[20] Touring the Western Slope in November, H. J. Holmes, editor of the *Avalanche-Echo*, happily noted that the "rising up" was materializing and that cattlemen and farmers from all over the area were prepared to make the Glenwood meeting "a great demonstration."[21] On the bitterly cold evening of November 28, at the Albany Hotel in Denver, an insurgent caucus drew up and passed extensive antitax resolutions. Discussing the insurgent attitude with newspaper reporters, Edward Taylor explained that "We have profound respect for Mr. Pinchot, but the rules enumerated [by him] for Colorado are Utopian."[22]

On the morning of December 4, two hundred grim cattlemen

crowded into the tiny Glenwood Hotel for the confrontation with Pinchot. Their leader, as always, was Elias Ammons, who began the meeting with an attack on the "obnoxious tax." In a long harangue, Ammons claimed, as he had at the Public Land Commission hearings in 1904, that he had been "picked out" by local forest rangers and others for economic ruin, which was to be accomplished through imposition of the tax.[23] He was followed by Gunnison lawyer Dexter Sapp who claimed, to loud applause, that stockmen should not be taxed to preserve timber to conserve snow and water for parts of the state they did not inhabit. Fred Light from Pitkin, a mining camp in the middle of the Gunnison Reserve, spoke long and bitterly of the "non-existence" of forests in the Gunnison and Holy Cross areas. More than some others, Light was heard by the cattlemen. Dismissed as a "tinhorn orator" by local rangers, he was recognized by his fellows as one of the most obdurate of all the insurgents.[24]

The protest droned on through the morning. When the cattlemen were finished, a handful of miners added their thoughts. Finally, a group of farmers spoke. Robert Steward of Plateau declared that "forest reserve regulations were as odious to the farmers as to the stockmen," and John Dittman, a Mesa farmer-rancher, solemnly warned Pinchot that local pioneers had suffered enough indignities to "cause an ordinary man to rebel."[25]

Throughout the morning Pinchot sat, urbane and unruffled, and listened intently to the cattlemen. Then, in the afternoon, they listened to him. For an hour and a half he spoke. Confident, effusing good fellowship, his rhetoric simple and persuasive, he seemed to beguile his audience. His message to the dissidents was simple: the grazing tax would be enacted and any cattleman who used the range would pay it. As uncompromising as Pinchot's position was and despite the fact that the cattlemen allegedly had come to Glenwood to make "a great demonstration," when the Forester finished his address, no move was made to dispute it. The ballroom remained silent.[26] That night Pinchot left Glenwood for Denver, then caught a train for Washington.

The next day, determined to salvage something from the meeting, the insurgents concluded it by passing resolutions declaring "unanimous and unalterable opposition to the imposition of any grazing tax" in Colorado. "The people of Colorado" had not asked for a tax and did not want it, read the resolutions. Such taxation would be borne unfairly by cattlemen living inside reserves, while those living outside on the nonforested public domain would be allowed to graze their stock without paying fees. Further, forest improvements allegedly to be financed by tax revenue were neither needed nor desired by those who would have to pay the tax. And, most importantly, no other class of citizens had ever been taxed while building their lives; any burden on cattlemen, as a group, was unconstitutional.[27] The resolutions were emphatic enough, but they had a hollow ring to them. No matter how assertive the insurgents might have been, the fact remained that the tax still would go into effect on January 1. Worse, they had had a chance to assail Pinchot, and they had not used it. As one disgusted newspaper saw it, the Forester had "thrown a wet blanket" on the insurgents, disarmed them, and embarrassed them.[28]

Despite their defeat at Glenwood, a small band of Colorado cattlemen travelled to Washington shortly before Christmas, 1905, to present their views to Roosevelt himself. The trip was beclouded with pessimism. It was widely thought that Pinchot, back in Washington after his trip to Glenwood, was "continually at work to defeat" the Coloradans "working against his pet scheme."[29]

The pessimism was justified. On December 17 the three men—Elias Ammons, Isaac Baer of Meeker, and cattleman-lawyer Frederick Ewing—joined senators Teller and Patterson in a visit to Roosevelt. Patterson, considered the group's most articulate spokesman, took the lead in attacking the grazing fee as an "intolerable usurpation of power," a "plain case of where somebody thought certain things should be done, and determined to stretch the law to order it done." But Roosevelt was

Gunnison County Stockgrowers Association.
Courtesy Denver Public Library, Western History Department

not swayed. His reply was blunt: the state of Colorado was "satisfied" with the new order, therefore it could not be considered unjust.[30]

The next day Patterson, in a final attempt to dissuade the president from levying the tax, met with him privately in the White House. The *Montrose Enterprise*, reporting the talk between the two men, stated that Patterson had won "a signal victory."[31] But he had not. After conferring with his attorney general and determining to his satisfaction that the tax was not unconstitutional, Roosevelt "frankly stated" to Patterson that he was "committed to the policy of exacting compensation on the forest reserves."[32] So, for the moment, the matter rested.

Savoring his "victory," in his annual message to Congress in December, Roosevelt announced that "the forest policy of this administration appears to enjoy the unbroken support of the people. . . . All organized opposition to the forest reserves has disappeared."[33] Replied Henry Teller: "My people shall not be trampled on as long as I can work for their protection."[34]

On January 1, 1906, the grazing tax went into effect on all Colorado reserves. Its rates were uniform and uncomplicated. Cattlemen were required to pay from twenty to thirty-five cents a head for cattle and horses for a "regular" reserve grazing season and from thirty-five to fifty cents a head for a calendar year. Sheepmen paid from five to eight cents a head for the regular season and from eight to ten cents for the entire year.[35] Grazing quotas established by the Forest Service were generous, ranging from an allowance of seven thousand head of cattle and horses on the San Isabel Reserve to forty thousand head on the White River and from no sheep at all on the Park Range Reserve (probably in deference to the particularly hostile attitude of cattlemen there) to sixty thousand on the Leadville.[36] By any reasonable gauge the rates and quotas were fair. But it was not the rate or quota scale that concerned the still-angry insurgents. What concerned them, as always, was the principle. Said the *Steamboat Pilot*,

the principle of the tax is wrong. . . . With all due deference to President Roosevelt, Forester Pinchot, and Secretary [*of Agriculture*] *Wilson, the fact remains clear cut and incontrovertible—the grazing tax for forest reserves is wrong. And all the sophistry of the administration and all the syncophancy of the partisan press cannot make it right.*[37]

To be sure, there were those who attempted to convince the insurgents that in Pinchot, Roosevelt, and Wilson they had "three good friends" who would "carry out in good faith" every promise they had made to the cattlemen—namely that the tax was for the benefit of the little man.[38] But the dissidents chose not to listen. They remained convinced throughout the remainder of the fight that, as one sympathetic newspaper phrased it, "their cause" was "just" and that there seemed to be "no good reason why they should not win in the end."[39]

As in the past, much of the reaction in western Colorado against federal policy was led by the combative Roaring Fork and Eagle River Stockgrowers Association and its president, Fred Light. At an unusually raucous January 12 meeting in Carbondale, attended by senators Teller and Patterson and Congressman Hogg, the association voted unanimously to adhere to the position taken by the Colorado delegation which had met with Roosevelt in December. Led in a heated discussion of their problems by Teller and Patterson, the cattlemen asserted that the grazing tax was but the beginning of a federal attempt to lock up the entire public domain. Warned one of the senators: "Stockmen ought not to lie down, as there will be a great effort made at this session of Congress to put all the public lands under the same [rental] rules. The trouble now is only a small infant compared with what may come in the future."[40] Hogg, for one, believed that already it might have been too late to stop the government. "The forest reserve system," he said, "has come to stay. I am sorry that it has. I am not a believer in it. . . . I do not like it. I think the whole thing is wrong from start to finish, but my thinking will not change it, because everybody outside the forest reserve counties is in favor of it, and the reserve counties are a mighty small drop in the bucket."[41] The cattlemen nonetheless passed resolutions declaring the tax illegal.

In mid-January the Roaring Fork and other state cattlemen's associations prepared to confront Pinchot again—this time in Denver during the annual meeting of the National Livestock Association. Discussing the objectives of the proposed conference with Pinchot, the *Denver Republican* insisted that most Colorado cattlemen were "very well pleased with the situation" on the forest reserves and "practically agreed on the main outlines of the Pinchot policy."[42] But the mood of the cattlemen belied the *Republican*'s words. The men who drifted into Denver were generally angry. The *Denver Record-Stockman*, analyzing their feelings, wrote that "the average stockman is growing tired of being regarded as an intruder and is weary of the constant fight" for his rights.[43] To recoup lost rights, the cattlemen apparently believed that they had to discredit Pinchot. But they had tried before and failed.

On January 29, a cold, blustery day in Denver, anticonservation cattlemen met with the Forester and grazing inspector Albert Potter. After a four-hour conference at the Brown Palace, the *Denver Republican* reported that all had been quiet and harmonious; rather than protest to Pinchot as they had planned, the cattlemen had listened passively while he explained that the fees were law and would not be annulled.[44] But the strident *Rocky Mountain News* reported that the Coloradans had met "amid a feeling of determination and enthusiasm that had never been manifested before." It noted that both Elias Ammons and John Springer had "excoriated" the grazing-tax idea and aroused a "heady response" from the cattlemen. Ammons had been particularly impressive, attacking the "grazing tax evil," charging that Colorado cattlemen had not been given a "square deal" by Roosevelt, and demanding that forest-reserve matters be left to "men who are sent to Washington by Colorado people, and not a lot of people who do not know a ranch from a pink tea party."[45]

The next day the cattlemen met again with Pinchot, with the Forester dominating the proceedings. As he had at Glenwood, he persuasively presented the case for the grazing tax, and, as they had at Glenwood, the insurgents listened without rebuttal. The *Denver Republican*, reporting on the meeting, effusively termed it a "love feast," the most "peaceful gathering ever known in the history of the livestock industry." Emphasizing the "magic influence" of Pinchot over the insurgents, the newspaper declared that

in truth, the stockmen were disarmed. . . . Mr. Pinchot is one of the most diplomatic men who has come out of the East. Aroused last spring when they were ordered to pay a fee for the use of the forest ranges, the stockmen came down to meet the terrible Pinchot, who stood as the representative of those who would rob them of their ancient privileges, and they were prepared to grow heated in debate and do battle. Instead of a fiendish individual, the stockmen met a suave, polished gentleman who is exceedingly friendly . . . and is ready to meet them halfway in all good suggestions. [The meeting] was gratifying.[46]

It was difficult to account for, but the *Republican* was right. For the second time in two months Pinchot had silenced the insurgents.

Whatever its results, the Denver meeting created controversy all over western Colorado. Statewide reaction, as measured by newspaper editorials, was varied. Some, reflecting the attitudes of their localities, believed that the cattlemen had been wrong all along and that Pinchot—rightly—had jarred them back to reality. The *Delta Independent*, which took a centrist position on conservation, wrote that the meeting had "proven to many [stock] growers that the policy of government toward them on the range is not as bad as many of them would imagine."[47] The *Walsenburg World*, spokesman for a plains city with much to gain from conservation, stressed Pinchot's display of "good will" at the meeting and editorialized that the meeting's net result was the permanent end of "all friction over public grazing." The "agreement" between the Forester and the insurgents, added the *World*, was one "of the happiest results of the meeting."[48] Even the *Yampa Leader*, a steadfast opponent of virtually every facet of conservation, called the meeting "wonderful."[49]

Other newspapers, however, maintained that the cattlemen had been "sold out" by their leaders, not backed down by Pinchot. The furious *Glenwood Avalanche-Echo* hurled charges at the cattlemen that they had "given up" and had been defeated because their key leaders, swayed by Pinchot, had deserted the "cause" to "curry favor" with him rather than fight him. The newspaper contended that "big cattlemen" with their "ability to control forest officers" had dominated the meeting from the start, supporting Pinchot both to secure better grazing "arrangements" than others and to maintain Roosevelt's enthusiasm for railroad regulation (something they sought and something that, so far, the president had pursued). It granted that Pinchot had been too crafty for the "average cattleman of the Continental Divide," too "diplomatic and genteel," and too "smooth" to be outsmarted. But the *Avalanche-Echo* still insisted that the cattlemen had undone themselves.[50] Among others, the *Gunnison News-Champion* agreed. Disgusted by cattlemen "falling all over themselves going around on the quiet to Pinchot to secure concessions the other fellows didn't know about," humbling themselves, and becoming "servile to the autocratic government," it issued a warning to them. It was a dangerous practice, said the paper, to curry favor with the government: "The history of the world does not show a case where the tyrant has failed to appear when invited."[51]

Soberly assessing the results of the Denver meeting, weighing all arguments, and sifting through the propaganda, the *Grand Junction News* accurately concluded that, after all, it had changed nothing. Defiance remained undiminished in the high country. There still existed—and always would exist—"much dissatisfaction" among those "pushed under the yoke of a government tax."[52]

When the National Livestock Association convened in Denver in late January, Colorado insurgents tried and failed to engineer an antitax protest movement. Despite attempts by Elias Ammons to put the convention on record against the tax, the anticonservationists found few supporters; even Ammons' own Colorado Cattle and Horse Growers Association failed to back him. On February 2 the convention repudiated the insurgents by passing resolutions endorsing the tax. Two factors may have been responsible for the decisive action: first, the fact that Murdo MacKenzie, a Roosevelt loyalist and president of the association, used his position to promote the administration's program and, second, the insurgents' humiliation at Glenwood.[53] Whatever the reasons, the insurgents had suffered a significant setback. Commenting on the situation, the *Denver Republican* remarked that "whether Mr. Pinchot is a hypnotist or governmental control of the forest ranges is so just that it pleads its own case, the fact remains that practically all the stockmen of Colorado have been won over to his side of what at one time threatened to become a bitter controversy."[54] If the *Republican* was right, the insurgents, looking to the future, might have seen the handwriting on the wall.

The spring and summer of 1906 passed with relatively little controversy over the grazing-tax issue.[55] For several months insurgents turned their attention to other matters, primarily the resurgent leasing idea.

In March, 1906, the Interior Department drafted a grasslands leasing bill and submitted it to Congress. Colorado insurgents were stunned. For seventeen months—ever since the Public Land Commission hearings of August, 1904—they had believed that the leasing concept was dead. Upon learning of the government's action, their immediate thought was, as the *Denver Record-Stockman* sadly stated it, that they could say "goodbye to the free range" forever.[56] Nonetheless, they mobilized to fight the bill as they had its predecessors.

The Interior Department's leasing bill was little different from others which had preceded it. It vested power in the federal government to lease grazing lands on the public domain, authorized the secretary of the interior to oversee the process and to withdraw and lease lands at his discretion, and it earmarked revenue for state reclamation projects. If the bill appeared innocuous to its backers, it was seen in a different light by its opponents. It even prompted the *Denver Republican* to denounce it: "A policy under which public lands are withdrawn," protested the *Republican*, "checks settlement, and to that extent is wrong except in the case of forest reserves."[57] Before insurgents could mount an attack on the bill, however, it died in Congress.

Two months after the death of the bill, conservationist Senator Elmer Burkett of Nebraska submitted a new measure in its place. Its provisions were simple: the bill proposed in vague terms that grazing districts be created throughout the West and be administered by the Department of Agriculture. What was controversial about the bill, at least to anticonservation cattlemen, was the fact that it would put grazing lands directly under the jurisdiction of Gifford Pinchot. Insurgents reverted to their oldest arguments. In April the *Routt County Courier* charged that the Burkett plan would allow the "rich man" "to lease the lands, and the man struggling to escape from poverty will be left in a worse rut than ever. There is but one way the small ranchman of the West stands anywhere near an equal show with the cattle baron, and that is to give him free range." "What right," it asked, had Pinchot's Forestry Bureau "to deprive [small ranchers] of that which they have always considered their own and by right of constant use have made their own?"[58] The capricious *Denver Republican*, swinging back to the administration line, sternly warned the antileasers that "they should not throw themselves across the path of the movement. . . . Defeat lies in wait for those who oppose it."[59] But the antileasing element remained undeterred, and to their satisfaction the Burkett bill was never reported out of committee.

Opponents of the Roosevelt administration and its leasing inclinations were given no opportunity to celebrate. On July 26, 1906, they were suddenly confronted with a brand new problem. On that date the president began withdrawing from entry all suspected coal-bearing lands on the western public domain. His ultimate objective: to subject them to federal leasing procedures.

Though he had given little outward indication of it, for a number of years Roosevelt had been concerned by the extent of fraud on western coal lands. For years, aided by archaic or poorly enforced land laws, speculators and corporations had taken possession of vast tracts of the public domain's coal lands. In many cases engrossment had been designed to control the coal lands themselves for monopolistic purposes. In other cases such lands were sought exclusively for speculative purposes. And, on occasion, coal entries were made in forest lands in order that the purchaser might gain control of all surface timber. Whatever their ultimate goals, Roosevelt, along with Pinchot and other conservationists working toward efficiency in the area of resource management, was opposed to the methods employed by coal seekers. In a 1906 policy speech he stated that it was "a scandal to maintain laws which sound well, but which make fraud the key" to resource development. "My own belief," he concluded, "is that there should be a provision for leasing coal."[60]

Mindful of the fact that a big-business-oriented Congress would not pass leasing legislation, Roosevelt determined to take action himself. By proclamation, beginning on July 26, he ordered the withdrawal from entry of all potential coal lands on the public domain. After examination and classification, the Interior Department explained, noncoal lands were to be restored to entry. Coal lands, however, would remain under the custodianship of the federal government "in perpetuity," to be leased at its discretion. To a disbelieving West, Secretary of the Interior James R. Garfield carefully explained that the leasing system would "induce development when needed, prevent waste, and halt monopoly."[61]

If Colorado insurgents were skeptical about the projected benefits of the government's plan, events over the course of the next two years reinforced their feeling. Between July 26, 1906, and January 1, 1908, the Roosevelt administration withdrew from entry 13,246,480 acres of public domain within Colorado's borders; 4,435,480 acres were never restored. Anticonservationists deplored what they considered to be the hypocrisy of the Roosevelt plan: in the name of "inducing development," the government had withdrawn over four million acres of habitable land. Having "lost" some eight million acres of land in forest reserves and being on the verge of losing more to grasslands leasing, insurgents immediately, almost instinctively, protested the loss of still more through coal-land withdrawals.

They challenged the withdrawals on economic grounds, arguing that if left in force they stood to damage the economies of numerous Colorado counties.[62] To an extent their fears were valid. In 1906, Colorado was producing in excess of ten million tons of coal a year in mines in fifteen counties. Its value came to some $12,735,616 in 1906 alone.[63] In those counties heavily dependent on coal mining for economic prosperity, perhaps federal withdrawals did promise to be damaging. And, logically, those counties with coal-land withdrawals *and* extensive forest reservations threatened to be damaged most of all.

Coincidentally or not, the area hardest hit by the withdrawals was the northwest quadrant of Colorado—that area roughly between Delta and the Wyoming border and Utah and the continental divide which contained both the Park Range and White River reserves.[64] A region long conditioned to opposing conservation in other forms found little difficulty in deploring the new withdrawals. For the most part, its ensuing outcry appeared to be a community effort, a melding of cattlemen, mining interests, small-town businessmen, and the press to "save" their communities. In Yampa, for example, where the government retired 1,442,000 acres of land from entry, leaving the city a virtual island in the middle of withdrawn territory, the outraged *Yampa Leader* charged that the withdrawals would

> *greatly retard the progress of this part of the state and* [*are*] *regarded by our people as a serious blunder on the part of the administration.* [*They are*] *looked upon as an act of the coal trust, which effort has been aided by the administration. The trust seems satisfied that much of this land contains much valuable coal deposits and wanted the treasure saved until it could get time to grab it. . . . The coal land of Routt County is a treasure of which the people have always been proud, and now to have a chunk of it grabbed right while we were in the middle of a conversation with investors and homesteaders, trying to induce them to come, invest, and help build up the country, well, it doesn't look good and the county don't feel good about it either.*[65]

The *Steamboat Pilot*, long an enemy of Roosevelt and his policies, lashed out at him in its most savage editorial since the conservation controversy began:

Once again, in this new reservation of coal lands, Routt County has heard from the great bombastic Teddy. . . . Oh, redoubtable Teddy, your executive methods win our keenest admiration by the acute and delicate finesse with which they are maneuvered to serve your ends. . . . About a year ago it was our timber that laid heavy on his tender conscience, for if timber were used to build up this part of the state, where oh where, in after years, could he find a suitable spot for his spectacular hunting expeditions? . . . Ha! I have it. Over in Routt County lies the choicest bit of land I know for my favorite sport. . . . Then straight away there goes forth an edict reserving all the choice timber lands of Routt County. . . . And now comes this new coal reservation with all the talk of preservation of coal and prevention of trusts. But we in Routt County know full well there is a nigger in the fence somewhere.[66]

Certainly conservationists saw merit in Roosevelt's action. As the *Denver Republican* said, "President Roosevelt's determination to save what remains of the public coal lands for the future benefit of the whole people is a worthy act, wise from a commercial standpoint and patriotic in its aim."[67] But in most coal-bearing areas of Colorado the feeling was growing that in all phases of conservation "department and executive rulings" were "coming to take the place of law." "If we are to have a dictator," said the *Steamboat Pilot*, "the expense of maintaining a Congress is unnecessary."[68] The whole affair, added the *Denver Times*, was a study in the misapplication of "arbitrary power," a classic example of "what an intolerable nuisance the 'Big Stick'" had become.[69]

Inevitably, perhaps, in the fall of 1906 the Colorado back country broke out in virulent protest against the entire structure of the federal conservation program. Unlike the wave of protest that had swept the reserve regions between 1897 and 1900—protest precipitated by the general question of reserve use—the new one was triggered by specific insurgent grievances: the grazing tax, mining and lumbering restrictions, coal-land withdrawals, and the projected federal leasing of the public range. Unlike the earlier outburst, too, the 1906 explosion (which lasted through the spring of 1907) entailed widespread and overt lawlessness and occasional violence. No single group dominated the protest; insurgent cattlemen stood in the forefront of most of the action, but they were joined on a more or less equal basis by homesteaders, miners and mining interests, timber cutters, and local newspapers.

No area of Colorado bred more defiance of federal conservation programs and laws than the Park Range Reserve in the far northwest corner of the state. In a day when most other areas of the Colorado range had been pacified by the federal government, the Park Range still stood out as one of the wildest, most lawless regions left in the West. From Steamboat to Yampa, from Meeker and Hayden north to Wyoming and west to Utah, the area was a lingering remnant of the old frontier where, literally, the strongest survived. The only law on the Park Range was determined by the cattlemen—generally the handful of barons who dominated the region. Disputes were settled as they always had been, not in courts of law but on the range itself. The result was murder, terrorism, and bloody range wars, usually aimed at sheepmen (who were presented with "dead lines" in the 1880's, beyond which they went only at their own risk), but frequently involving small cattlemen as well.[70] When the government created a reserve in 1905, imposed grazing restrictions, and attempted to parcel out land to cattlemen and sheepmen alike on a basis "satisfactory to both interests," stockmen—primarily the small operators—balked.[71] The 1906 grazing tax only served to anger them further.

In the fall of the year, infuriated by both the grazing fee and the government's decision to allow sheep grazing in Whiskey, Big and Little Red, and Crane parks, Park Range stockmen initiated what amounted to small-scale guerilla warfare against local rangers attempting to enforce the law.[72] The center of insurgent activity was the rugged Brown's Park region near Yampa, where Ora Haley's Two-Bar Ranch dominated the county. Self-styled "rolling juggernaut" and one of the most persistent foes of conservation in the state, Haley flatly refused to pay the tax. When local rangers attempted to collect it, he scattered his herds across the reserve and defied federal authorities to count or tax them; when the rangers attempted to round the cattle up for count, Haley's men sabotaged the roundups—even, on occasion, stampeding cattle through ranger camps. The arrogant Haley, who "kept up a moving row" with the government in his attempt to keep the local range "free and open for the Two-Bar and nobody else," consistently defied local forest supervisor Harry Ratliff, a "stubborn forester who refused to be dominated and insisted on serving the Forest Service instead of becoming a tool for the Two-Bar outfit."[73] Their clashes caused friction on the Park Range for years.

On several occasions Haley formally accused Ratliff and his rangers of rustling Two-Bar stock, and at least once Haley caused Ratliff to be arrested, for allegedly stealing a horse. When Ratliff persisted in enforcing the grazing tax, Haley personally rode to his office and threatened him with "disastrous counterblasts." Ultimately, the rancher hired gunman-sheriff Bob Meldrum of Baggs, across the state line in Wyoming, to challenge Ratliff. Weeks later, in a classic showdown on a Baggs street, the ranger outdrew Meldrum: the "unexpected move completely nonplussed the marshal, his killer instinct vanished for the moment. Meldrum stared dazedly as Ratliff removed the gun from Meldrum's holster, shoved it under the waistband of his own pants, and walked away." In time Haley and other range autocrats came to the realization that "the 'tenderfeet' government employees were boys that could take it rough."[74] Local cattlemen never ceased their antagonistic activities (although two of the largest outfits, the Sevens and the Two Circle Bar, either came to support the tax or to offer only passive resistance to it), but they never succeeded, either, in taking over the range again.

To some extent, activities on the Park Range might have been precipitated by the local anticonservation press. The *Routt County Courier*, for example, constantly encouraged insurgent cattlemen to stand their ground and to spurn any gestures of "friendliness" on the part of the federal government. Cautioned the *Courier*: "You must not put your heads into the lion's mouth because he seems gentle."[75] The *Steamboat Pilot*, as it had for a decade, continued to call for resistance to "the utter ignorance of Lord Pinchot" who "operated out of a luxurious office in Washington" and knew "nothing about range conditions" in northwest Colorado. "The whole miserable business," said the *Pilot*, "is rank imbecility."[76]

On the White River Reserve to the southwest, where anticonservation sentiment had existed since 1891, feelings remained essentially the same. One reason was the recent coal-land withdrawals. From the fall of 1906 through the spring of 1907, dozens of meetings were held protesting the action, climaxed in February by "one of the largest mass meetings" ever held in Rio Blanco County. There settlers from five counties adopted resolutions rejecting the withdrawals on the grounds that they established unnecessarily powerful federal control within the boundaries of a sovereign state and, at the same time, promised to enrich large corporations at the expense of "small operators and individual [settlers]."[77]

The government's primary problem, however, was cattlemen. Federal officials and proconservation stockmen insisted that insurgents had been "pacified." Cattleman George Swigert of Satank told the *Glenwood Post* in 1906 that "the square and honorable treatment accorded the people by Mr. Pinchot" had eliminated "many of their fears and restored their confidence in the administration."[78] And reserve supervisor Sidney Moyle added that "scarcely any objection to the forest reserves or the grazing tax" existed among local settlers. They were, said

Moyle, "favorably inclined" toward both.[79] Just as in Idaho, where in 1905 the government had claimed opposition to forest reserves was "melting," only to find stockmen openly violating reserve-use laws,[80] the cattlemen's actions belied the conservationists' claims. "We ain't a bunch of rattle-brained farmers," said one insurgent. "We are men of sober sense and we will make Mr. Pinchot come to time."[81]

At Rifle on February 11, 1907, the Grand River Cattlegrowers Association called a meeting of stockmen from all over western Colorado to discuss the fee and to consider the feasibility of ignoring it. The mood was clearly defiant in a crowd which included even a number of defectors from the Pinchot camp—cattlemen from the Grand Junction area who had become "disgusted with his methods" and were now "among the bitterest" opponents he had.[82] At a stormy day-long meeting in the Rifle City Hall, the insurgents concluded that until federal courts rendered a decision on the constitutionality of the grazing tax, they would not pay it. The *Gunnison News-Champion*, scarcely concealing its jubilation, called the Rifle "revolution" one of the "greatest conventions of homeowners ever gathered" in Colorado, a meeting which proved "the determination of those sturdy Americans" to maintain the fight against conservation.[83]

Other meetings followed—at Yampa, Meeker, McCoy, and other communities. Some stockmen, fearful of federal reprisals, condemned the tax, but consented to pay it. Others, notably those comprising the Rifle Stockgrowers, the Eagle Valley Stockgrowers, and the Grand and Eagle River Stockgrowers, voted to ignore it. At McCoy in June all insurgent cattlemen in northwest Colorado met one final time to condemn a system run by "tyrants" which did nothing but interfere with the efforts of honest men to "build up the country." They voted unanimously to defy federal authority and not pay the tax.[84]

Throughout the turmoil much of the local press spurred the insurgents on. To the east of the White River the *Meeker*

Herald exhorted them to "remember that by presenting a solid front in opposition to the obnoxious measures of eastern visionaries," they could "win out in the present fight."[85] And the *Glenwood Avalanche-Echo*, becoming more reactionary by the day, even devoted itself to crude poetry:

Wise old guy this Baron Pinchot,
Seeks to fence in all the earth,
While we sit here and watch his doings
In a manner full of mirth.
Wonder if when he gets through here,
He will journey up to the skies,
And build a fence around the sun,
No telling, how he flies.
But while you're building fences
Of barbed wire and the like,
Remember that the cowboys
May decide to go on strike.
Maybe when they're through with you
And you their wrath have felt,
Your pet scheme will be blasted,
And your scalp hang from their belt.[86]

Years after the conservation furor had ended, one veteran ranger looked back on life on the White River and commented that it was "remarkable . . . that the users of the forests so quickly and so completely accepted the supervision of the forests by forest officials."[87] Judging from the atmosphere of 1906 and 1907, however, he had forgotten much.

To the east of the Park Range and White River reserves, across North Park on the divide, controversy also plagued the Medicine Bow. The primary problem there, as elsewhere, was the grazing tax—a symbol of unwanted federal interference to large numbers of cattlemen, who "talked long and loud" against it.[88] On the Medicine Bow, however, the government's most

A lumber mill in the Medicine Bow Forest Reserve.
Courtesy Denver Public Library, Western History Department

serious problem was posed by defiant timber cutters. Led by insurgent lumberman Robert Sherwood of Estes Park and H. J. M. Mattis of Fort Collins, the timber cutters had operated on the Medicine Bow for years, largely unimpeded by federal rules and regulations. When the government established restrictions in 1905, they reacted by ignoring the laws. After a series of confrontations in 1906 with resident ranger Herbert Wheeler and after Wheeler threatened them with banishment from the reserve, the lumbermen resolved to take action against him. When Sherwood and a band of lumbermen arrived at Wheeler's cabin one spring day to drive him from the reserve, the ranger, rifle in hand, ordered them away. As Wheeler himself recalled it later, Sherwood "got so mad he jumped up and down, wildly cursing the [Forest] Service." But, "after going white in the face with anger," he and the others left. The timber cutters largely obeyed the law from then on.[89]

Almost as contemptuous of reserve laws as lumbermen were the Medicine Bow's quarrelsome miners. Fearful that the government's policy of selling large quantities of lodgepole pine and spruce timber to the highest bidders would eventually strip the forests of vital mine timbers, they resolutely opposed federal policy.[90] In so doing they but followed a pattern established elsewhere in the West. Whether in Idaho or southwestern Montana, where they vigorously protested reserve restrictions, or elsewhere, insurgent miners reflected a common feeling.[91] And on the Medicine Bow, as elsewhere, they were strongly supported by much of the local press. "If Uncle Sam owns the forest reserves," said the *Steamboat Pilot*, "so does he own you and me."[92] To miners and others the inference must have been clear.

In the northwest quadrangle of Colorado no reserve was more agitated than the Holy Cross. Cattlemen, who had grazed their herds in local forests for a quarter of a century before the government stepped in with restrictions, were particularly belligerent.[93] The feeling of Red Cliff rancher John D. Mims was prevalent:

> *The idea that anyone in the peaceful pursuit of private enterprise can [under federal regulations] be prosecuted as a trespasser on his own land is repugnant to the principles of American liberty and the spirit upon which our institutions are trying to stand. . . . And I am chagrined that our great government, through Pinchot, has become so cheapened as to say to you and me that we are aliens in our own country.*[94]

One of the early Holy Cross rangers, describing relations with local stockmen, later wrote with great accuracy that cattlemen "resented governmental interference, and their resentment fell on the heads of the Forest Service employees who had to enforce its regulations."[95] The years 1906 and 1907, certainly, were filled with such confrontations.

Headed by Fred Light, called by one paper "the most cantankerous of all the kickers against the forest reserves" in Colorado, the Roaring Fork and Eagle River Stockgrowers Association took the lead in provoking trouble on the Holy Cross.[96] Throughout 1906 and 1907 the Roaring Fork dissidents led an antitax movement that finally culminated at Basalt on February 22, 1907, in an outright refusal to pay the tax at all. A handful of rangers attending the meeting vainly attempted to dissuade them, but, as a local newspaper reported, the ranchers "raised their voices to swell in protest" as they joined fellow insurgents on the White River in open violation of the law.[97] Not until the Forest Service issued strict orders to its rangers to hold such cattlemen in trespass, making them liable to prosecution, did they relent. Even so, however, the reserve remained, in the opinion of the rangers themselves, the "hotbed of the West."[98] The dominant attitude remained, as the *Eagle County Blade* wrote, that "the fellows who spilled tea in Boston Harbor were not the only ones who had a righteous cause for revolution."[99]

Many of the cattlemen responsible for unrest on the Holy Cross also caused trouble on the Leadville to the east. Ironically, perhaps, the most outspoken insurgent was John D. Mims of Red Cliff, chairman of the Eagle County Republican Central Committee. In a graphic reminder to the national administration that anticonservation insurgency was more than partisan politics, Mims led a countywide denunciation of Roosevelt's "forest folly," charging that grazing permits in the reserves went to cattlemen on the basis of "how good" they had been in the past and "how good they promised to be in the future."[100] Joined by disgruntled local lumbermen, angered by a recent federal directive banning the further cutting of timber on the reserve for use in local mines, and miners, Mims and fellow insurgents brought several years of severe unrest to the area. Referring to their troubles, the *Eagle County Blade* called for the "overthrow" of Pinchot in terms that no federal official could easily afford to dismiss.[101]

To the east of the Holy Cross, across the upper Arkansas River Valley on the South Platte Reservation, the government

William Kreutzer, the "dean" of Colorado's Forest Service rangers.
Courtesy Denver Public Library, Conservation Library Center

A cartoon attacking Pinchot and his ranger corps, from the *Leadville Press*, October 23, 1908.

Courtesy Denver Public Library, Conservation Library Center

found its policies under fire from both homesteaders and cattlemen. The situation was not new; homesteaders and timber cutters had violated the reserve since its inception, and cattlemen had almost decimated local rangelands. In 1902, South Platte rangers had made the situation more tense with a recommendation forwarded to the secretary of interior that reserve ranges be closed to grazing entirely and that cattlemen ignoring federal restrictions "be dealt with as trespassers."[102] In 1906, when the tax was levied, cattlemen virtually took over the reserve. As in other western states, New Mexico, for example, where stockmen remained virtually unchallenged on federal forests, they largely continued to do as they pleased.[103] Only the diplomacy and dedication of head ranger William Kreutzer prevented a complete take-over. Kreutzer, a roughhewn ex-cowhand who had spent his life in the western wilderness and who saw his job, according to one author, as the "pursuit of the Holy Grail," contained the stockmen in time and halted their activities.[104] The restoration of peace, however, was beyond Kreutzer or anyone else.

On the neighboring Pike Forest Reserve, miners supplanted cattlemen as the primary troublemakers. Their chief complaint was that the ranger force understood little about them or their needs and had reported adversely on mining claims for a half-dozen years, "not giving the mining men a fair chance."[105] Perhaps nowhere in Colorado was "mining fever" any more prevalent than on and near the Pike. In 1906, Cripple Creek, on the southern edge of the reserve, was (along with Creede) one of the West's last authentic boomtowns. Its mining district—including Victor, Goldfield, Anaconda, and Independence—was considered to be, as late as 1911, "the richest mining field in all the world." In 1906 an aggregate of some $190 million in gold had come out of the district, and it was widely believed that "not half of the wealth" had yet been tapped.[106] In 1892, when the Pike was established, Cripple Creek was less than a year old, with most of its mining done from placers and its future questionable.[107] By 1906, however, it was famous enough to have been visited by Roosevelt himself (in 1901, the same year Gifford Pinchot had been rebuffed there by the Trans-Mississippi Commercial Congress) and prosperous enough to bridle at any federal restriction placed on mining in nearby forests.

On the Gunnison Reserve in the central Colorado Rockies, miners in the Gunnison-Crested Butte region also reacted to federal interference. But if any organized resistance was carried out, it was done by local cattlemen angered both by the grazing tax and governmental protection of sheepmen. Insurgent opinion, as voiced by spokesmen for the Gunnison Stockgrowers Association, was that federal "exploitation" of Gunnison County "pioneers" was "uncalled for and unjust."[108] And on more than one occasion cattlemen translated their feelings into violent action. So dangerous were they that each "ranger was obliged to carry a six-shooter to emphasize his authority." At all times, and especially when attempting to collect grazing fees or protecting sheepmen, district rangers were obliged to be on guard against cowboy gangs intent on seeing them "laid in the bush."[109] Before he went to the South Platte, ranger William Kreutzer had several such confrontations. In one instance, coming across the slaughter of a herd of sheep by a band of cowboys, "one of the raiders cocked his gun, poked it against Bill's stomach, and backed him around the park. Some of the raiders wanted to hang him . . . but the saner members of the group objected. So great was their anger and frustration, however, that [Kreutzer] thought they might have done him in if he hadn't escaped from the guard set over him."[110] It was a typical incident, repeated time and again across the Gunnison. As often as not arguments between rangers and cattlemen continued to be "settled with a gun" through the years.[111]

Much of the local discontent, as on certain other reserves, was generated by the activities of the insurgent press. What the *Glenwood Avalanche-Echo, Steamboat Pilot, Eagle County Blade,* and *Routt County Courier* were to the northwest, the *Gunnison News-Champion* was to its area. Warning its people that federal "grafters and bureaucrats" would bind them "hand and foot" unless they participated in "the general fight being made on the President's mistaken policies," the *News-Champion* constantly isolated Pinchot and his program for special condemnation. Had there ever been, it asked, "such an example of the Pharisee spirit in national affairs? . . . It leads us to expect no relief until the shoe begins to pinch hard enough to arouse our citizens to a realization of the high-handed manner in which our fundamental principles of government are being overridden." It remained the opinion of the newspaper that the source of most local trouble was the grazing tax, symbolic of the "gross ignorance" of a federal bureaucracy that impressed on

Cattle grazing in the Montezuma Forest Reserve near Telluride, Colorado.

Courtesy Denver Public Library, Western History Department

the West an "un-American carpetbag system of government" guided not by common sense but by "maudlin sentiment."[112]

In southwestern Colorado antitax sentiment also surfaced on the Montezuma Forest Reserve. Cattlemen there feared that the tax combined with the passing of the winter range could destroy the region's stock industry entirely.[113] For that reason, like fellow cattlemen on the Gunnison and elsewhere, they regularly threatened to "lay rangers in the bush" if they enforced the tax.[114]

Fortunately for the Forest Service, the Montezuma was patrolled by veteran rangers able to cope with the malcontents. At one point, for example, when Disappointment Creek cattlemen refused to pay the grazing tax, ranger James Lowell was sent to collect it. Fully aware that he might be "as good as dead," Lowell rode into the back country unarmed. "His weapons were soft talk, reasonableness, a persuasive argument that this business was part of the job he had to do. No word came from [him]. More than a week went by before he rode back to his headquarters. He was unscathed, and in his hip pocket were the signed applications for permits to run stock in his district. Every man entitled to the permit had signed up."[115] Trouble cropped up again less than six months later, and ranger Herbert Wheeler was dispatched to pacify the cattlemen. At a tense meeting at Disappointment Creek in the late spring of 1907, as Wheeler himself later reported, a brash rancher named Pat McKenna

started a harangue against the government and interference with the stockmen. In his talk he said the boys had been talking, and the first ranger that came by that day would be laid in the bush. He seemed to stir up enthusiasm. . . . But I said in the meeting that if a ranger was laid in the bush, two would come to take his place, that they were dealing with the United States government, and there would be no foolishness about it.[116]

Wheeler defused the situation. In time, so the Forest Service claimed, local cattlemen came to realize that federal regulation had "given a stability to the [cattle] business which it did not possess before."[117] The claim was debatable; antitax sentiment might have diminished, but it was never snuffed out entirely.

If the government was able to neutralize local cattlemen, it found more difficulty in controlling the Montezuma's timber cutters. Early in 1907, when President Roosevelt added a million acres to the reserves, they carried their protest directly to him, claiming that the action damaged their industry. In an angry letter to Philander Knox, Roosevelt's attorney general, Frank S. Clark of the Telluride Land and Lumber Company complained that large-scale timberland withdrawals on the Montezuma threatened his company and others with extinction. His company, he said, supplied mining timbers to the booming

Ouray and Silverton districts; if it failed and other companies failed with it, the mines could be forced to shut down. In time the entire mining-oriented economy of western Colorado could collapse. "This state of affairs is not peculiar to Telluride," said Clark.

> *I saw the same thing in San Juan County, and have heard the same story from several other mining districts. This may not seem like a very important political issue, but here in Colorado it has already lost almost as many friends of the Republican party as any question that has come up since the silver question. It is not that we disapprove of Roosevelt's policy of protecting the forests and managing them honestly . . . but we certainly do object to the government, after taking possession of practically all the merchantable timber in the West, administering it in such an arrogant, blind, and foolish manner.*

"I am a pretty good Republican," concluded Clark, "so I am ashamed to see a Republican administration . . . go in for paternalism so strong as to work a real hardship on the [people] of this state."[118]

When Knox forwarded the letter to his chief, Roosevelt answered:

> *I know that on the one hand there is always danger that our agents [rangers] may be a little over-strict, but on the other hand my experience is that mine owners and lumber men . . . care primarily to get the mines worked in the immediate present and are willing to sacrifice the good of the rest of our people for the future if their immediate objectives can be attained. I do not blame them very much, for a man's interests often render him honestly blind to other considerations, but I have to take that fact into account.*[119]

So the matter rested.

Though protest from the lumbermen did not subside for years, the Forest Service insisted throughout the period that lumbering was conducted profitably on the reserve. It maintained that the addition of territory and the vigilance of local rangers in protecting it "neither stimulated nor hampered lumbering to any extent." And it concluded that the curtailment of false mining patents led to an actual increase in prospecting and created a wider demand than ever for timber, thus stimulating the lumber industry rather than damaging it. The reserve had been "decidedly healthy" for all local industries.[120] Bitter lumbermen and miners, however, never agreed. Speaking for them, the *Rico News* summed up what appeared to be local sentiment:

We believe that there is the greatest danger ahead to our . . . interests. What the state of Colorado needs is her resources developed. We want actual settlers who are interested in developing her resources. . . . There are many notable wrongs which have been done by the governmental attempt to handle the lands and to manage our affairs. Colorado cannot nor should not stand for it any more.[121]

Southeast of the Montezuma, on the San Juan withdrawal, the situation largely was the same. Cattlemen, angered by the grazing tax and (as on the Gunnison) the rangers' protection of sheepmen, violated reserve laws, harrassed rangers (one was ludicrously charged with the crime of slaughtering sheep—an action undoubtedly taken by cattlemen), and aligned themselves with dissident miners. Joining the alliance was the *San Juan Prospector*, which unqualifiedly justified their actions:

The entire West is justly indignant at President Roosevelt's forest reserve policies . . . because they establish a system as obnoxious and repressive as English landlordism in Ireland. . . . The government's chief policy seems to be to squeeze every cent it can out of settlers who have made their homes near forest reserves. . . . Uncle Sam has become a penny-pinching landlord, preying on a class of pioneer citizens . . . trying to develop the wilderness.[122]

Even in far western Colorado, where conservation was more warmly welcomed than anywhere else in the state, insurgents—usually cattlemen—operated in violation of reserve laws. On the Uncompahgre Forest Reserve, for example, the attitude of many local pioneers was, as one historian has stated it, "not always in accord with existing regulations . . . and at times [it was] openly defiant and antagonistic." Cattlemen, in particular, resented domination by "government officers of inferior knowledge."[123]

On the Battlement Mesa Reserve only ranger William Kreutzer stood between insurgent stockmen and virtual anarchy, and his days were filled with confrontations. On one occasion when Kreutzer requested Mesa Lake cattlemen to move their herds to fresh ranges on Buzzard and Muddy creeks in order to allow old ranges to build up, many flatly refused. Said one: "I'll be damned if I'll drive my cows forty miles to range just on the say-so of some tenderfoot ranger." Only after riding a killer bronco that local ranchers feared was Kreutzer able to persuade them to move their herds. On another occasion, when a forest fire exploded on Grand Mesa, Kreutzer was forced to fight it alone, "with a fire tool in one hand and a six-shooter in the other."[124] In the spring of 1907, while on patrol near Cedaredge, he was faced with a minor rebellion by local citizens who "had decided that no more government agents would be tolerated there." They sent two cowboys to "escort" him away:

They, the community, gave him thirty minutes to pack up and hit the trail. . . . With pleasant words and outstretched hand, he walked up to the punchers. His hand darted out, jerking a gun from its holster. He fired it over their heads, ordering the two cowboys to reach. . . . He told them he . . . would tolerate no more interference from the valley settlers . . . and he was never threatened with eviction from his official domain again.[125]

Peace never fully arrived on the Battlement. The optimistic *Delta Independent* expressed its belief that, despite the hostile atmosphere, insurgent cattlemen would one day come to feel "very kindly toward the forestry department" and "the manner in which Forester Pinchot [met] the grazing situation."[126] But they never did. In 1906 they virtually hounded Battlement supervisor John Craig off the reserve. Explaining his action to newspaper reporters, Craig wearily said, "I am simply worn out."[127] Nor did anticonservation forces allow Kreutzer and others to forget that they had "declared open season on rangers." Kreutzer, pistol under his head, never slept in the same place twice.[128] Thus did conservation take root on the Battlement.

As important as forest reserves, grazing fees, and coal-land withdrawals were in fostering discontent in the mountain country, no single issue galvanized insurgents of all areas like the leasing question. Dormant throughout the second half of 1906, the leasing furor exploded again—for the last time—in the early months of 1907 and ran concurrently with the trouble on the forest reserves.

After the demise of his leasing bill in Congress in 1906, Senator Elmer Burkett of Nebraska introduced another in the Senate on January 8, 1907. Insurgents all over the state attacked it immediately. In Denver the *Rocky Mountain News*, bypassing Burkett, castigated Roosevelt in an editorial that set the insurgent mood for the next five months:

> *The people of Colorado cannot approve the system of leasing to which the President has given his sanction. Men who a few months ago regarded him as the incarnation of all virtue and wisdom are now coming in hundreds to pledge themselves to resist paying for their rights of pasturage on the public domain, and to fight the President's pet project in every way. . . . These men are in a condition of revolt against the federal government.*[129]

The quixotic *Denver Republican* agreed. "The public lands," it said soberly, "are for the people to make homes upon, and not for cattle and sheep when homesteads are in demand."[130]

Reaction to the Burkett bill was even more adverse in the range country. Like the *Rocky Mountain News*, the *Telluride News* in western Colorado laid the blame squarely on Roosevelt. "President Roosevelt has always been regarded in the West as a friend of this section, but never before has so serious a blow been aimed at the development, progress, and prosperity of the West as his effort to secure enactment of laws for the withdrawal of public lands and leasing of same."[131] The *Eagle County Enterprise* requested that the government "let the cattleman range his herds until the homesteader comes" and "leave the fence down and the way clean."[132] And the *Montrose Enterprise* maintained that leasing was no panacea for the ills of the range. "Every bit of land calculated to support a family must be used for that purpose," it said. "America should be a country of homes"—not a national leasehold administered by the federal government.[133]

While state newspapers debated the leasing bill, insurgent cattlemen took their case before the Colorado Cattle and Horse Growers Association at its annual Denver meeting on January 21, 1907. By 1907, however, proconservation elements in the organization were stronger than ever before. When the meeting opened they were fully prepared to resist the opponents of leasing, and, to the insurgents' surprise, sitting with them was Gifford Pinchot.

When insurgent leader Elias Ammons opened the convention with the declaration that he and his followers would provide "strictest opposition" to the Burkett bill, he was challenged immediately. John Springer, speaking for the leasers, warned Ammons that there was "no use in going against the federal administration." There was "a man in the White House" who believed in a "square deal" and who was "seeking the greatest good for the greatest number." He would see that the cattlemen got a "square deal" themselves.[134]

On the second day of the convention, January 22, Ammons clashed with Pinchot himself. Before a full house at the Albany

Hotel, the small, gaunt cattleman launched into a stock anti-leasing speech. The *Denver Times* recorded the moment:

> *In an earnest and eloquent plea,* [*Ammons*] . . . *denounced the* [*leasing*] *measure. . . . "This is a question between the nation and the state. It is a question of whether we are going to have control of our own lands or the government is going to become a landlord and place it under a system of tenantry. Do you want it? True patriotism begins around our own firesides, we must be loyal to ourselves first, and if we are loyal to our own interests we will be loyal to the nation. Do you not realize what you are doing when you lie down and let the government come in and usurp your rights? Will you turn over this land to a prince* [*Pinchot*] *under a system as foreign to our principles as is the government of Russia?"*[135]

Pinchot took the floor after Ammons' speech, calmly replying that while he agreed in the full protection of all men's rights, leasing—like forest reserves—was necessary and inevitable. The obdurate cattlemen, he said, needed to recognize the fact: "The wisest thing the cattlemen could do would be to break this bronco themselves."[136]

Despite the Forester's counsel, Ammons' address apparently helped the antileasers' cause. During the early course of the convention the leasers had picked up substantial momentum; several state cattlemen's associations (mainly from the Delta-Montrose area) had lobbied for a formal endorsement of the Burkett bill, and even the association's conservationist-dominated public-land committee leaned toward the adoption of a leasing resolution which it proposed. But when time came for a vote, after Ammons' plea and after some delicate parliamentary maneuvering on the part of the insurgents, the resolution was tabled without a vote. The association remained on record as opposed to leasing. The insurgents were jubilant. The *Glenwood Avalanche-Echo* crowed that "Gifford Pinchot is down and out so far as his efforts to control the public grazing lands of the United States is concerned. Mr. Pinchot boasted that he could handle the stockmen of the West . . . but he failed. . . . Now Colorado cattlemen are singing, 'Great is E. M. Ammons, who put Mr. Pinchot to rout.'" For their part, the happy cattlemen of the Roaring Fork Valley—the same men leading the antigrazing tax movement in northern Colorado—rewarded Ammons with a boisterous victory banquet.[137]

In late January, a few days after the Colorado Cattle and Horse Growers Association meeting, Senator Burkett introduced a leasing amendment to the pending 1907 Agricultural Appropriations Bill in Congress. Apparently beset by doubts that his independent leasing bill could indefinitely survive the assaults of western insurgents, his reasoning may have been that if one bill were defeated, the other might survive. Whatever the reason for his action, it had one immediate effect: it set off another chain of disturbances on the Colorado range. "It's plain as a pike staff," fumed the *Gunnison News-Champion,* the new leasing proposition was "monstrous," "treachery in its most raw and rotten form."[138]

Beginning at a giant rally of five hundred angry stockmen at Craig on February 20, "discussions" on the Burkett bill were held throughout the rest of the month in every community west of the divide. At the Craig enclave it was reported that only "two or three" of the five hundred spoke in favor of leasing, although others expressed support for some sort of grazing plan as long as the administration of local lands remained in the hands of the cattlemen themselves. Claiming to represent the "sentiment of a great majority of the stockmen, farmers, and citizens of the western slope," participants in the Craig rally passed resolutions harshly condemning the entire Burkett plan.[139] Other stockmen's and farmer's groups concurred. The Western Slope Fair Association and the Farmer's Club of Garfield, Eagle, and Pitkin counties passed antileasing resolutions at large rallies. Civic and commercial groups—including the Denver Chamber of Commerce, the Denver Real Estate Exchange (both of which had favored forest conservation in the past), and the Colorado State Commercial Congress—followed suit. Ultimately all were made happy. The original Burkett bill was killed in congressional committee in December, 1907. And on February 23 the Burkett amendment for the Agricultural Appropriation Bill was stricken from it on a point of order. For the moment, again, the leasing idea was stopped.

Looking back over the activities of 1906–1907, it is not difficult to see that both the antireserve and antileasing movements served as a fairly accurate barometer of much of the state's feeling about conservation in general. Because of the diversity of the dissident groups involved (many of them, like farmers and cattlemen, antagonistic to and incompatible with each other in normal times), because of their relatively large numbers, and because of their presence in virtually every area of Colorado, they gave substantial credence to the idea that the anticonservation movement was more than the crackpot crusade of a handful of embittered malcontents. Whether on forest reserves protesting against grazing fees or on the open range resisting leasing, whether fighting against mining and lumbering restrictions and coal-land withdrawals or for forest homesteads, it was a fact that large numbers of diverse people believed, as Elias Ammons articulated it, that if conservation succeeded, it would "put half this state under federal jurisdiction" and possibly destroy its sovereignty. Colorado would become "two systems of government," wrote Ammons to Thomas Patterson—one system run by "its people" and the other controlled by "some bureau in Washington." When Ammons declared that "the businessmen and the small stockmen and . . . homeseekers" opposed such a system, most assuredly he spoke for many.[140]

As important as the 1906–1907 turmoil was in the Colorado backcountry, one salient fact should be remembered about it: it did not signify—in retrospect—as serious a repudiation of conservation as might have been thought at the moment. The movement was indeed angry, and it did embrace large numbers of people—probably more than at any previous time during the conservation controversy. But, at the same time, similarly large numbers of pioneer citizens did not join in the protest, preferring, instead, to continue supporting the Roosevelt-Pinchot program. Because of its unprecedented hostility and its pervasiveness, the protest movement was widely construed, even in Washington, to be a massive, statewide repudiation of federal resource policy. But certain conditions and events proved that it was not that all encompassing.

All across northern and western Colorado, for example, several major newspapers consistently took the government's position during the furor. And they, in turn, were supported by pioneer settlers who approved of their stance. One of the papers, the *Steamboat Sentinel*, argued that "if the government had started this [conservation] move a few years sooner, Routt County would already be ahead in more ways than one. It would have prevented the entire timbered regions of the county from being gobbled up by the speculators and corporations, to the detriment of every settler in the county." Referring to its crosstown rival the *Pilot*, the *Sentinel* concluded that the forest-reserve situation in Colorado had been "ludicrously misinterpreted and misrepresented" by insurgent zealots seeking private profit from public resources.[141]

In Glenwood Springs, perhaps the hub of all anticonservation activity in the area, the *Glenwood Post* never wavered in its support of federal conservation policy. Its principal target was the *Avalanche-Echo* and its editor, H. J. Holmes, whom it likened to a "surgeon who daily probes and irritates a wound which nature would quickly heal if given a chance." Said the *Post*: "A malodorous atmosphere, a poisoned brain and distorted digestion will often paint on a canvas monstrosities in shapes and colors all its own. And herein lies the basis of all those silly attacks [on conservation] that have about as much effect as a school boy bouncing a rubber ball off the Rock of Gibraltar."[142]

Farther down on the Western Slope, in the proconservation Gunnison River Valley, other segments of the press largely agreed. The *Delta Independent* continued to believe that forest reserves and the grazing tax "would bring a benefit" to the state "rather than work a hardship" on it. The paper admitted that the tax, in particular, was "like a red flag flaunted in the face of a bull," but it argued that the tax would afford valuable benefits to all classes of stockmen. As for leasing, the *Independent* maintained that the tax would work "so great a benefit to our [cattle] industry" that it should have been endorsed by all cattlemen.[143] Finally, the influential *Montrose Press* added its voice to those advocating conservation. Its position was that those who disobeyed reserve laws were committing "anarchy" and should be dealt with as such. Forest reserves and the grazing fee both helped "the little man, the salt of the earth" and as such deserved the support of all pioneer citizens.[144]

While mining and lumber interests rarely were found in conservationist ranks in 1906 and early 1907, cattlemen were. For all the tumult on the reserves, significant numbers of stockmen continued to resolutely support conservation. For every insurgent cattleman who refused to pay the grazing tax, another not only agreed to pay it, but perhaps asked for additional timberland withdrawals. For every stockman intent on laying rangers "in the bush," another offered his co-operation. Such actions greatly undermined the idea held in some quarters that insurgents were "taking over" the state.

For all the many instances of ranger-cattleman friction, many cases also existed of their co-operation. In March, 1906, the government notified all state stockmen's associations that they could draw up committees to advise local forest officers on grazing matters, and the action thawed hostile relations in many areas. As far as some cattlemen were concerned, the action seemed to underscore the fact that "the forest officers desired the co-operation of the stockmen" and that it was possible to work in harmony.[145]

In the Uncompahgre-Battlement Mesa area, for instance, where cattlemen long had been more skeptical of forest reserves than had farmers (and where William Kreutzer experienced all of his troubles), the Montrose County Cattle and Horse Growers Association appointed a committee of three to confer periodically with local rangers concerning "all differences rising from grazing regulations."[146] Ultimately, Uncompahgre stockmen even petitioned the government for the incorporation of all grazing land between the Uncompahgre and Battlement reservations into one or the other of them. Other important groups, notably the Delta County Livestock Association, concurred, and for it they received a letter from Pinchot thanking them for their concern.[147] Overall, the mood in the Uncompahgre territory was conducive to the pursuit of conservation. "Cattlemen here are feeling very kindly" toward it, said the *Delta Independent*, "and are expressing themselves as more than pleased at the manner in which Forester Pinchot is meeting the situation."[148]

Even in the heart of anticonservation territory—on the northern reserves—much evidence existed to suggest that proconservation sentiment still was widely prevalent among stockmen. On the Medicine Bow, for example, it was reported that the neighbors of one Andrew Norell—arrested by rangers for grazing cattle on the reserve without paying the tax—"pooh-poohed with indignation the idea of leniency" for him and "demanded that he be prosecuted."[149] In the White River-Park Range region the *Glenwood Post* reported that after their initial outburst against the government, local cattlemen were "taking a saner view of things" despite the efforts of the *Avalanche-Echo* to keep them "stirred up." Even Fred Light bought a permit, said the *Post*, and declared that he intended to "live up to the rules and render every possible assistance to the forestry officers."[150] John Howard of Wolcott, in an interview with the *Yampa Leader*, spoke for many fellow stockmen when he said insurgents like Light had "indulged in a lot of foolishness." Concluded Burns rancher John Edge: "Our experience on the reserves has been very satisfactory and we have been very well treated. . . . I intend to pay my tax like a little man and maintain my priority on the range. . . . I may say also that I have perfect confidence in Mr. Pinchot and President Roosevelt, both of

been more fruitful than this," insurgents still chose not to believe.[155] Still resentful of the ranger corps with its alleged "bossism" and "one-man rule," contemptuous of "tenderfeet" and "unstable theorists" and "pernicious carpetbaggers" who "ruled" the reserves from the East, and fearful of the establishment of "tenantry" on the land, they still refused to accept the Roosevelt doctrine.[156] "Come now boys," bellowed the *Routt County Courier*: "Now is the time to act. Now is the time to show whether you really have that fond feeling [for the state] you said you had. . . . Come out strong. . . . Work for our country's interest as it is shown in the hearts and homes about you. Let's come out strong from now on until the danger is past."[157] The cry had been heeded in the past. Little reason existed to believe that it would not be again.

IX. Watershed

Throughout the tumult on forest reserves and rangelands in Colorado and other western states in 1906 and 1907, many of the states' representatives in Congress mobilized to carry on the work of anticonservation there. Significantly, for the first time since the conservation controversy had begun, they possessed sufficient strength to seriously challenge the government's executive branch. The reason was the addition of substantial numbers of fellow congressmen to their ranks.

During the first decade and a half of the conservation era, only a handful of insurgents—like Henry Teller and Thomas Patterson—had sat in Congress. Isolated, disorganized, spurned by most easterners, and ignored even by many westerners, for almost fifteen years they had fought conservation largely alone. Throughout late 1906, however, as anticonservation agitation reached new proportions in areas all over the West, the sentiment of some congressmen—especially in the Senate—began to favor the insurgents. Some of the converts were western moderates. Others were eastern and midwestern conservatives such as Senator Henry Cabot Lodge of Massachusetts and representatives Tawney of Minnesota, Mann of Illinois, Hemenway of Indiana, and Fitzgerald of New York. Their union with western irreconcilables—Teller, Patterson, Thomas Carter of Montana, Weldon Heyburn of Idaho, Charles Fulton of Oregon, Clarence Clark of Wyoming, Samuel Piles of Washington, and a large coterie of representatives—marked the beginning of what historian John Ise has called an anticonservation "party" in Congress.[1]

The objectives of the westerners' new allies were diverse, but they all aimed at embarrassing Theodore Roosevelt and damaging his conservation program. Some were motivated by the apparently sincere belief that the forest-reserve administration under Pinchot had become too costly for the government to continue. Others feared that business interests they represented in the East—railroads, mining, and lumbering concerns—would be damaged by any further withdrawal and conservation of exploitable natural resources in the West.[2] Beyond that, however, the anti-Roosevelt, anticonservation mood of the group was rooted more in politics than in economics. The president, with what George Mowry has called his "energetic use of the executive power, his impulsive personal actions, and his yearly clashes with Congress" on a wide range of issues, had, very simply, antagonized Congress. In 1907, a lame-duck executive bereft of patronage power and possessing little ability to influence future elections, he made a perfect target not only for insurgent westerners intent on the abolition of conservation, but antiadministration easterners and midwesterners bent on political revenge.[3] The latter group may have cared little about anticonservation per se, but it was as good a tool as any of them possessed to carry out their political designs.

If certain easterners and midwesterners used the conservation issue to hurt Roosevelt, the motives of insurgent westerners were not so subtle. They cared less about damaging Roosevelt than in wiping out his program. Regardless of their states, their language was the same; just as Patterson and Teller spoke for much of the insurgent West, so did other congressmen speak for much of Colorado. Thomas Carter, for example, was perhaps even more anticonservation than his Colorado colleagues. A man who had maintained as early as 1897 that the federal creation of forest reserves showed "contemptuous disregard" for the public will, Clark tenaciously held to his old beliefs.[4] Marcus Smith of Arizona, whom Roosevelt contemptuously dismissed as "a fussy person of no consequence," argued—as did many Coloradans—that so many forest reserves existed in the West that "very little room" existed "to move around without a challenge to halt."[5] Charles Fulton of Oregon, like Patterson in particular, loathed the Forest Service—a "bureau . . . composed of dreamers and theorists" who sat in "marble halls" and dreamed of conservation, to the detriment of the "lowly pioneer" attempting to carve out "a home and dwelling place" in the West.[6] William Borah and Weldon Heyburn of Idaho substantially agreed, particularly Heyburn, the "Objector." Characterized by John Ise as "the archenemy of the reservation policy" and by Gifford Pinchot as an "enemy of ours," Heyburn consistently took the position that forest reserves constituted a "violation of the contract of statehood" and an "infringement upon the rights of citizens to select their own homes." Collectively the insurgents all agreed with Heyburn that an "outrage" had been "perpetrated."[7] And by the time the second session of the Fifty-ninth Congress convened in December, 1906, they were prepared to avenge it.

In their assault against conservation, insurgent congressmen focused mainly on the Agricultural Appropriations Bill which came up before the Senate in January, 1907. Utilizing debate over it as a sounding board for their own views, they launched "a full attack on federal resource policy, . . . dredged up every economic, political, and personal argument, polished by a decade of usage, and hurled them against the entire structure of conservation."[8] Coloradans among them concentrated, first, on the leasing question, specifically on the then-pending Burkett amendment to the appropriation bill. Congressman Robert Bonynge of Denver declared that he was "opposed to any measure of that kind" and that he would do his "utmost to defeat it." Franklin Brooks of Colorado Springs, in a letter to Rifle cattlemen, added that they would "kill this thing."[9] Henry Teller, an archenemy of leasing, clearly defined his position in a letter to the *Denver Republican*. Leasing, said Teller, was "the most extraordinary proposition ever presented to an Anglo-Saxon, self-governing people. Such a system exists, if anywhere at all on earth, only under the Russian bureaucracy. . . . The system will either reduce our people to a set of servile peons or bring about a condition of resentment and irritation that will be intolerable."[10] When Teller fell ill, however, it was left to Thomas Patterson to fight the amendment.

From the beginning of Senate debate Patterson was put under heavy pressure from his constituency to oppose the leasing rider. The Denver Chamber of Commerce, for example, urged him to use his "best efforts to prevent passage" of the amendment, and Colorado Cattle and Horse Growers Association President Fred Johnson urgently wired him that "nine-tenths of the people in the state" were "opposed to any amendment to land laws" at the moment. Even pro-Roosevelt Republican Governor Henry Buchtel forwarded a request to Patterson that he implore Congress to "postpone all considered measures which would interfere with our citizens acquiring title to the public lands" in order to "give the people of the western states opportunity to be heard."[11] Leaning in an antileasing direction to begin with, Patterson resolutely followed the course suggested by Buchtel.

During Senate debate on the Burkett amendment, Patterson time and time again took the floor to denounce it. On February 21, two days before the amendment was killed by the Senate, stricken from the appropriations bill on a point of order, Patterson issued a final denunciation of it: "Why should stockmen," he said,

be compelled to pay tribute to this new-fangled method of dealing with the public lands? The early settlers of Indiana, Illinois, Nebraska, and Kansas had free range. . . . but after they have used their range, after their states have been settled, after their resources are developed, after all this, they start a movement . . . intended to cripple the mountain states . . . that does in fact cripple them and shuts them out of the race of prosperity on equal terms with the other states. . . . Grazing and

Thomas M. Patterson, an anticonservation senator from Colorado.
Courtesy Denver Public Library, Western History Department

leasing is a matter that has been discussed in every county and town in Colorado, and I can truthfully say that almost without exception those who favor the leasing of grazing lands have done so against the most urgent protest and the strongest opposition that the mass of people in the state could make manifest.[12]

When the leasing fight was over, Patterson immediately turned to other issues.

Joining other insurgents, the senator next attempted to reduce the size of Gifford Pinchot's salary (funded annually through the bill). "There has been a glamour and romance attempted to be thrown over this whole forest reserve business," said Patterson. "The man at the head . . . is raised to the attitude of a great benefactor of the human race. . . . Mr. Pinchot is a very good man—but not much better than a good many others. He is a man who rides a hobby—a hobby that if ridden with judgement might accomplish some good, but I am satisfied that Mr. Pinchot is riding his hobby to a fall."[13] By a narrow margin the Senate awarded Pinchot a salary raise—from thirty-five hundred to five thousand dollars a year. But Patterson and others could not have been too unhappy. They had made their point.

The anticonservation faction also made an issue of the size of appropriations earmarked for the Forest Service for fiscal 1907–1908. After operating on a budget of one million dollars in 1906–1907, Pinchot requested an increase of nine hundred thousand dollars. As one historian has written, for a bureau as unpopular as the Forest Service to request such an increase in the face of an irritated Senate was to "invite trouble."[14] Trouble was precisely what Pinchot got. Patterson stepped in, using the occasion not so much to contest the increase as to complain about the evils of federal interference in the lives and affairs of Colorado's pioneer class. "As I have said," Patterson repeated,

> *those who are thrusting* [*forest reserves*] *upon us are the representatives of states that have grown into mighty empires. . . . If our mountain states were like them, we would not complain. But, like the senators from states whose limit has perhaps been reached, we might if we were not too broad for such littleness, attempt to foist an unwelcome and distasteful system upon weaker states. . . . I protest, in common with the people of the state I represent, that under the so-called forest reserve system we do not want more than a fifth of our state taken from the people and turned into a federal preserve.*[15]

Pinchot received his request for expanded appropriations. Interestingly, Patterson was at odds on that particular issue with many of his western colleagues. They supported larger appropriations mainly because a large percentage of the funds would be spent in the western states themselves, helping to develop wilderness areas.[16] Beyond that point, however, there was no further disagreement among either western insurgents or their eastern allies.

On February 23, Senator Charles Fulton of Oregon moved an amendment to the appropriation bill providing that "hereafter no forest reserve shall be created, nor shall any addition be made, to one heretofore created, within the limits of the states of Oregon, Washington, Montana, Colorado, or Wyoming, except by an act of Congress."[17] The action was momentous. If enacted into law the amendment promised virtually to destroy the progress of the conservation movement in America. For his part, the bullish Patterson said that

> *we are opposed to the reserves . . . and I think I am within the truth when I say that 90% of those in Colorado have been dissatisfied with* [*them*] *and make, I think, loud and well-founded complaints. . . .* [*The Fulton*] *amendment we are heartily in favor of, for we do not want any more forest reserves in Colorado. . . . So indignant today are the people of the western portion of the state I represent about the . . . forest reserves that they are in a state of rebellion.*[18]

Some were not as satisfied as Patterson about the action. Heyburn and Carter, for example, demanded that the Fulton idea be made retroactive to include at least some reservations made in the past. Dissuaded by Patterson from taking such action, they nonetheless made it clear that they would expect it to be taken in the future.

Western conservationists (Francis Warren of Wyoming, Francis Newlands of Nevada, Reed Smoot of Utah, Fred DuBois of

Idaho, and Californians George Perkins and Frank Flint) banded together with pro-Roosevelt easterners and midwesterners (Jonathan Dolliver of Iowa, Knute Nelson of Minnesota, Albert Beveridge of Indiana, John Spooner of Wisconsin, and Joseph Proctor of Vermont) in an attempt to defeat the Fulton amendment. But such a tenuous coalition was not strong; ultimately they found it impossible to overcome the insurgents. After a bitter debate punctuated by western threats to filibuster for the reduction of reserves already created, conservationist senators capitulated. On February 25, without even a voice vote, the Senate passed the bill with the Fulton amendment intact.[19]

While western anticonservationists celebrated their victory, Roosevelt pondered his next move. The dilemma he faced was apparent. He could not afford to veto the appropriations bill; it was too important. But on the other hand, its enaction promised acute disruption in the conservation movement; Roosevelt most certainly understood that the Congress could not be counted on to create any more reserves. Whether or not the vast tracts of unreserved timber remaining in the West would have fallen into the hands of the "land grabbers, in whose interest [so conservationists said] the bill had been drawn up" in the first place, was speculative.[20] But Roosevelt was not prepared to take chances. No sooner had Congress passed the bill than he and Pinchot "almost gleefully" devised a plan to neutralize the impact of the Fulton amendment on the West.[21] For several days, while insurgent westerners impatiently awaited the presidential signature, Pinchot and Roosevelt plotted the withdrawal of some seventeen million acres of timberland in the states covered by the amendment. Then, on the morning of March 4, Roosevelt dramatically proclaimed the creation of twenty-one new national forests in six western states (Colorado excluded). Only then did he sign the Appropriation Act.

The president's action left the insurgent West mute. Later, however, when the shock wore off, "the opponents of the Forest

Service," as Roosevelt later recalled in his autobiography, "turned handsprings in their wrath."[22] Predictably, most protest against the "Midnight Reserves" (strikingly reminiscent of Grover Cleveland's action and the response to it a decade earlier) emanated from states traditionally most bitterly opposed to conservation. In Washington, for example, a Seattle newspaper echoed a thought long familiar in parts of Colorado: "The federal government," it said, "assumes the attitude of the alien landlord, holding perpetually for its own uses millions of acres of land in this state, drawing revenues from them for expenditures elsewhere, and paying no taxes on its vast holdings." Much like Charles Thomas and Alva Adams and other governors of Colorado had said in other contexts, the governor of Washington declared that Pinchot had "done more to retard the growth and development" of his section than "any other man." And the feeling of them all was that "recent abuses of power" had "grown to the point" that "bitter revolt" impended against the entire conservation program.[23] Many Coloradans understood the feeling. Only weeks before Thomas Patterson had spoken of a "state of rebellion" in his own region.

Colorado's reaction to Roosevelt's action was milder than that elsewhere. The reason was that while large additions had been made to existing Colorado reserves (Holy Cross, Uncompahgre, Park Range, Montezuma, Medicine Bow, and San Juan in particular), no new ones had been created. Nonetheless, many insurgents used the occasion to display their disgust with conservation. One Colorado Republican, writing to Governor Buchtel, criticized Roosevelt himself: "Now mind you, I am a strong Roosevelt man, but he does get off on some things, and one of them is this fool forest reserve system."[24] Characteristically, the abrasive *Steamboat Pilot* editorialized that

it is remarkable that with a boasted "Western man" for President the land policy of the present administration has been the most burdensome and restrictive in all the history of the public lands. The whole theory of the [*government*] *is that every settler is going to rob the government. . . . And then the precedent is set that the public lands are to be disposed of . . . dependent on the whim of the chief faddist in the Agriculture Department [Pinchot]. . . . Very few of the autocratic monarchs of the world would so dare to set aside the will of the people this way.*[25]

In a half-humorous vein the *Denver Field and Farm* complained that if the president continued to "nationalize" American land in the future as he had in the past, soon the only burial grounds left in the nation would be on forest reserves. Then the old cowboy song would have to be changed to

Bury me not on the range,
Where the taxed cattle are roaming,
And the mangy coyotes yelp and bark,
And the wind in the pines is moaning;
On the forest reserve please bury me not,
For I never would then be free;
A forest ranger would dig me up
In order to collect his fee.[26]

In March, 1907, the attitude toward federal conservation was accurately summed up in an editorial by the *Denver Record-Stockman*. As long as governmental authorities sat in Washington and dictated "rules and regulations that set at naught the statutes of the states," it said, the West would "fight to the end."[27]

In the turbulent spring of 1907 the Colorado state legislature stepped into the conservation picture. For a number of years the body had generally ignored the national dimensions of the conservation struggle, preferring to deal with such matters primarily within the borders of its own state. By 1907, however, it had become increasingly difficult to divorce local from regional and national problems. In the eyes of some legislators Colorado had become engaged in a corrosive quasi-civil war with the government of the United States, one which, in the words of two insurgent state senators, had caused "irreparable injury" to the state.[28] Concerned by what it saw—the debilitating social and economic effects of the conservation battle, the rising militance of certain citizen groups, and what might have been construed in some quarters as a general breakdown of law in certain parts of the state—the legislature resolved to seek some remedy to the problem.

On March 20, 1907, two weeks after Roosevelt's proclamation of the Midnight Reserves, Colorado state Senator Rodney Bardwell introduced a resolution into the legislature calling for a meeting of western states and federal officials in Denver to discuss the conservation problem. Predictably, the resolution isolated the government and its forest reserves as the primary source of trouble. "Assuming all the rights of a private land-owner," it read, the government had "undertaken the active administration of the lands composing the forest reserves," illegally "utilizing them for the benefit of the government" at the expense of the people of the state. Upon withdrawing from entry a quarter of the total area of Colorado for reserves, the government had disregarded its "implied obligations to the state" by

entering into active possession of these lands, with the expressed determination of developing their resources for the benefit of the general government, thus depriving the state and its citizens of the benefits which would accrue from the use of these lands in the manner established by custom and practice in the older states, and, in addition, engaging in business in competition with our citizens.

With that indictment, the resolution concluded that "the action of the Federal Government in thus usurping the rights of the states and its citizens to develop and acquire title to these public lands and to utilize [their] resources . . . as part of the assets of the state, we believe to be contrary to the spirit and the letter of the act of Congress creating the state of Colorado."[29] The senate passed the resolution with only two dissenting votes.

While the Colorado House approved of the content of the Bardwell resolution, it disapproved of its stringent tone. It amended the text, softening it somewhat, and returned the resolution to the senate—only to have it rejected. The senate, dominated by insurgents such as Bardwell (who, ironically, represented the proconservation counties of Denver, Adams, Logan, Morgan, Phillips, Sedgwick, Washington, and Yuma), Horace DeLong (Mesa and Delta), Dexter Sapp (Pitkin and Gunnison), and Edward Taylor (Eagle, Garfield, and Rio Blanco)—appeared ready to settle for nothing less than a harshly worded condemnation of federal conservation policy.

On March 30, Representative John Lawrence of Saguache (a center on insurgency for a decade) introduced a substitute resolution calling, in more temperate terms, for a meeting of western states and federal officials "for the purpose of discussing the relation of the states to the public lands, and, if possible, agree upon some policy in regard to these lands to be urged upon the general government, that will look toward a more rapid settlement by citizens. . . ." On the same day of its introduction, the resolution was unanimously adopted by both the house and senate and was signed on April 1. On April 27 the call for a public-lands convention was formally issued by Governor Buchtel.[30] The place was to be Denver and the time, June.

The convention's official call clearly mirrored the thoughts of western insurgents. At issue were all facets of conservation, but the focus was on the forest-reserve system in particular. The primary complaint was, as it had been in the past, that the widespread federal control of land within the boundaries of sovereign states was unjust and that the extension of any system which threatened to "hinder the development and acquirement of title to these lands by citizens or the adoption of a policy contrary to that which has recognized the right of the state to encourage settlement and development under the existing laws, might prove disastrous to the prosperity of this section of the country."[31] The response of western governors to the invitation offers an interesting illustration of how the West as a whole viewed the convention's stated objectives. Some agreed with the basic complaint, and others did not, but almost all seemed to advocate a general clearing of the air. Joseph K. Toole of Montana, generally considered to be antagonistic to conservation, wrote that he hoped the convention would "result in the accomplishment of its purposes." Albert Mead of Washington concurred, along with Bryant Brooks of Wyoming. On the other hand, several governors hoped that the convention would not deter the work of conservation. George Chamberlain of Oregon, for example, hoped that no action would "be taken by the convention looking to a modification of any reservation." J. H. Kibbee of Arizona, along with James Gillett of California and Frank Gooding of Idaho, voiced the opinion that many western citizens were

heartily in favor of the policies of the national administration relative to the public lands. There has been in the past such a prodigal waste of our natural resources and such fraudulent abuse of its generosity concerning the acquisition of its public lands, that a proper public spirit demands a remedy for those evils if there can be one—at least some policy to prevent further like abuses.[32]

In April, as the convention's format began to take shape, proconservation elements began to fear that insurgents were less interested in promoting an honest exchange of ideas than in turning the meeting into a one-sided "attack on President Roosevelt's land policies."[33] They were worried, for example, about the composition of the convention's "program committee"—those men responsible for selecting topics and speakers. With Bonynge and Teller on it and Teller as its permanent chairman, conservationists feared the program would be weighted against conservation. When the committee issued an *Address of the Programme Committee Outlining the Object of the Meeting* on May 29, they were more convinced than ever.

According to the committee, the West wanted to deal with several basic questions: Did the federal government possess "the constitutional right to hold the public lands within the borders of a new state in perpetual ownership and under municipal sovereignty without the consent of the state?" When new states were admitted into the Union in the nineteenth century with all the rights and privileges of the older states, "did not the agreement include the right to acquire the public lands for its citizens under the laws of the United States?" Given the fact that the withdrawal of large tracts of western public lands had been justified as a "public necessity," did a "public necessity," in fact, exist? Did the federal government possess the "constitutional capacity" to engage in "merchandising timber and coal in competition with the citizens of the state?" If the general government did possess the constitutional power to "embark on an extensive and monopolistic scale in the development and merchandising of the resources of the public lands," was such action in the interests of the "progress and development of the states?" Finally, would the leasing system, if enacted, "retard the settlement, development, and gradual absorption of the public lands into private ownership?"[34] It may have been argued, as, for example, the *Laramie Republican* did, that Teller and his insurgent allies had deliberately chosen subjects in opposition to the Roosevelt administration.[35] But, by the same token, the committee had been assembled not by Teller but by Buchtel—a conservationist and Roosevelt loyalist.[36] If conservationists were unhappy, they had only the governor to blame (though Buchtel hardly could have avoided taking the action he did, inasmuch as Teller was "perhaps the most distinguished" of all western leaders as well as "senior Senator of all the region west of the Missouri River").[37]

Beyond the nature of the program, conservationists also worried about the allotment of delegations to the convention. According to the original call, each state was allowed ten official delegates. Beyond that, each chamber of commerce, board of trade, real estate exchange, commercial group, or association of stockmen, lumbermen, foresters, horticulturists, or irrigationists was allowed five delegates apiece. Conservationists felt that the convention's insurgent organizers would make no attempt to strike a balance between pro- and anticonservation factions.

For that reason, even before proceedings began, cries of "rigging" arose from the conservationists' camp. "There will be a hot time in Denver when the public lands convention gets to work," predicted the *Denver Republican*. "Information has reached Washington that the enemies of the government's public land policies have 'rigged' the convention preparatory to making a bitter attack on President Roosevelt."[38] The *Denver Post* concurred that the convention was and would continue to be in the hands of a handful of cattlemen bent on turning it into a "sideshow" to embarrass the president.[39]

For his part, Teller brusquely denied all charges. Pointing out the fact that the convention had been authorized and called by a Republican governor (although it had been instigated by a Democratic legislature) and approved of by a number of Republican governors and other officials, he implied that the rigging charges were a smoke screen designed to discredit, in advance, what would surely be criticism of "the rather remarkable [land] policy" of Theodore Roosevelt.[40]

Real or imagined, the insurgents' activities worried conservationists and presented the Roosevelt administration with a dilemma. Ideally, with little to gain and much to lose, Roosevelt might have preferred to ignore the convention entirely. But he doubtless realized that such a position would constitute, in western eyes, tangible proof either that he was callous about western problems—as many westerners had charged all along—or that he was afraid to meet insurgents face-to-face in debate on his land policies. On the other hand, the possibility existed that if the president acknowledged the importance of the meeting, if he sent his best men to defend federal policy at it, and if, somehow, the policy were upheld, the conservation movement actually might profit. After extended consultation with Forest Service agents and conservationist friends in Colorado and after careful analysis of comments in the western press, Roosevelt decided to dispatch a federal task force to participate in the convention. Because federal strategy depended entirely on a massive, resolute show of strength, conservationists immediately began maneuvering "friends" of the administration into convention seats. Insurgents, cognizant of the fact that the Roosevelt men were highly "effective" in "the art of persuasion," immediately protested.[41]

Teller was the first to question the motives of the "small army of representatives" sent to Denver by Roosevelt to "plead his case before the convention."[42] But the anticonservation press was more intemperate in its charges than Teller. The *Gunnison News-Champion*, for example, cynically wrote that,

> *fearing that the coming convention will criticize the administration's Russian policy for the West, the administration supporters are straining every nerve to control it. However, the sentiment among men of all parties is so overwhelmingly against a policy of landlordism, exploitation, special privilege, arbitrary checking of agricultural and mining development, of considering every western man a thief, of carpetbag government, that there is every indication the convention will administer a severe rebuke to the President's ill-advised policy anyway.*[43]

The *Glenwood Avalanche-Echo* warned the insurgents that "Teddy and Pinchot are now packing this convention. Unless the stockmen stand solidly together, their wishes will never be aired and the purpose of this convention will be thwarted. . . . In fact, the Washington gang is going to try hard to turn the convention into a political meeting. They know their case is hopeless. . . ."[44] The skeptical *Eagle County Blade* worried aloud that while "the representatives of the West" would "rent the hall and pay for it," the convention would be "dominated by federal officeholders" who would "dictate its expressions and make its records."[45] When an ex-forest-reserve supervisor, a member of the convention's credentials committee, was caught attempting to infiltrate the vital resolutions committee with "government agents," the insurgents' fears appeared at least partially founded.[46]

Throughout the uproar, conservationist charges to the contrary, at least one important fact remained beyond dispute: Colorado's official delegation to the convention was not dominated by the insurgents. The makeup of the delegation—four active conservationists, three anticonservationists, and three "neutrals," all appointed by Buchtel—graphically illustrated the ideological division that had polarized the state for so long. Conservationists included Jared L. Brush of Greeley, a lifelong Republican and friend of the administration; Earl M. Cranston, Republican United States district attorney from Denver; and Republican politicians Frank McDonough and William H. Dickson, both of Denver. Insurgent spokesmen included Charles D. Hayt of Denver, a Republican judge; R. G. Breckenridge of Monte Vista (near the San Juan Forest Reserve), Republican speaker of the Colorado House of Representatives; and D. C. Beaman, a Republican and chief attorney for the Colorado Fuel and Iron Corporation (which largely dominated the mining industry in Colorado). The neutrals were Frank Goudy, a Republican lawyer opposed to leasing yet strongly in favor of the forest-reserve system; John F. Vivian of Golden, Republican register of the state land board; and E. R. Harper, Colorado's lieutenant governor.[47] The delegation, said Buchtel, was representative and balanced. Although it was entirely Republican, Buchtel said that its activities would be totally apolitical—as there was "too much at stake for bickering."[48]

Among Colorado's unofficial delegations, the insurgents probably sent more men to Denver than conservationists did, but the margin was not large. Most of the insurgent groups were composed of stockmen—the same men responsible for what discord existed in the mountain areas of the state at the moment. They fully intended to bring their protest to Denver. In one newspaper interview, White River rancher Patrick Heron stated his determination to speak out against local rangers who had allegedly forced him to pay his grazing fee at a time when his wife was ill and his child dying. Similarly, three other White River cattlemen—G. W. Beardslee, Patrick Sullivan, and Thomas Moran—prepared to protest that they had been coerced into paying grazing taxes on the White River Reserve whether they ran cattle on it or not. They claimed that rangers had threatened them with arrest if they went to Denver to protest, but that they intended to go regardless.[49] Besides cattlemen, mining interests planned to be well represented at Denver. A handful of citizens from the Montezuma Reserve planned to dispute the inclusion of mineral land in the withdrawal; to curtail mining activities, they said, was "to make a hobby interfere with progress" and to damage the economic structure of the region in "no small way." D. C. Beaman, a member of the official Colorado delegation, prepared for the meeting by stating that reserves made "life miserable" for miners and small settlers. William Eggleston and Dr. Edward Sirois, both owners of mining property in the Pike Reserve, declared that it was "absurd to make an ignorant ranger the judge of value of a mining property." Their assertion was, as Sirois stated it in an interview, that "a trust under the Forester is no better than under a Rockefeller. All the good friends of the West ought to take a stand against the present system, which is radically wrong, opposed to the welfare of the western states, paralyzing all progress here, and causing so much evil and hardship."[50] Conventioneers from all over the state shared the feeling. As one insurgent newspaper grandly stated it, hundreds of men who had "the same blood surging through their veins that inspired their forefathers of '76 to stand up and fight for their rights" planned to stand up and fight for similar rights in the summer of 1907.[51]

The insurgent attitude, however, was not shared by all. A substantial number of unofficial Colorado groups—primarily stockmen's associations—stood solidly against the anticonservationists. From Pueblo and Colorado Springs, from the Montrose-Delta area, and even from northwestern Colorado, large numbers of cattlemen mustered to defend the Roosevelt policies. From the Uncompahgre-Battlement region, where one disgusted Delta rancher expressed surprise that a man of Buchtel's intelligence would have catered to the insurgents in the first place (by sending the invitation to the federal government), most cattlemen seemed to adopt the position of the Montrose delegation—that they would not oppose Roosevelt's program.[52] The entire Colorado Springs delegation sternly warned the insurgents that they risked a "clash" if they attempted to "control the convention with an anti-Roosevelt policy."[53] In northwest Colorado a surprisingly large number of stockmen from Routt County promised to support the administration—"to the shame of the rest of the county," said the *Routt County Courier*.[54] Expressing the feelings of them all, the *Aspen Democrat* warned insurgents that in their zeal to affect "radical changes" in federal land policy, they needed to steer clear of radicalism themselves—for their own good.[55] The convention, concluded the *Denver Republican*, needed to be fair in its dealings with conservation and "not be unduly magnified into a scheme to bring the Washington administration into disrepute over its land policy."[56]

The divisions experienced by Colorado delegations, of course, were experienced by other states too. While every state sent insurgent contingents to Denver, many others were proconservation, and some were split between the two factions. As Elmo Richardson points out, for example, the New Mexico delegation favored some form of federal jurisdiction over western natural resources, yet at the same time it opposed leasing. Other delegations, notably those from California, Oregon, Utah, and Texas, endorsed conservation completely.[57]

In a flurry of excitement the Denver Public Lands Convention was gaveled to order at the Broadway Theater on the morning of June 18, 1907. As delegates from all over the West massed in the June heat, the *Denver Republican* noted the apparent preponderance of insurgents—particularly in Colorado delegations—and predicted that "it is almost certain that politics will crop up early in the proceedings" because "a certain element from the Western Slope seems determined to stir up trouble."[58] The newspaper was right on both counts: the insurgents did "stir up trouble," and Roosevelt's emissaries fought back fiercely.

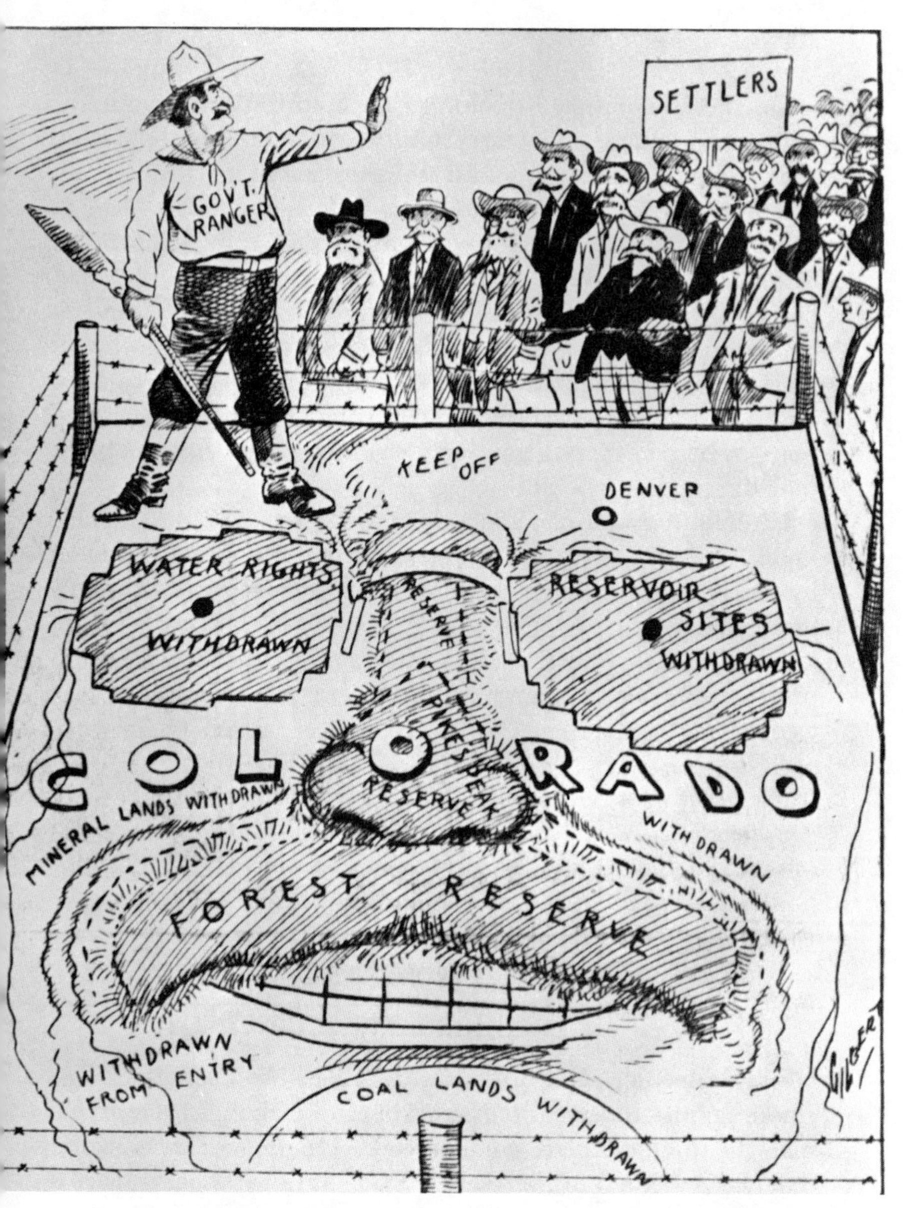

An anticonservation cartoon printed during the 1907 Public Lands Convention by the *Denver Times*, June 17, 1907. Notice that the withdrawals are drawn in the shape of Roosevelt's face.

Courtesy Colorado State Historical Society

On the convention's opening day both anticonservationist and administration forces carefully and emphatically stated their cases. Following an introductory address by Governor Buchtel, Senator Carter of Montana followed with the keynote speech. To "yells of approval" from the crowd, he exhorted it to action: "If the people of this country are to be held in terror," he cried, "now is the time to resent it." The administration immediately countered Carter with Secretary of Interior James Garfield. In a thoughtful, broad-ranging address which touched every point of the conservation controversy, Garfield outlined the government's position with candor.[59] On that note the morning session ended.

In the afternoon of June 18, Commissioner of the General Land Office Richard A. Ballinger pursued the theme put forth by Garfield. As a westerner, Ballinger appealed to insurgents more than other members of the Roosevelt group; they were particularly hopeful that he would take their side, and to all outward appearances, they had good reason for optimism. As a historian has said,

like a good many other citizens he was a little scornful of the conservation zealots, and remained closer to the old school of thought which was not yet ready to endorse the growing opinion that conservation was almost a matter of life and death to the nation. . . . As between the forces seeking to develop the West and those working for the preservation of the natural resources, his heart was with the former.[60]

Despite his alleged anticonservation bias, however, Ballinger stood against the insurgents. Maintaining that "as a western man" he stood ready to "challenge at all times . . . any assertion that the President of the United States is not in hearty accord with the best interests of the citizens of the Great West," he emphasized his belief that the public lands had to be protected at any cost. "The clamor against government vigilance," he concluded, "comes not from the settler who wants to secure a home. . . . It comes from those who are enflamed with a speculative lust for the great natural resources of mountain, forest, and plain."[61]

Shortly after lunch, Henry Teller strode to the podium, pale and agitated, for the afternoon's major address. In a long, sometimes eloquent, sometimes demagogic speech "frequently interrupted with vociferous cheers" from the crowd, the compelling, silver-haired senator set forth the insurgent case. On the primary theme of western land and its settlement, Teller contended, as he had for decades, that "the chief desire should always be to get the unoccupied land into the hands of men who want to live upon it. . . . There is no glory in following the plow unless a man follows it upon his own land. It is our duty to see that every man gets his land and that it is not tied up by the government." On the subject of forest reserves he argued vehemently that no timberlands had ever been destroyed in Colorado "but what the timber did not go to the benefit of the people." Pounding a fist on the rostrum, Teller shouted that "I am not very much in favor of forest reserves. . . . We cannot remain barbarians to save timber. I do not contend that the government has the right to seize the land, but I do contend that we have the right to put it to the use that Almighty God intended." Teller correctly gauged the mood of many delegates in speaking as he did. The *Denver Republican* commented, somewhat uneasily, that the senator had "struck a popular chord, and was cheered and applauded . . . in his attack" on conservation.[62]

Of as much importance, perhaps, as the first day's speeches, was the "packing" controversy that paralleled them. Insurgents continued to accuse Roosevelt forces of encouraging delegations (such as those from Texas) traditionally opposed to the grazing interests of Colorado, Wyoming, and Montana to counter them in the convention.[63] And they accused them, further, of infiltrating other western delegations with rangers and land agents. As one angry newspaper explained, the administration had "every federal officer, no matter what his rank, that could possibly be there as a lobby" in the Denver meeting.[64] On the other hand, however, conservationists maintained that the convention's organizers were discriminating against them both by refusing to allow their speakers to be heard and by refusing to issue credentials to conservationist delegations. By the end of the first day the credentials committee had accredited 386 delegates from Colorado and 145 from Wyoming, while virtually ignoring proconservation states such as Nebraska, which was allowed two delegates, and South Dakota, which was given three. On the surface, at least, conservationist charges seemed accurate.

On June 19 the convention braced for another stormy session. At dawn the city awoke to banner headlines on Thomas Patterson's *Rocky Mountain News* calling for the convention to "Oppose Uncle Sam As Landlord" and to give a "Stamp of Disapproval for Roosevelt Land Policy."[65] At the same time the *Denver Post* eloquently editorialized that the people of Colorado

> must *have freedom. We* must *have our colossal land and waters. We* must *have room for many millions, but the room must not be closed up and bricked up by National policy. The genius of growth must not be buried alive, in a wall, by the federal government. . . . We are not a colony or a dependency or a reserve territory; we are a sovereign state, and we want to people our lands and use our waters and open our mineral fields* now![66]

Both papers renewed their charges of packing. The *News*, for example, steadfastly maintained that "the entire army of land registers and clerks, forest outriders and all manner of government officials and local officeholders" were "in the game" as delegates to subvert the people's will.[67]

During the morning's proceedings, insurgents subjected Roosevelt's representatives to what the *Denver Republican* called a "grilling," couched in "both temperate and intemperate language." Following a blistering antiforest-reserve speech by

Senator Thomas Walsh of Montana, the insurgents sent Robert Bonynge and Ethelbert Ward, a Denver lawyer and member of the executive committee of the Colorado Cattle and Horse Growers Association, to the podium. In a relatively unemotional dissection of the reserve problem, Ward conceded that Congress did possess the power to pass conservation laws but only if consented to by those states affected by them, only if state sovereignty was not impaired by them, only if they did not abridge state laws, and only if they did not result in the discouragement of homesteading.[68] Bonynge followed with a brief address in which he condemned the federal creation of forest reserves. "Just as a reserve is created," he said in conclusion, "a homesteader will avoid it because . . . impediments and obstacles are thrown in the way of speedy development."[69] The congressman then gave the floor to other speakers, all of whom criticized federal policy, and saved most of his invective for a later time.

Although Murdo MacKenzie (allegedly speaking for the National Livestock Association, which was not permitted to take the floor) condemned the program committee for packing the program with speakers who made "attacks on government policy," it was conservationist Irving Hale, a leader in the Colorado State Forestry Association, who made the afternoon's featured speech.[70] Shortly before the convention, Hale had published an article in a state magazine lamenting the fact that "Colorado's glory of the forest" was "fast becoming a glory" that was past. But, he had also written, the "havoc" could still be "checked and the forests partially restored by the Government forest reserve policy—another diadem in the Roosevelt crown."[71] At the convention Hale repeated his contention that only Roosevelt could save the West from itself.

In the afternoon, too, the packing controversy reached its peak. Conservationists, increasingly irritated by their treatment at the hands of the credentials committee, angrily challenged the insurgents in a series of confrontations on the convention floor. After a heated debate punctuated by several brief fights, delegate totals were revised. Colorado's number of delegates

Gifford Pinchot addressing the Public Lands Convention in 1907.
Courtesy Colorado State Historical Society

was increased to 513 and Wyoming's to 178, but at the same time delegations from proconservation states were increased proportionately even more (Nebraska's delegation, for example, was raised to 33 and South Dakota's to 26). Arguments over accreditation diminished but did not cease. Open antagonism existed, but neither side moved to close the breach.

On June 20, when the delegates massed for the final day of the convention, the insurgents still appeared to be in command of the proceedings. They seemed to believe that their movement had crested. The *Gunnison News-Champion* happily

wrote that at that point "men of all parties" seemed to be "well-nigh unanimous in condemnation of the policies of Roosevelt and Pinchot—a surprising and gratifying fact."[72] The *Saguache Crescent* added that the convention, which had been "conceived and planned on a square deal" and at which the anticonservation West had had "no undue advantage," had gone exceedingly well. Conservation questions had been "fairly and freely discussed," and the westerners had won many converts to their cause.[73] Many remained unconverted, however, and kept up their criticism of insurgent tactics. Roosevelt loyalist A. E.

DeRicqles spoke for most of his allies when he "regretted" that Teller had taken a position "in opposition to the President of the United States," that agencies such as the Denver Chamber of Commerce had propagandized to "make this country believe that all Western people were opposed to the policy of the President," and that "no opportunity was given to the other side of the question in any shape or form."[74]

The convention's last major address was given by Gifford Pinchot on the morning of June 20. Confident and urbane as always, almost elegant in a black tailored suit, Pinchot walked across the floor to the podium, ignoring catcalls from the crowd, and confronted the assembly: "If you fellows can stand me," he quipped, "I can stand you."[75] The central theme of his address was the value of the forest-reserve system to the nation. On the subject of the grazing tax he explained, as he had so many times in the past, that the government would "give the small man in the grazing proposition the best of it every time." In response to accusations of arrogance and demagoguery, he quietly replied that he "resented them with every fiber of my being." In conclusion he asked the cattlemen and others for their co-operation in the matter of conservation: "Speak to your people," he said, "that they may go forward."[76]

When Pinchot returned to his seat, cheered "lustily" by the crowd, a handful of insurgents immediately took the floor to attack his speech. Led by Robert Bonynge, who took violent exception to Pinchot's assertion that the controversial Midnight Reserves had been withdrawn before the passage of the Agricultural Appropriations Act, they assailed him with every argument at hand.[77] For the insurgents it may have been the convention's greatest single moment—particularly Bonynge's attacks on the Forester, "whose popularity was lowered several degrees" as a result.[78] The congressman was followed to the floor by John Shafroth and Thomas Patterson, two of Pinchot's most persistent critics. Unrolling a map showing the extent of the forest-reserve network in Colorado, Shafroth made his point with uncharacteristic gentleness: "I recognize the work Mr. Pinchot has done for all of us," he said, "but I think the people who live here know better than he what needs to be done." The choleric Patterson was not so kind. He ended the morning's session with a searing attack on forest reserves (a problem which one newspaper reported "loomed before his eyes like the yellow peril").[79]

With two days of conflict behind it, the convention prepared, finally, to adopt resolutions expressing its sentiment. On the afternoon of June 20 the resolutions committee (which was not and had not been under the domination of Colorado insurgents) presented a package of twelve proposals for consideration, all of them prepared either in conference, where each state was represented by one delegate, or taken under consideration from the floor. Collectively they included several highly important provisions. Section two, for example, stated that "the people of the West are unalterably opposed to any change in the wholesome and beneficient policy of treating the public lands of the nation as a trust to be disposed of in all cases to actual settlers for the cultivation and the making of homes." Section three specified that forest reserves should be created only when they did not "withdraw from actual settlement land suited to settlement." Section six demanded that all nontimbered lands within federal reserves be withdrawn immediately and restored to entry. In reference to the grazing issue, section seven stated total opposition to leasing. Section eight specified that all agricultural lands contained in forest reserves be opened to homesteading. And section twelve urged that all withdrawn coal lands be restored to entry at the earliest possible moment.[80]

The nature of the resolutions stunned insurgents and conservationists alike—and for the same reason: no matter what they called for, no matter how they were worded, the proposals were, all things considered, astonishingly mild. The Roosevelt men, of course, had expected the worst; after years of anticonservation and antigovernment agitation in and around Colorado and after three straight days filled with harsh, occasionally violent insurgent talk, they had anticipated resolutions radically opposed to federal land policy. But while the resolutions *were* critical and while they *did* call for changes in federal policy, they were so moderately *worded* as to be practically meaningless. Hardcore anticonservationists, dismayed by the generous tone of the resolutions despite the fact that they had made no apparent attempt from the floor either to force radical provisions on the resolutions committee or to alter the language of those provisions already adopted, warned conservationists not to be misled. "No, Mr. President," said the *Steamboat Pilot*, "don't let this deceive you. The West is going to fight your grazing policy, the absurd extent of your forest reserves, and your coal land program. . . . It is useless not to fancy that the resolutions of the convention did mean all they said and with a stronger emphasis than was given them."[81] By then, however, such displays of defiance had a particularly hollow ring to them. The fact was that in the very heart of insurgent territory, in the midst of a convention packed with enemies of conservation, moderation had prevailed. Insurgents could deny it all they wanted, but it was a fact, immutable and irrefutable.

As time approached for the convention to vote on the resolutions, many delegates left the convention. Conservationist delegations, apparently satisfied that the resolutions were the best they could hope for, left even before the proposals were even officially submitted.[82] After the presentation, small bands of insurgent cattlemen and a few homesteaders joined the trek, drifting out of Denver through the June heat, back to the mountains. If their feeling was that opposition to the resolutions would be useless, they were right. In the early evening of June 20, by a voice vote, the convention passed the proposals. Without fanfare the meeting was gaveled to a close. The rest of the delegates departed, said a California newspaper, "roaring as mildly as a sucking dove."[83]

Predictably, controversy lingered in the wake of the great Denver debate; instead of answering questions, it merely posed more. And in the process, the debate sent insurgents and conservationists, cattlemen and politicians, and journalists and federal administrators in search of the meaning of it all.

In general, western opinion was divided over the results of the convention and the larger question of its significance. In Wyoming, for example, the *Laramie Republican* believed that the resolutions had been too harsh. Advocating leasing as the only way to break the stranglehold of "big sheepmen" on the range, the paper felt that the proposals, as mild as they may have been, should have been less biased in favor of the insurgents. On the other hand, however, men like Congressman Frank Mondell, who hailed the coal-land provision in particular, and newspapers like the *Centennial Post*, which maintained that the Roosevelt administration had consistently acted according to its "own ideas" and "in the absence of law," supported the substance of the resolutions. In California the *San Francisco Chronicle* took the position that the convention had been an insurgent victory; the West at last had impressed upon the East the fact that it would not share its wealth with "states that have eaten their cake" and now wished to "share with those who have scarcely had a chance to nibble theirs."[84] The *Seattle Post-Intelligencer* agreed, taking particular exception to Ballinger, Washington's native son. In Oregon the *Portland Oregonian* demurred, calling the convention a "frizzle," and the *Salt Lake Tribune* and the *Arizona Gazette*, among others, adopted the same position. Lashing out at the "meanly selfish and exceedingly unpatriotic" motives of the insurgents, the *Gazette* concluded that the convention had not represented the "real attitude of the West."[85]

Post-convention debate in Colorado mirrored the divisions of the larger West. Insurgents, of course, proclaimed victory over the Roosevelt administration. The *Denver Field and Farm* editorialized that "not since the Boston Tea Party have the people of the nation come out in such open revolt against the administration of our government" and won. Despite the intimidating presence of "presidential thimbleriggers" and "political pikers" placed in the convention by conservationists, the insurgents had "proceeded to flay the administration alive." The newspaper claimed that it was "sorry for Baron Pinchot—

his face was so red."[86] The *Basalt Journal* agreed that despite the presence of federal lobbyists, "the overwhelming sense of the convention was against . . . any form of governmental control and extension of the forest reserves. . . . It was the sentiment of the West and not Colorado alone that there be a halt called on the government setting aside the balance of the public domain."[87] The *Meeker Herald*, a bulwark of anticonservation sentiment in northwest Colorado for fifteen years, insisted that, despite the tone of the resolutions, the convention achieved "much good." Roosevelt, said the *Herald*, had "followed the advice of the visionary Pinchot and selfishly interested schemers long enough;" the convention would most certainly force him to "modify his course."[88] In Denver, the *Denver Post* gloated over what it called an "unqualified" insurgent victory:

> *The main thing accomplished was the refreshing evidence that divinity which doth hedge about Theodore Roosevelt can be torn away and the truth exposed by his fellow citizens. . . . Coldly, calmly, with determination, the majority of the convention proceeded to carry out its purpose [of discrediting conservation]. . . . Roosevelt practically is dictator in these United States. But out West in Colorado—in Denver—we solemnly met and called him down.*[89]

If insurgents were happy with the convention and its results, Colorado conservationists merely registered revulsion. The *Pueblo Chieftain* indignantly declared that

> *of all the hot air and buncombe conventions in the history of the West . . . the Denver Land Convention was certainly entitled to preeminence. . . . The convention developed into a protracted struggle between some Democratic politicians seeking political capital and a few range barons on one side, and a few Republican officeholders on the other. . . . So far as the real sentiments of the people of the West are concerned, the convention was a complete failure.*[90]

A cartoon from the *Denver Post*, June 21, 1907, depicting the "defeat" of conservation at the 1907 Public Lands Convention in Denver.
Courtesy Colorado State Historical Society

Condemning the intemperate "roasting of Pinchot and Garfield," the meaningless talk about "tyranny, landlordism, bureaucracy, etc.," and the pursuance of a "cut-and-dried anti-administration program," the *Colorado Springs Gazette* (owned by Pinchot's friend Clarence P. Dodge) summed up the Denver meeting as "a fizzle." "Perhaps the most regrettable thing about it," it concluded, was "that the impression is sent broadcast that this convention represents the real attitude of the West. . . . As a matter of fact, there are far more people in the West who support the administration policy than there are those who oppose it."[91]

In Denver the *Denver Republican* printed numerous letters deploring the actions of the insurgents. In a typical letter appearing on June 22, one writer bitterly complained that anti-administration Coloradans—a "little band of political harpies continually feeding on the good nature of more honorable citizens for their political prestige"—had brought "mortification" and "discredit" to the state. "How long," he wrote, "is every gathering for the public weal to be marred by the intrusion of these marauders? Are their devious mechanizations to be permitted to become a running sore on every public movement launched in this state, making the commonwealth ridiculous in the eyes of the nation?" His conclusion—that the anticonservationists were the "shame that rests on Colorado"—was shared by many.[92]

In reality, of course, Colorado insurgents had won very little in Denver. Though they failed to realize it or simply refused to admit it, three factors had damaged, if not destroyed, their cause.

First, they had overestimated their own importance at the convention. The insurgent press, as Everett Dick has written, "filled the country with strident anticonservation propaganda, giving the impression that the country from the Rocky Mountains westward was seething with indignation against . . . conservation. As the howling of two coyotes sounds like a whole pack to the tenderfoot, so the press made it appear that the whole West was in revolt against the administration."[93] To a great extent it appeared as though insurgents mistakenly believed statements made by their own newspapers—the *Rocky Mountain News*, *Glenwood Avalanche-Echo*, *Gunnison News-Champion*, and others. Then, perhaps, because they overestimated the extent of their movement, their influence, and their strength, they approached the meeting not in a spirit of cooperation but of arrogance and cockiness. Thus they invited animosity and repudiation not only from federal officials and conservationist groups but from the apparently large numbers of moderates who attended the convention not to protest but to hear the president's men, to determine precisely where—as one newspaper put it—"the states . . . are at" in the conservation scheme, and to solve existing land problems stemming from it.[94] True, the insurgents comprised the majority at the convention, but it was a tenuous majority. And while they may have manipulated many of the meeting's proceedings, they never attained complete mastery over them. In the end, partly because of their attitude, partly because of misconceptions of their power, they succeeded in doing themselves more harm than good.

Second, the packing controversy had undermined the credibility of almost all the convention's actions. Its attention drawn time and again to the insurgents by conservationist cries of "packing," the wary public ultimately dismissed the entire convention as an abortive western conspiracy, as the "land grabbers' last stand."[95] Most importantly, the public tended to discount the convention's anticonservation resolutions—no matter how moderate they might have been—as a meaningless by-product of the conspiracy. Whether or not the insurgents had, in fact, packed the convention, or had tried to, was a moot point. The public consensus, fueled by the claims of the Roosevelt administration, was that they had.[96] Worse, insurgents had gone about their work clumsily. It seemed to be true, in the final analysis, that "had Pinchot himself tried to introduce a note of discord into the proceedings, he could not have been more successful than the organizers, intent upon seeing that their views be publicized as the viewpoint of the whole West."[97] Seeking a mandate, the insurgents, instead, had hastened their own downfall.

Finally, beyond the packing crisis, the insurgents had been irreparably damaged by the tone of the resolutions. What they had sought at Denver was a defiant, emphatic declaration of western rights and grievances; what they received and presented to the nation—resolutions totally devoid of anger—hardly lent credence to their cries of oppression. The American nation, already skeptical of western radicalism in any form—whether populism or anticonservationism—was not to be convinced, on the basis of the resolutions, that the entire West opposed the Roosevelt land program. On the basis of evidence presented to it by the Denver convention, there was no conceivable way the nation could conclude that, as the *Rocky Mountain News* had once stated, the West was in a "condition of revolt" against the federal government. Gifford Pinchot, writing to a friend a few days after the convention, happily reported that "We had a great time and we were by no means eaten up. The resolutions were absolutely harmless." Because they were, they—and the convention itself—had "no perceptible effect either on the Roosevelt administration or the American people."[98]

One question which continued to haunt Colorado insurgents long after the convention had ended was why the resolutions turned out as they did. The obvious answer was that the insurgents simply had not dominated the critical resolutions committee as they had other parts of the convention. They had planned—possibly schemed—to make the convention in every sense a reflection of their views, but, for whatever reason, they had failed to manipulate the convention's most important committee. Early in the proceedings they apparently saw the oversight. During the first day's debate they complained that "the resolutions committee was not as radical as expected," and they blamed it on infiltration by "government agents."[99] But the resolutions were less the product of outsiders than of native westerners—like committee Chairman Frank Goudy of Denver—more moderate than radical and bent on proposing anticonservation resolutions that the Roosevelt administration might respond to in good faith rather than in anger.

Whatever its effects, the Denver Lands Convention was a watershed in the history of the conservation conflict in the American West. On one side of it lay fifteen years of insurgent hopes, and on the other side of it the hopes lay shattered. The blistering Colorado June of 1907 marked the end of an era in the history of the state. Though the anticonservation movement there was not dead, it would never again be as strong and as vibrant as it had been in the past. If the pendulum had ever swung in favor of the insurgents in Colorado, now it swung away. They had had their day. It would not come again.

X. End and Beginning

In the late summer of 1907, as the conservation conflict receded in the West, the state of Colorado might well have looked back on its recent past in an attempt to determine precisely what the significance of the controversy had been. Certainly no western state had grappled with the problem more persistently—or with more internal chaos—than had Colorado. And yet, despite all of its travails, it still had failed to establish a clear-cut consensus on the conservation question. If anything, the Denver convention, which had been designed to answer questions, had only given rise to more. Still, one thing was certain: the back of Colorado insurgency had been broken. Though the movement was not dead, it was no longer viable.

In a state attempting to make sense of the sixteen-year-old struggle that apparently had come to an end, one primary question had to be, How had the conservationists ultimately won the state, especially after insurgency had seemed so strong for so long?

From the very beginning of the era, though they could not have known it, the insurgents were destined to lose the conservation fight. To begin with, probably at no time did they constitute a majority of the state's citizens. If at any time they took on the appearance of a majority, the appearance was largely illusory. As Gifford Pinchot wrote, the volume of insurgent protest often obscured the fact that their numbers were relatively small: "Those who were for [conservation] made far less noise than those who were against it."[1] Absorbing the daily rantings of the *Glenwood Avalanche-Echo* over the course of two decades, one easily might have received the impression that Colorado in general was "simply boiling over with indignation against the President, Mr. Pinchot . . . and everyone else concerned with forest protection."[2] But such an impression, as the Denver convention showed, would have been false. As long as the vast arid sections of the state needed mountain water safeguarded by healthy watersheds and as long as those sections, anchored by populous urban centers such as Denver, Colorado Springs, and Pueblo, supported conservation, insurgency simply could not dominate. It had its strongholds, but they were rural and relatively small; and the population of all of them combined, even assuming that it had been uniformly anticonservation (which it was not), barely equaled the population of a single proconservation center like Denver.

Not only did the insurgents fail to establish themselves as a majority group in Colorado, but they remained, from the beginning, fragmented even among themselves. The dilemma of the cattlemen was a case in point. Regressing from a state of relative cohesion at the beginning of the conservation era to a state of bitter disunity by 1907, the cattle industry provided a graphic example of the extent of internal division in the western insurgency. Other key industries, too, found themselves vulnerable to division. While large timber concerns supported conservation, for example, small timber cutters did not, and while large mining operations often cast their lot with the government and its "gospel of efficiency," independent miners and prospectors did not. In any event, as long as the major resource-use groups differed so radically among themselves about conservation, insurgents could not have hoped to dominate the state.

The nature of insurgent leadership also may have contributed to the movement's eventual decline. Whatever their intentions, many anticonservationist leaders occasionally drifted into demagoguery during the conservation debate; and while the popularity of individual men such as Teller, Shafroth, Taylor, and Ammons remained unimpaired, their collective intemperance almost certainly alienated some segments of Colorado society. If not before, their machinations at the Denver convention cost them some support. At all times the possibility that Colorado statesmen, like politicians anywhere, acted in only mock concern for the people had to be considered, and events like the Denver debacle seemed to confirm the probability. No longer did pious statements—such as that of Thomas Patterson that "there is too much paternalism, too much government, too much interference with the private affairs of the people"—have much meaning.[3]

Finally, even had the insurgents controlled the state, they still would have faced one final, insurmountable obstacle: Roosevelt, Pinchot, and the might of the federal government. One important factor in the demise of insurgent fortunes was the perennially widespread personal popularity of Roosevelt. To bewildered insurgents it must have seemed that he could do no wrong, that no matter what action he took "against" the state, he still retained "many friends" and much support for his policies.[4] Even at the Denver convention it was reported that Roosevelt's enemies held him in "high esteem," and while they might have attacked his policies, they did not attack him.[5]

If Pinchot never shared Roosevelt's popularity, he nonetheless held his own against anticonservationist leaders, and, to a great extent, it may have been their chronic inability to overcome him that crippled their movement. On countless occasions—in Cripple Creek, Glenwood, Denver, and elsewhere—they attacked him, but not once, not even in their home territory, did they succeed in discrediting him. The forester was served well by his "resiliency, by which he could nimbly bounce back after being unmercifully pounded," and his "boldness, reasonableness and good humor" which "effectively destroyed the black image which many westerners had of him."[6] Pinchot's courage and tact and Roosevelt's popularity formed a combination that no insurgent group could have hoped to overcome—

at least not in Colorado. The two men, backed by a skillful group of scientific conservation planners, an efficient Forest Service, and a zealous ranger corps, ultimately were able to overcome division in their own ranks (caused by the Muir group) and make inroads into Colorado.

A second major question that Colorado attempted to answer in 1907, if it had not before, was which side had been right in the conservation conflict and which had been wrong.

From the viewpoint of the conservationists, both in Colorado and elsewhere, the insurgents were wrong, their goals unjustifiable and indefensible.[7] To the conservationist mind, the insurgents' cardinal fault was their inability to see that resource waste was "one gigantic problem" which had to "be solved if the generations, as they came and went, were to live civilized, happy, useful lives in the lands which the Lord their God had given them."[8] As resource planners perceived it, insurgent elements, steeped in frontier anti-intellectualism, rejecting the "rational, the logical, the analytical approach to resource problems," and accepting instead the "unstated major premise" of the times that "everything would come out all right," only invited national disaster. While men like Henry Teller and Elias Ammons reflected "faith in a greater future, despite all odds and reason," the conservationists assumed that only they fully understood reality. As Gifford Pinchot wrote, summing up their collective philosophy: "The conservation of natural resources is the key to the future. It is the key to the safety and prosperity of the American people, and all the nations of the world, for all time to come. The very existence of our nation . . . depends on conserving the resources which are the foundations of its life."[9] The final judgment of conservationists, those in Colorado as well as elsewhere, was that anticonservationism was wrong and unpopular, a movement promoted only by "selfish interests" who had been "neither logical, reasonable, nor politic" in their "fight" against the government.[10] Conversely, only those who had fought for land and resource preservation were the champions of the people, defenders of the nation's "splendid heritage" for the use and enjoyment of "future generations."[11]

Colorado insurgents did not—could not—agree with the assessment. To the very end of the conservation period, even after the 1907 debacle, they continued to defend themselves. "Uncle Sam is you and I," said one embittered pioneer in 1907:

> *a few years ago in northwestern Colorado he . . . said to the prospective settlers, come and settle and develop the land. . . . So the settlers came to wrestle with the wilderness. They conquered, and as they were about to emerge from their trials this same Uncle Sam* [*originated conservation, withdrew land from entry, and imposed grazing taxes*]. . . . *Is that your boasted "square deal?" It is only blind partisanship* . . . [*and*] *rank injustice.*[12]

In truth such a position was not entirely unwarranted. The insurgents, for example, might have had valid reasons for opposing the preservationist ideas of men like John Muir and Hamlin Garland. Moralistic and self-righteous, the preservationists unreservedly condemned pioneers who found "God's trees" "rejoicing in wildness" and destroyed them. Indiscriminately labeling such men and groups as "vandals" and "destroying angels," Muir and his followers sought nothing less than the total reservation of the western public domain.[13] At no time, however, did the wilderness cult fully understand the nature of pioneer life. It did not or would not understand the importance of settlement to frontiersmen, and, unfamiliar with the exigencies of pioneer life, it did not realize the fact that access to local resources was the key to survival. If land devastation was wrong, total land reservation was no less so. Even Pinchot conservationists agreed to that.

By the same token, insurgents had sound reasons for denouncing "Pinchotism." As several historians have pointed out, the men who masterminded the conservation movement—Pinchot and his coterie of resource planners—were "men of science, not economists," who did not reflect the dominant economic faith of the early 1900's and who never fully understood the aspirations of landless pioneer entrepreneurs.[14] Alluding to the problem in a 1906 Senate speech, Henry Teller complained that "areas as great as many of the states" had been withdrawn "without any application from anybody in the state of Colorado." Now, said Teller, "these areas are dedicated to solitude and silence. Nobody can go in. A man cannot even take his gun and go in there without the permission of the forest reserve people. No taxes are paid. There are valleys there that would support a population big enough to maintain a school and a church that we are absolutely prohibited from touching."[15] Among those who did not understand the pioneers' compulsion to settle, the temptation was to dismiss such statements and such desires as hypocrisy. But on the other hand no one could say, categorically, that Teller and others like him were not sincere.

If the withdrawal of western land distressed insurgents, its unilateral administration by conservationist planners compounded the feeling. Essentially the Pinchot group believed that the efficient preservation of natural wealth could be accomplished only by technicians like themselves, not by western legislatures, economic interest groups, or individual citizens. So, ignoring the fact that many such grass-roots groups disliked the idea of "integrated planning" and "central direction" and shared a "violent revulsion against the scientific, calculated methods of resource use adjustment" favored by conservationists, the planners "rarely, if ever" permitted westerners to help decide policy questions.[16] Cleveland's action in 1896, Roosevelt's Midnight Reserves in 1907, grazing fees, mining restrictions, lumbering restrictions—all such actions invariably antagonized local groups interested only in local problems and in finding local solutions to them. To a nation or any part of it raised on the concept of localism, such departures from it seemed, at least, dangerous. And perhaps they were.

The dictatorial attitudes of Roosevelt and Pinchot contributed to the frustrations of localities. Pinchot unquestionably was a domineering man. So was Roosevelt. And because of this attitude, they grated on the feelings of independent westerners. Roosevelt, for example, "advocated direct as opposed to representative government" and often acted by presidential proclamation. His program emphasized power flowing from the top of government, from the executive branch, thereby minimizing local institutions and grass-roots groups. Roosevelt almost never co-operated with local groups; he cultivated them, used them for what help they could give him, then ignored them. In part his attitude was based on his concept of the presidency—that the chief executive should take the lead in initiating action for the public good, regardless of the attitudes of local interest groups and even Congress. But, on the other hand, Roosevelt may have negated local power out of fear of late nineteenth-century radicalism. He hated populism and "rejected Western Insurgency" from the beginning as its extension.[17] Such an attitude, obviously, did not lend itself to fairness and objectivity in dealing with the West.

If conservationists feared western radicalism, insurgents had cause to fear what they might have called conservationist "counter-radicalism." Samuel Trask Dana has written that the enthusiasm of both Roosevelt and Pinchot was "so contagious as to inspire among their followers an almost fanatic devotion both to the men themselves and the causes they espoused."[18] Such "fanatic devotion" frightened and repelled many westerners who believed they found evidences of it in virtually everything the conservationists did. Most offensive, from the beginning to the end of the conservation era, were government rangers, who even Roosevelt admitted were often "over-strict" in their dealings with local pioneers.[19] In Colorado, where Roosevelt and Pinchot were a "real inspiration" to them, rangers pursued conservation with a zeal that often bordered on the obsessive.[20] "What I've done," wrote one to his supervisor, "was all done for the Forest Service. . . . I have tried all these years to bear in mind that it is the cause of forestry and conservation and not me personally that is of concern."[21] Earnest and conscientious they may have been and a service to their nation as well, but such devotion had bad effects as well as good. In some cases, at least, insurgents were justified in denouncing methods utilized by rangers, land agents, planners and others in attempting to achieve their objectives.

While Colorado insurgents may have played the role of villain in 1907, today one cannot necessarily approach them as such. They may not have been right, but then, again, neither were they completely wrong. And the same holds true for the conservationists: they were not wrong, but at the same time they were not entirely right. In the final analysis the two groups can be evaluated objectively only if the conservation movement itself is put in its proper perspective, something that Coloradans could not do in 1907, and not dealt with as some kind of historical morality play. Samuel P. Hays, explaining the pitfalls of conservation historiography, has written that the conservation controversy, "cast in the framework of a moral struggle between the virtuous 'people' and the evil 'interests,'" has been distorted by historians depicting preservationists, such as those in Colorado, as defenders of "spiritual values and national character" and their opponents as antipatriots.[22] "It is easy, writing about the landscape," adds Roderick Nash,

> *to fall into the rhetoric of moralism—the "good guys" versus the "bad guys". . . . [but] such a representation unjustly uses the emotions of the present to describe the actions of the past. It fails to employ historical sympathy, to understand the past on its own terms. . . . Certainly early Americans made mistakes in using the land, but . . . rather than shaking moralistic fingers, conservation historians would do well to attempt to understand why men acted as they did toward the environment.*[23]

Perhaps the study of Colorado has helped to undermine the mythology of "good guys" and "bad guys" and facilitate that understanding.

The great debate over national resource policy which reached a climax in Denver in 1907 had touched on some of the most provocative problems in American life. Over the course of nearly two decades the controversy had raised many of the most significant questions of the time: Was the American frontier receding, as Frederick Jackson Turner had suggested, and if it was, could the nation—in terms of ideals, traditions, and institutions—survive the transition from agrarianism to industrialization and urbanization? Would the disappearance of the wilderness, with its primitive beauty, undermine the spiritual and emotional strength of a society caught in the transitional process? Would the dissolution of material abundance lead to national economic disequilibrium and to a lessening of political independence? If the wilderness was vanishing, could it be saved and conserved for the esthetic and material use of future generations without encroaching on the traditional rights of the existing one? Could large-scale resource planning be undertaken without overriding the rights and aspirations of individuals and localities that sought participation in policy making? It might have been argued in 1907 in Colorado and elsewhere that none of the questions had been answered, and the argument would have held much validity. But more important than unfound answers was the simple fact that society at least had sought them. And in so doing it set patterns and precedents regarding man and his environment that have endured to this day.

What, then, of our own environmental problems? Is it conceivable that one generation might look at the actions of another, assess its position in regard to the environment, and take positive, logical action to solve those problems? Is it possible for us today to examine mistakes made in the past that we might avoid repeating them now and to evaluate past successes that we might emulate them? In other words, did the battle for the western wilderness teach us any lessons? Realistically, answers to such questions may be difficult to come by. But soon we shall see. As Colorado enters the late 1970's it faces environmental problems of unprecedented magnitude. The first conservation controversy caused deep and lasting social and economic problems for the state and its people. The second promises at least the same.

Overshadowing all other issues today, of course, is the "energy crisis." Nothing in a half century has so polarized Coloradans as the question of impending national fuel and power shortages and whether or not western natural-energy sources should be tapped at an accelerated rate to alleviate those shortages.

Opponents of conservation, or at least of "excessive" conservation, have become outspoken. Beginning with the indisputable fact that the West today possesses enough subsurface deposits of coal, oil shale, and natural gas to alleviate at least part of the crisis, they are able to present persuasive arguments in their favor. Their central theme is that Americans are at that point in their history where they must opt for one of two things: either for the continued impoundment and preservation of western wilderness for esthetic and social considerations or for the stepped-up exploitation of the region for the purpose of finding and utilizing energy sources for a nation seriously in need of them. No longer, they say, can Americans have both worlds—pristine wilderness *and* ample energy production.

If we take the former option, say anticonservationists, we must reconcile ourselves to drastic and permanent alterations in our national life-style. At the 1973 meeting of the American Mining Congress in Denver, Charles F. Barber, chairman of the American Smelting and Refining Company, clearly stated the case against "excessive" future conservation. Underscoring the fact that "we've come to the end of the era of abundance so far as natural resources are concerned" and are "entering an era of scarcity," Barber stated that the United States would be unable to sustain high "standards of living" if it endorsed any "reduction in the quantity of basic resources which will be consumed." Our society, he concluded, will continue to demand such standards, impeded only by environmentalists "making demands [which are not related] to the energy requirements of achieving those demands."[24] In the context of the first conservation era such a statement is weighted with irony. Rooseveltians argued that the quality of life could be maintained only through the careful conservation of natural resources; but today we may argue that the quality of life is sustainable only without it!

Present-day conservationists dispute the view. They also fear its attractiveness. "The demands for energy, minerals and natural resources to keep on living in extravagant, wasteful ways will be intense" in the future, says one; "so will be the pressures to stampede over environmental considerations of protecting the soil, forests, rivers, lakes, air, and prairies to meet those demands."[25] It is not, of course, that environmentalists oppose the production and distribution of energy. Rather it is that they fear, first, the attitude of the federal government in the matter, and, second, the exploitive process itself—the physical means by which man would get at energy resources.

With reference to the former, they suspect the "boomer" attitude of the federal government (which once again has been placed in an adversary role with respect to Colorado and much of the West). The government has adopted the position that "national energy interests override state and regional concerns about social, environmental, and economic impacts" of energy-resource development. Speaking before eleven western governors in Denver in January, 1975, for example, chief of the National Energy Council Rogers Morton bluntly said that "no president, no government, is going to stand by and let electric power production not meet demands. If the plants are not built [because of state objections], there is a federal responsibility to do something about it." His conclusion was that "if the states don't want the federal government to take charge," they would have to develop programs of their own that would provide for the dispersal of energy all over the country. Much as James Garfield held in 1910 that Colorado could not say that "its water was for the use of Colorado, but for the use of the whole country," Morton held in 1975 that western energy supplies were to serve "not only the states, but the national interest."[26]

In general, proconservationists have not hesitated to express their fear of federal coercion in the area of resource development. Colorado Governor Richard Lamm, for example, has stated his belief that Colorado faces "increasing danger" of the government "coming in and telling us how, what, and where to develop our natural resources." Reading into Morton's words the implied threat that—for "cause"—the government could override the Constitution's Tenth Amendment, he has pointed out that "the federal preemptive power does exist" and could be used if the West fails to act "properly" on its own.[27] Lamm and other conservationists might declare, as he has, that "the West can't become a coal bin for the entire nation," and that westerners cannot allow "the rape of Colorado [and other states] to satisfy the energy needs of the rest of the nation." But they doubtless realize, too, that the federal government "holds the ultimate trump cards" in the hand.[28]

With reference to the question of the exploitive process, controversy surrounds the question of how natural gas, oil, and coal can be extracted from western land without destroying it. In the case of natural gas, proponents of its usage contend that such "unlocking" can be achieved safely and without environmental damage through controlled subsurface nuclear blasting. Conservationists have vigorously objected to the idea, principally on the grounds that radioactivity released by the firing of nuclear devices would adversely affect both surface plant and animal life and underground water courses.[29] As in other days when conservationists bridled at the activities of timber combines and cattle kings, now they resist others. During debate over the 1973 Rulison Shot near Rifle and Project Wagon Wheel near Big Piney, Wyoming, they vehemently expressed their feelings. "Despite the fact that there is an energy shortage," said Wyoming Senator Clifford Hansen in support of opponents of the Wagon Wheel project, "I propose to be guided in my thinking . . . by what appears to be best for the people of this state."[30] Hansen spoke for large numbers of Coloradans, too, and in so doing he sounded not at all unlike an Edgar Ensign.

The debate over oil shale, too, has created extensive controversy in Colorado and its neighboring states. Advocates of maximum energy production maintain that the opening up and mining of the massive northwestern Colorado-southwestern Wyoming-northeastern Utah oil-shale field could provide between one and five million barrels of oil a day for a nation in the midst of a severe oil shortage. Beyond providing new sources of fuel, they add, extensive shale mining would create new jobs, add to local, state, and federal tax revenues, and swell the population in northwestern Colorado to 280,000 people by 1987.[31] In the fall of 1974 millionaire oil developer John M. King said that the nation would "fall into a disastrous depression" if it failed to proceed with "an all-out crash program to develop Colorado's oil shale deposits." No doubt, too, many Coloradans and others agreed with his conclusion that "esoteric theories" about the impact of oil-shale development on the Western Slope would become "rather moot" if an energyless nation fell into depression.[32]

Despite the obvious economic appeal of such an argument—one fundamental to anticonservation attitudes at the turn of the century—conservationists so far have rejected it. Operating in agreement with Undersecretary of the Interior Hollis M. Dole that "the mining of oil shale is going to create horrendous environmental problems," they have united in opposition to the leasing of oil-shale lands by the Interior Department to private corporations in Colorado, Wyoming, and Utah.[33] They have done so on several grounds. First, they have contended that federal leasing would enrich certain large oil companies and allow them to monopolize the infant industry. Second, they have maintained that leasing inevitably would lead to the abuse of public lands lying adjacent to leased lands; in January, 1975, for example, they charged that the Interior Department was illegally allowing the Rio Blanco Oil Shale Project the use of forty-nine hundred acres of public land lying near its base of operations.[34] Third, they have said that companies involved in shale-oil recovery have failed to find ways to minimize their social impact on communities facing the influx of large numbers of people.[35] Finally, arguing along purely ecological lines, conservationists have said that recovery projects often tend to proceed with their operations before calculating their environmental impact on any given region. A single oil-shale mining and refining operation on the Western Slope, they assert, would consume at least three million gallons of water daily and generate a volume of rock dust a mile square and eight hundred feet deep over its economic life. Despite the fact that "the potential for environmental damage . . . is tremendous" under such circumstances, conservationists feel that developers have not been cognizant of it; either they have failed to draw up environmental-impact studies in advance of their actions, or they have drawn up such studies and then ignored them.[36] Although such charges are not completely fair—in that most oil companies involved in oil extraction *have* sought ways to minimize environmental damage—they are not, by any means, completely inaccurate either. And because of that fact, conservationists continue to oppose much of the oil-shale recovery program. Just how much was recently illustrated by the once-anticonservation *Rocky Mountain News*. In an editorial highly reminiscent of those published by proconservation newspapers during the crisis years of the first conservation era, it stated that

we cannot afford, even to provide badly needed fuel and energy, to tear up Colorado's land, pollute its water, extend to the limit its natural resources or create ill-planned, shoddy construction and employee boom towns. . . . And Colorado must be prepared to have its own say about what happens to its resources, its land, its water, and its population growth and not sit back and let federal agencies and industry dictate Colorado's future.[37]

The critical conservation showdown of 1907 was precipitated in part by the question of coal. In 1977 the question is as important as it was then. Whether discussing the conventional mining of coal or the commercial conversion of western coal reserves into synthetic heating gas, conservationists and anticonservationists have clashed again and again over the subject.

Proponents of coal mining, like ex-Colorado congressman Wayne Aspinall, argue that "the mining industry is satisfying the demands of the people of this age."[38] Specifically, of course, they point to the fact that coal is the present and future key to adequate national electrical-power production. In normal times perhaps no objection would be raised to such a contention, but today, because the quickest and most economical method of coal extraction is strip mining, opposition indeed has arisen. As in most conservation matters, some of the opposition is valid and some of it is not.

In January, 1973, state Senator John Bermingham of Denver made a statement which seems to sum up the conservationists' attitude about the mining of coal in Colorado. Worrying aloud that excessive development might "tear up western Colorado to let people in Los Angeles drive around," he challenged the state legislature to decide whether or not it wanted Colorado to be "torn up for other parts of the country." Just as Henry Teller might have responded to his antagonists, Senator Hugh Fowler of Littleton replied that with eight hundred years' supply of coal reserves lying within the borders of the state, such resources needed to be converted to the "needs of the people."[39] Conservationists, however, have not yet been converted to Fowler's way of thinking. Although they may be resigned to the fact that Colorado "has no choice but to furnish coal to the nation," they feel that the state *does* have a choice as to whether it will be ravaged in the process or not. Their primary fear is that coal exploitation will result in a "physically and socially ravaged Appalachia," and their solution to the problem lies in unremittant opposition to strip mining.[40]

The strip-mining furor, which has been present in the West for several years, began to accelerate in late December, 1974, when President Ford vetoed a bill which would have largely controlled surface coal recovery. Ford's action was based, not illogically, on the belief that the bill would have caused an 18 per cent cutback in the nation's coal output within three years—something clearly "unacceptable at a time when the nation can ill afford significant losses from this critical energy source."[41] The veto, however (ironically executed while Ford was vacationing at Vail), has outraged conservationists convinced that it "opened the way for serious damage to the environment of Western states."[42] The *Denver Post*, labelling Ford's action "heartbreaking," recently editorialized that it would free coal companies to engage in "quick and careless destruction of the land." Concludes the editor of the *Valley Press* at Hayden: "They're rippin' the country apart . . . gutting the country and raping the land."[43]

Certainly the problem has no quick and easy solution. On one hand coal men argue—and will continue to argue—that "if the folks back East can't get the power for their TV's and their air conditioning and their toasters and percolators and all, and their lights go out, it . . . would be a hell of a thing." They will continue to complain as bitterly as their turn-of-the-century counterparts that "in the last ten years, we have learned to explore minerals in ways that have almost zero environmental effect, but we have been excluded from one federally owned tract after another. Why? Because, people say, you're going into a beautiful forest, you're taking machinery, you're making noise. . . ."[44] On the other hand, however, conservationists are likely to oppose the coal industry just as they have in the past, especially as long as strip mining is largely unregulated. As one young Montanan said recently—in words that could be echoed by many Coloradans, "we feel, all of us, that this is our last stand, that there's no place, now, that we could go to live the kind of life we've built. If we tear up this land and dam the rivers and dry them up and muck up the air with smokestacks and fill it full of people and ticky-tacky houses, there just won't be anyplace left, not in this whole country; there won't be anything left."[45]

As serious as it may be, the energy crisis probably has not stirred up any more controversy in Colorado in recent years than has the bitter debate over land development. During the years of the first conservation controversy one of the most divisive questions was to what extent Colorado's land should be settled. Conservationists argued that settlement should be pursued with caution, sanity, and an eye to the future. Anticonservationists countered that without healthy, aggressive settlement then, at the moment, there literally would be no future. Today the same arguments still prevail. Now, however, their backdrop is different: the Colorado land boom of the 1970's has placed them in radically different and increasingly important perspective.

Any perceptive Coloradan knows today's facts. The state is growing at an almost frighteningly rapid rate, heading toward a projected population of some four million people by the end of the century (a gain of nearly two million people from 1972). With only 280,000 acres of Colorado wilderness protected by law, the rest of the state's land has become fair game for developers. The result is that some three million acres of land currently are under development: Front Range cities from Fort Collins to Colorado Springs have become more crowded by the day, pollution and water scarcity have become commonplace, and what once was open space has largely disappeared into subdivisions, roads, ski resorts, and utility corridors. Should current developmental trends continue, says the Colorado Land Use Commission, there will be an "adverse impact on the natural resources" of the entire state, resulting in "long-term economic deterioration" and a radical reduction in "the quality of life of the majority of Colorado citizens." Conservationists may understate the point when they say that "unrestricted growth can be . . . calamitous."[46]

Development of the Colorado high country today takes two basic forms, both of them controversial and both possessing serious inherent dangers to the state. One, of course, is recreational development, whose popularity is attested to by burgeoning ski resorts along the continental divide. To both the individual entrepreneur and the skiing community at large,

Colorado's winter recreation explosion has been a bonanza. Any individual or community marketing what one observer has called the "Colorado skiing experience" can expect extensive economic return in sales of clothing, equipment, transportation, food, lodging, and entertainment as well as actual "on-the-mountain activity." Beyond that, on a nonconsumer level, investment funds flowing into any region to finance ski-area development (and related construction of such things as restaurants and condominiums) greatly accelerate the overall economic growth of that region.[47] Economic experts say that by late 1975 the nation had ten million active skiers, a number increasing to twenty million by 1980.[48] Colorado will have its share of them.

One measure of the ski industry's health in Colorado is its attendance figures. The 1974–75 season, for example, even coming in the midst of economic hard times, drew 4,800,000 skiers before it ended. Revenue for the season was estimated at $141,500,000 (up from $127,000,000 spent on 4,304,000 ski visits during the 1973–74 season). During the holiday season alone, from December 21, 1974 to January 5, 1975, some 940,000 ski visits (President Ford's among them) were counted on Colorado slopes, and the revenue coming from them was substantial. As for "secondary economic benefits," Robert Pattridge, editorial-page editor of the *Denver Post* has wondered how many of the skiers have consumed beer and steak from Coors' brewery and Ken Monfort's Greeley cattle plant, called home on Mountain Bell, and stayed at the Brown Palace Hotel.[49] His point, even for conservationists, should be well taken.

Areas heavily dependent on skiing activity fiercely defend the idea of continued expansion. In Vail, Aspen, Steamboat Springs, Crested Butte, and elsewhere, emphasis clearly is on further development. Part of the prodevelopment argument is economic. One advocate, focusing on such points as the flow of out-of-state revenue into Colorado (an estimated 80 per cent of Colorado ski-area revenue comes from outside the state) and gasoline and sales tax expenditures, says that "Colorado natives may curse the visitors for clogging highways, lift lines, pubs and motels. But we should be appreciative of them. Especially in these troubled [economic] times." From Vail and Breckenridge, where one developer says that skiing "turned the economy around," to Steamboat, where another adds that it changed a faltering Routt County economy "for the good," the consensus of ski boomers is that their viewpoint is essential to the overall prosperity of the state.[50]

Another part of the developers' argument is that the expansion of skiing projects, especially into rural areas, invariably improves the overall quality of life in those areas. Pointing out the fact that the entire Vail Valley had no sewage district before the development of a ski area there, one developer has remarked that "it's not just growth we're talking about—it's an improved community."[51] Telluride is a case in point. There, before developers carved a ski area out of the mountain valley south of town, the city had a population of only 436; it had no doctor or dentist, no hospital (its only hospital had been converted into a museum), no drug store, and few young adults willing to grow up and remain in such an atmosphere. Today, however, Telluride has a doctor, two lawyers, new retail stores, a proposed library, and a total population of nearly 900 people.[52] They point to the transition of the community as "proof" of what the ski industry can do in terms of enhancing the quality of everyday living for year-round residents as well as for skiers.

Conservationists do not believe that the ski industry necessarily produces either economic or social benefits. To those who emphasize improving the quality of life, one Coloradan has suggested a look at the "brown band of smog devouring the air" in the White River Valley or the "downtown traffic" on Vail Pass. "It's about time," he said, in a letter to the *Denver Post*, that "skiing . . . is deemphasized and Colorado's natural wilderness emphasized."[53] Even those who feel that ski developments are not inherently bad maintain that more caution should be exercised in terms of their expansion. As Richard

Lamm has said, even admitting that most projects apparently have gone to lengths to protect local environments as much as possible, "while [developers'] intentions seem impeccable, they simply may be incapable of assuring, at this point, mitigation of the serious problems" they face. "I have to question even well-planned developments if they are simply in the wrong place or if there are too many of them."[54]

In recent years conservationists have been particularly skeptical of such proposed "super resorts" as Copper Mountain near Dillon, the Wolf Creek Ski Area near South Fork, the Marble and Telluride projects, and Powder Mountain on Grand Mesa. Until recently their primary target was the Marble Ski Area project in the Crystal River Valley (the scene, ironically, of some of the most heated fights of the first conservation era). In November, 1973, they won a signal and perhaps precedent-setting victory when the Forest Service refused to allow the project to expand onto 624 acres of federal land because the developers allegedly had not submitted an adequate drainage plan.[55] At the present time, however, they have turned their attention to the controversial Beaver Creek "winter sports area" near Vail.

In late January, 1975, the United States Forest Service designated the Beaver Creek area between Vail and Eagle in White River National Forest as a "winter sports site." The net effect of the proclamation was that it opened the area to extensive future development. Vail Associates, Incorporated, began seeking a permit to construct ski trails on three thousand acres of national-forest land near Avon. In addition, while projecting a permanent population of some thirteen thousand people in the area by 1995, the Eagle County commissioners approved development plans that could bring an estimated forty thousand people into the region on peak ski days. Prodevelopment forces justified the designation on the grounds that Vail Associates had undertaken a "thorough and sensitive analysis" of environmental conditions in order to prevent the occurrence of problems. They maintained, too, that recreational development had begun in the upper Eagle Valley long before the Forest Service took action.[56]

Conservationists reacted angrily to the declaration. Governor Lamm, for one, filed an official appeal of the decision with the Forest Service, and Colorado Senator Gary Hart called for a review of the matter. At issue, specifically, were a number of wildlife, water, air pollution, and land-use questions, paramount among them the question of precisely how a twenty-seven hundred-acre area could support a population of forty thousand people (five times Eagle County's present population). A larger issue, however, was that of federal versus state power in this or other Colorado land matters. Any situation pitting a proconservation governor and senator against a seemingly anticonservation federal government was strange to Colorado, but that is precisely what had developed. The state accused the government not only of trying to "ram the [Beaver Creek] designation through without a full airing of environmental questions" but also of circumventing and ignoring state land and planning agencies in the process. The *Rocky Mountain News*, which used to blast Theodore Roosevelt, accused the Forest Service of "blatant cynicism" in its Beaver Creek decision and theorized that the service's "slavery to the multiple-use concept of forest management, which in practice has meant commercial development wherever possible," lay behing it.[57] Rhetorically asking whether or not the urbanized Gore Valley (Vail) "would be what it is now" if the Forest Service had not mistakenly allowed large-scale development there years ago, the Colorado Division of Planning implied that Beaver Creek would inevitably become another Vail.[58]

After a year-long "investigation" of the Beaver Creek project, the Lamm administration withdrew its objections to it. Underlying state acquiescence to the original plan was the fact that, between January, 1975, and February, 1976, the Forest Service had allowed the state to participate extensively in the drafting of a crucial environmental assessment report relating to Beaver Creek. Finally, satisfied that the environment would be protected by new guidelines reducing air and water pollution and lowering development density, and that the state had not been bypassed in the decision-making process, Lamm gave his approval to the project. The Forest Service responded in March, 1976, by reapproving its original designation.[59]

The Beaver Creek furor, however, did not subside, nor is it likely to soon. Too many environmentalists remain convinced that the assessment report—however much the state may have participated in its drafting—was premature, superficial, and based on faulty assumptions about the area and its environment.[60] Until they change their minds, arguments undoubtedly will continue between them and the skiing industry, if not over Beaver Creek then over another project in another place at another time.[61] In a sense, of course, the arguments never ended in the first place. The players may be different in the 1970's, but the stakes are the same as they were nearly a century ago.

The second developmental form, and one of potentially more consequence than skiing development, is that of both residential and "leisure" housing construction in the high country. Often in conjunction with the building of new ski areas such as Beaver Creek (as, for example, the $24 million Steamboat Village project near Steamboat Springs), condominium colonies and sprawling housing projects are springing up across Colorado with almost incredible speed. In the San Luis Valley alone three hundred thousand acres of land are under development, as is practically the entire south side of Mount Blanca. Some fifty-four hundred acres of the Arkansas Valley at the foot of Mount Elbert are under option for development. The approaches to beautiful Rocky Mountain National Park are "strewn with an astonishing number of houses," along with mobile homes by the hundreds.[62] Colorado City, Sangre de Cristo Estates, Woodmoor, Wild Horse Mesa, Snowmass, Dillon, Breckenridge, Winter Park, Steamboat—from New Mexico to the Wyoming border land development has become perhaps the most vital economic and environmental concern of the 1970's.

Conservationists, convinced that current construction patterns have both damaged mountain environment and put the state on the road to overpopulation, have become increasingly emphatic in arguing for saner land use in Colorado. Ex-governors John Love and John Vanderhoof both have gone on record in favor of land-use planning as a "basic need" if Colorado is to achieve the "wise and prudent use of [her] natural resources, the most fundamental of which is the land."[63] Countless people have adopted the slogan, "Don't Californicate Colorado," and to the real-estate interests' cry "Own a piece of Colorado!" they have replied, "Think small."[64]

As others before them did, neoconservationists have taken vigorous action to save Colorado. They secured a vote by the people of the state to eliminate the 1976 Winter Olympic Games from the state, arguing that environmental damage inflicted on the Western Slope would be followed by a massive influx of permanent settlers and a multiplication of housing developments.[65] The city of Boulder has moved to curb local mountain housing developments by seeking zoning resolutions that would reduce mountain density and require more environmental considerations by developers.[66] The city even has debated the feasibility of establishing a local population ceiling. The Colorado Land Use Commission, employing its "emergency powers," has begun rigorous examination of land developments in Clear Creek, Douglas, Gunnison, Saguache, and other counties.[67]

None of this is to say, however, that environmentalists have gained any kind of ascendency in Colorado. Opposition to them has been and continues to be powerful. For every Coloradan intent on "undevelopment," or what Lamm has called "mindless Chamber of Commerce promotionalism," another sees the urgency of a "Sell Colorado" emphasis.[68] The city of Buena Vista, for example, has launched a major campaign to lure development to its region. The community of Delta, at one time a center of conservationist activity, has done the same, as has Club 20, a group of prodevelopment counties in western Colorado. "We need a lot more than clear air and scenery" to attract people, industry, and homebuilding, said one member, and countless Coloradans certainly agree.[69]

Perhaps the highlight of the recent confrontations between land developers and conservationists was the state legislature's debate of land-use bills in 1973 and 1974. When a comprehensive land-use bill (S. B. 377) was introduced in the legislature in April, 1973, it fared poorly. Despite the support of then-Governor Love, the proconservation press, legislative conservationists such as John Bermingham, Joe Schiefflin, and Lamm, and a large segment of the public, it was shelved on the last day of the session.[70] Apparently it failed because of some of its specific provisions. Particularly obnoxious to opponents of the bill was a provision creating a five-member state-land commission to review any land development involving air pollution, oil shale, clear-cutting of timber, water diversion, strip mining, highway location, ski-area construction, airport location, and nuclear explosions, and to impose its own restrictions where localities failed to act in the "public interest." Like other Coloradans in times past, many today still fear the investment of power in any central authority—in this case in a land commission. Land developers and chambers of commerce opposed S. B. 377 for obvious reasons. But much of the reaction against it (most of it emanating from the Western Slope) stemmed from fear that the bill and the commission would undermine local control of local land and resources.

Conservationists were deeply distressed by the failure of the bill. In a particularly incisive editorial in the *Rocky Mountain News*, one of them lashed out at the "small minds" that killed it. Maintaining that the bill's "chilling presence laughs at us as we stumble through the motions of trying to cope with development," Richard Schneider wrote that

legislators threw away a bill that would have provided central, statewide land use controls coupled with important local decision-making. Lawmakers discarded a bill that would have established well-thought-out land use policies and goals for the state. They discarded a bill that would have allowed the state to tell industry precisely what is expected of it when it opens up shop in Colorado. More important, . . . there would have been some sense of coordination had Senate Bill 377 passed, a feeling that Colorado was directing its own destiny.[71]

Although a different land-use bill did pass in 1974, conservationists have not been particularly happy with it. One has said that "it falls so short of the mark it's embarrassing to think about," mainly because under its provisions Colorado's land-use controls still rest with county commissioners and town councils rather than with any strong central authority. Lamm, the bill's author, has dismissed it as "unworkable" (after its gutting by senate Republicans before passage).[72]

What might happen next is difficult to predict. One thing, however, is certain: action of some sort is imperative. One fact that neither side can ignore is that Colorado is the nation's seventh-fastest-growing state. Another is that, under the circumstances, development—mainly in the area of leisure housing—can destroy the state if left unattended. In any event, both groups might do well to consider a recent experience of *Denver Post* environment editor Dick Prouty. Returning from a trip along the Front Range from Denver to New Mexico in April, 1973, he reflected on what he had seen. The masses of billboards near Pikes Peak and stone quarries along the Rampart Range ("an open sore on the forested foothills") disturbed him enough, but the most dismaying aspect of his trip was the extensiveness of the land development he saw. Entering the San Luis Valley, he wrote that he was profoundly shocked:

The West is gone! On the west side of [*La Veta*] *Pass the once sprawling foothills and then the flat basin of the San Luis Valley are no longer scenic, open land stretching off to the mountains on the horizon. Like tan tape worms, roads have been bulldozed across the land. There isn't a sign of a house to go along with these 'housing developments.' Just the scars on the land and some roadside signs: '$50 down and $25 a month.' For what? . . . We stop in the developer's office. Wall-sized maps* *pasted with radiant orange stickers attest the sale of the operation. Every sticker is a sale. There isn't a vacant lot left. I wonder at our lust for land.*

We go up on one of the roads. It's a giant rockpile, bulldozed through lovely pinon, pine, juniper and Utah cedar. The view is almost limitless. So is the checkerboard pattern of roads. Home on the range. The old song comes back. But no range is left in the eastern San Luis Valley. . . .

Where can you go now and see open land? South Park? No. Middle Park? No. North Park? A little. . . . Where is it going to stop? When you can't look at cattle grazing on irrigated pastures anymore because they've been subdivided?

There seems to be no area of the state free from the land syndrome. It's too much of a good thing. Take a look at Colorado. It will dismay you.[73]

Were the negative aspects of energy-resource development and ski-industry development added together with this grim view of land use in general, the problem Colorado faces today and tomorrow would be apparent. Even given the economic prosperity which surely would, which already does, result, those responsible for planning land use still would have to take the negatives into account. If they do, Colorado will profit. If they do not, lessons from the past will not have been learned, and the state will remain sadly and dangerously divided.

Colorado's third and final source of environmental friction in the mid-1970's has stemmed from the activities of what Roderick Nash might call the wilderness cult. Spiritual descendents, in a real sense, of Thoreau and John Muir and others like them, many Coloradans today agitate for more wilderness rather than less, and, also like their predecessors, they argue one particular point: that "scenic and spiritual values . . . take priority over economic ones, that the people are entitled to have [natural] places undisturbed by works of man," that, in fact, without the forest and the river and the mountain meadow man cannot hope to survive in his own world.[74] Such reasoning has always drawn criticism in a "pioneer-oriented," land-conscious society, and in Colorado, since at least 1964 when Congress passed the Wilderness Act, criticism has mounted steadily.[75] Today, polarized by the energy crisis and the land boom, conservationists and anticonservationists are further apart than ever on the question of wilderness and its role in American life.

The current wilderness debate is a classic case of history repeating itself: it is to Colorado in the 1970's what the forest-reserve debate was in the 1890's and the early 1900's. For example, the stage is the same—the national-forest regions of the state. As of the fall of 1973, 14.3 million acres of Colorado timberlands came under the administration of the Forest Service, 830,993 acres of it in established wilderness areas or in primitive areas under study for wilderness "potential." Some 9 million acres of federal land, however, are not included under any kind of restrictive designation. It is these lands that are so sought after by conservationists and anticonservationists—and usually with the same kind of desperate energy that marked the activities of the two groups during the first conservation period.[76] Even a cursory analysis of their attitudes today indicates that neither side has changed perceptibly since the day that Elias Ammons first confronted Gifford Pinchot.

In southern and southwestern Colorado several projected wilderness areas have been the subject of extensive debate in recent years.[77] In all cases conservationists have strongly supported the idea of land segregation. Concerning Powderhorn, for instance, claiming the existence of one of the "largest undisturbed alpine tundra areas south of the Yukon," conservationists fear that the encroachment of "civilization" into its interior would disturb the "irreplaceable ecosystems found there." Developers, however, refuse to accept such arguments. Where contested land is rich in resources—as at Hermosa Creek where both City Service Company and Humble Oil are exploring for base metals—its wilderness potential becomes inconsequential.[78]

Primary focus in that part of Colorado is on the proposed Weminuche Wilderness, a tract of 346,833 acres of "clear lakes, fast moving streams, tranquil meadows, and rugged mountains" northwest of Durango in the San Juan National Forest.[79] First sent to Congress for consideration in February, 1972, the proposal thus far has failed to pass both houses (though passage seems imminent in 1977). The reason has been an acrid debate over mineral and timber rights in the region. Only recently Colorado Representative Frank Evans, sponsor of the measure, reported that "sentiment expressed . . . in Colorado overwhelmingly supported designation of the wilderness area." Others, however, continue to argue that large tracts of mineral land and harvestable timber should be excluded from the territory. If not, they conclude, no wilderness designation should be made.[80]

In the extreme western part of Colorado the situation is largely the same. Considering the area's long and sometimes extreme proconservation heritage, it should come as no surprise to find a substantial number of land segregationists still working for wilderness expansion. Their targets include the Palisades near Gateway, Little Dominguez Hideaway near Delta, and Mount Sneffels, Uncompahgre Peak, Cow Creek, Dolores Peak, and Wilson Peak near the Uncompahgre and Wilson Mountains primitive areas. The chief contest is over mineral lands. In the case of the Uncompahgre, its area has yielded $300 million in mineral wealth since the 1870's (some $19 million worth in 1969 alone). In the spectacular Wilson Mountains mining success has been almost as significant. Low grade copper deposits, in particular, have prompted recent heavy exploration and drilling by Texas Gulf, Incorporated.[81] To it and other companies, conservationist agitation obviously is ominous. Should the areas receive wilderness status, mining activities in them would be sharply curtailed. In fact, in that the preservation-oriented Wilderness Act prohibits all but the most primitive mining techniques in the segregated areas, mining might be stopped entirely.

It is noteworthy that the conservationists' main impediment in securing wilderness expansion has been the United States Forest Service. In western Colorado, for example, when conservation groups requested the reservation of three massive wilderness areas totalling 172,000 acres, the Forest Service only proposed five smaller areas totalling 80,130 acres. According to service spokesmen, mineral values in the area pared from the original 172,000 acres outweighed its wilderness potential. Such reasoning left conservationists with the distinct impression that the service had catered to state mining interests in making a decision favorable to them. Indeed, the Colorado Mining Association went on record as being "pleased" with the action. As for conservationists, they remain puzzled at the federal government's action. Speaking for the Wilderness Society, regional director Clifton Merritt has said that "Forest Service officials at policy-making levels have ignored significant [proconservation] public input except when it happens to support their views. It seems unfortunate that the Forest Service has placed very uncertain mineral values above known wilderness values."[82] In fact, if the Forest Service's action with regard to Beaver Creek was questionable, its action involving Western Slope wilderness planning may be even more so.

Northern Colorado, too, continues to experience environmental tension. In other times the Park Range, Medicine Bow, and White River forest reserves saw more than their share of conflict (particularly the White River, where the conservation controversy actually began). Today it continues, not only at Beaver Creek but beyond it in the interior of the region. All that has changed from times past is the fact that mining interests rather than cattlemen lead the reaction against conservation.

Conservationists have been attempting to prompt federal examination of a relatively large number of acres in the region for possible incorporation into wilderness units. They hope to enlarge the Rawah Wilderness, for example, because of its "overcrowding" by hikers, backpackers, and others.[83] Similarly, they aim at the extension of the Mount Zirkel Wilderness west of the Rawah and wilderness designation for the pristine Encampment River drainage system surrounding it. On the fringes of Rocky Mountain National Park, finally, they seek to add Comanche Peak, Deserted Village, Neota Creek, and two units of the Never Summer Range to the wilderness system. In all areas, cognizant of the fact that wilderness designation would block timber harvesting and ski developments and that it would allow only that mineral development that promised minimum impact on the land, developers from the mining, oil, gas, lumber, and ski industries have resolutely fought the conservationists' plans.

The most graphic example of modern-day environmental values in conflict has been the debate over the 212,716-acre Flat Tops region north of Glenwood Springs and southwest of Steamboat Springs. The Flat Tops, a massive flattened dome of geologic strata capped with lava, lies at the heart of Colorado's first and most controversial forest reserve—the White River. In 1891 anticonservationists fought its reservation on the grounds that it would stunt settlement and curtail cattle grazing. Today its adversaries are water-power developers who had hoped to back water up into the proposed wilderness area for use in shale-oil development, coal gasification, and the generation of electric power. The debate has pitted them—primarily the Rocky Mountain Power Company—against environmentalists who have claimed that the impoundment of water would adversely affect area wildlife and irreparably damage the wilderness designation. The controversy intensified in December, 1975, when President Ford signed a Flat Tops bill into law. Interestingly, Ford signed the bill with reluctance, arguing, as developers had, that wilderness areas should not be created where the "evidence of man's activity" was clearly apparent.[84]

In the sprawling central Colorado Rockies west and southwest of Denver, conservationists and anticonservationists have linked up in some of their bitterest confrontations. On one hand, because the area features some of Colorado's most magnificent mountain settings, it has long been a target of wilderness advocates. On the other, because of its vast mineral deposits (gold, silver, copper, zinc, lead, and uranium) and lush range, it has just as long been a magnet for developers. Greatly irritated by the fact that two prime areas—West Elk and Maroon Bells-Snowmass—already are effectively locked up in wilderness units, developers have fought every attempt on the part of conservationists to have the system extended.

Of the many contested areas in the region (including Buffalo Peaks southeast of Leadville, Lost Creek in the Tarryalls, Aspen Ridge and Brown's Canyon near Salida, another Beaver Creek—southeast of Cripple Creek—and the Mount Evans-Mount Bierstadt region), several have generated particular controversy. Debate over the proposed enlargement of the West Elk and Maroon Bells-Snowmass wilderness areas has caused friction between developers and conservationists because of the area's already widespread copper-mining activities. In a similar vein much discussion has taken place over the future of timberlands contiguous to the Mount of the Holy Cross (in the middle of the old Holy Cross Forest Reserve) where logging, water and skiing development, and mining already have begun to mar a setting more suitable—according to one report—for escaping the "sights and sounds of civilization." Of particular concern to conservationists, finally, is the Indian Peaks region, stretching from Rocky Mountain National Park south to Corona Pass near Boulder. In a region already plagued by overpopulation (an estimated two thousand people visit its alpine wilds each weekend), transmontane highway planners, oil and natural-gas developers, and water-project planners have put its wilderness "usefulness" in serious jeopardy. Conservationists argue that further civilization in the Indian Peaks vicinity might limit its primeval environment to the extent that it would become useless to city inhabitants looking for weekend sanctuary.[85]

Perhaps the most controversial area in the entire state—Eagles Nest—is situated in the same troubled region. Its story largely is the same as elsewhere: the proposed wilderness area, now under consideration by Congress, has become a virtual battleground between environmentalists and developers (chiefly water-rights developers and advocates of hydroelectric power plants). At stake are 133,915 acres of "virgin forests, cascading streams, deep clear lakes, and abundant wildlife."[86] The contest for Eagles Nest is particularly critical because it involves water rights owned by the city of Denver. Environmentalists argue that inclusion of the Eagle-Piney water system in wilderness zones will not damage the city; rather, the entire project would both "preserve the best of the wilderness" and still allow Denver to recover 93 per cent of the water originally earmarked for diversion into its system.[87] Opponents of positive congressional action, however, dispute the argument. In a recent referendum, Denverites convincingly voted in support of the concept of transmontane water diversion from Eagles Nest.

Controversy began in May, 1975, when the United States Senate passed a bill prepared by Colorado's Floyd Haskell (and supported by Colorado representatives Tim Wirth and Patricia Schroeder) to establish a wilderness unit of 128,084 acres in the Gore Range, near Vail. Denver water-rights developers were incensed. Because unit boundary lines were drawn too low on mountainsides to allow water to flow naturally down the eastern slope to Dillon Reservoir and then to Denver, they maintained that a pumping system would have to be built to elevate water some 950 feet *up* to Dillon. They estimated the cost of pumping 170,000 feet of water a year at $136 million; electrical power—derived from burning one million tons of coal a year—would light homes for 750,000 people over a twelve-month period.[88]

In April, 1976, when the House passed a rival bill drawn up by Colorado Representative James Johnson, battle lines formed, with Colorado environmentalists pitted against the Denver Water Board. Conservationists, believing that Johnson's bill protected the Gore wilderness better than Haskell's did, supported Johnson's call for a 130,480-acre unit. The board countered by projecting the cost of building and maintaining a pumping system at $50 million over forty years. After supporting a Forest Service proposal to segregate only 87,755 acres, it finally called for the release of 11,000 key acres from which large amounts of water could flow naturally downhill to Dillon.[89]

In June, 1976, a House-Senate conference committee weighed the two bills and adopted most of the components of the Johnson measure. The net result was a proposal considered certain of passage in both House and Senate, to create a 133,915-acre wilderness. Importantly, the acres sought by the Denver Water Board were not eliminated. Antagonism mounted between environmentalists, who contended that developers failed to "compare the overall costs of spoiling one area to save a few dollars for another area," and developers and water users, who continued to argue that "the environmental argument is phoney."[90] In another day Denver largely stood with the conservationists because conservation promised water to a growing metropolitan area in need of it. In modern times, though, in supporting anti-conservation (or, more fairly, limited conservation), the city has given credence to points made by the Henry Tellers years ago: if resource demand is vital to any civilization and supply is imperative to its survival, civilization comes before conservation. The argument was critical at the turn of the century. In Colorado in the late 1970's it still is.[91]

As for the future, where Colorado will go from this point is impossible to say. Cynics might argue that rapproachment between environmentalists and developers simply is not possible in a state such as this where so much wilderness and so much space is to be had. Looking at the current wilderness debate they might conclude that we have learned nothing through the years—that we triggered the conservation conflict in the 1890's fighting for the forest, that we have come full circle over seventy-five years of time, and that we are fighting for the forest still. Whether the cynics are correct or not is a point of conjecture. Whether the conflict continues or not is a matter of critical concern.

To a great extent the direction Colorado takes in the future will depend on the environmental policies and programs of Richard Lamm during his last two years in office. To this point it seems apparent that he has largely abandoned the virtual development-at-any-price policies of his predecessors, John Love and John Vanderhoof, and that he will continue to seek substantial environmental protection for a state long dominated by the ideal of development. Anything less would be surprising for two reasons. First, during the gubernatorial campaign of 1974, in which he unseated Vanderhoof, Lamm made environment the overriding issue of the election. He argued against energy-resource exploitation by outside forces, and although he maintained that he was not antigrowth, he argued vigorously that growth had to be controlled. Without doubt, even given the impact of the Watergate scandals, which helped propel Democrats into office all over the nation, Lamm won because of his environmental views.[92] Second, many of his actions since he took office have been "environmentalist" in nature.

On the question of land use, for example, Lamm has adamantly maintained that Colorado would benefit from strong state and national land-use laws. To that end he supported an ill-fated national bill written by Senator Henry Jackson of Washington in May, 1975, and has since worked toward the "streamlining" and "clarification" of Colorado's own land-use policies. His priorities have consistently included the preservation and expanded development of agriculture, encouragement of tourism without exploitation of natural resources, diversion of population growth from the Front Range corridor, changes in the Subdivisions Regulations Law "to make it a more effective tool for dealing with the real estate consequences of high growth," and a severance tax on minerals to "help pay for some of the costs of growth" in those communities impacted by the rapid development of the mineral industry. As of this writing, because of the divisiveness of the issue, Lamm intends to defer his call for a newer, better land-use bill until 1977.[93]

In the area of energy-resource development and its potential impact on Colorado, Lamm has been particularly active in staking out the state's position with relation to the federal government. His blunt statement that "we're not going to let any exploiter rip us up and rip us off" could stand by itself. So, too, could his often-stated contention that, while Colorado resources should be developed, development should be carried out under state, not federal, control, and that under no condition should exploitation "leave the West as a sacrifice." "We're not going to stand in the schoolhouse door or try to isolate Colorado from the law," he has said, "but we mighty well intend to make the federal government justify its every effort to tell us what's good for us."[94]

Lamm's first action was to call for the creation of a "regional energy agency" to safeguard western environmental and economic rights, that western states might not be "swamped by the overwhelming political and economic power of the East."[95] The agency, established as the Western Governors' Regional Energy Office in February, 1975, ultimately was charged with drawing up and promulgating a comprehensive energy-development policy for the entire West. At the same time, lobbying for western interests in Washington, it helped persuade Congress to change pending energy-development legislation on more than one occasion (it helped amend a pending coal-leasing bill, for example, to allot Colorado some 50 to 60 per cent in royalties instead of 37½ per cent). Calling western participation in federal planning a "life and death" issue, Lamm has characterized the working of the energy office to date as a "bonanza" for the region.[96]

In the fall of 1975, Lamm, acting largely alone, scored another success of sorts. Acting in opposition to a proposed congressional bill to provide $6 billion in federal loans to synthetic-fuels developers, Lamm personally testified in Washington that such loans would invite large numbers of oil-shale and coal-gasification operations into the West. Convinced that mushrooming fuels development, funded by ample federal monies, would ravage the region, he counseled caution. Passage of the bill "in some states," he said, "could prove to be the single most important piece of legislation in two centuries."[97] In the end Lamm was able to force into the bill his own "bottom-line" demands—guaranteed impact money for the states, qualified veto power for the states, and guaranteed compliance with state and local laws by development projects. Though the measure eventually died in Congress—passed by the Senate but killed by the House—Lamm's personal success with regard to it was significant. Said the *Denver Post*: "Governor Lamm has shown leadership Colorado can be proud of."[98]

At no time has Lamm focused his concerns exclusively on the federal government. Time and again he has maintained that Colorado should develop its own energy policy and energy-policy commission and that it has "got to be tough" in imposing strict energy standards on itself.[99] But for the most part, right or wrong, he continues to perceive the federal government as more dangerous to Colorado than Colorado is to itself. His operating assumption continues to be that "the federal government is determined to develop more energy just as fast as it can, and it faces a terrible temptation to override the interests of the states" in the process.[100] In light of this "threat" Lamm has operated in a very particular way in the past. Presumably he will maintain the same course in the future.

As logical and state-serving as Lamm's actions might appear, not all Coloradans have agreed with them. He has attracted criticism from a wide spectrum of the state's citizens, from prodevelopment forces and environmentalist groups alike.

His most vociferous critics are those who have charged him with being "antigrowth." His opposition to the construction of Interstate 470 through the southwest Denver area in 1975 was a case in point. Those in favor of the highway claimed that failure to build it would stunt development in the southwest metropolitan area—and increase traffic congestion and air pollution in the core city. At the same time, Coloradans across the state became outraged by Lamm's frequent collisions with energy-resource and land developers. While they may have concurred that caution was warranted in dealing with developers, they were more concerned about the possible loss of development-related jobs in the state. The consensus seemed to be, as one critic stated in an open letter to the governor, that Colorado "does not need your fantasy." "This is a blood and guts practical old world we have," said another, "with little room for dreamers."[101]

Ironically, most of Lamm's criticism has come from environmentalists, his original constituency. Many incidents have apparently damaged his credibility in the environmentalist community: his support of a controversial thirteen-page "sell Colorado" article in a mid-year issue of *Business Week*, his approval of a nuclear-enrichment plant at Pueblo, and his backing of the Narrows reclamation project on the South Platte despite its criticism as "inadequate" by the Environmental Protection Agency. Even his stand on the synthetic-fuels loans was condemned as vacillation.[102]

Perhaps the most serious issue has been Beaver Creek. Originally Lamm withheld approval of the project, even firing several members of the Colorado Land Use Commission when they supported it. Later, however, after his objections had been met, Lamm withdrew his opposition, and the project was approved. Although Lamm forces maintained that revised guidelines guaranteed extensive protection of the land and that Lamm's original concerns had been more about the lack of state participation in the planning process than about the project itself, his critics were convinced that he had sold out. With no little bitterness they charged that, no matter what restrictions were placed on growth, the project would still be a "catalytic force" behind the urbanization of the entire Gore Creek–Eagle River region. "Does Colorado benefit by a few thousand more acres of ski area at Beaver Creek, not to mention God knows how many thousand more condominiums?" asked one. "The Lamm administration is going to have to learn how to say 'no.'"[103]

It may be that Lamm will find it difficult in the future to mollify the environmentalists. At the same time, it will be difficult for him to appease developers contemptuous of him and the so-called "no-growth stooges" in his administration. He likely will remain a man in the middle; and how well he bears up in that role will determine how healthy Colorado remains under his tutelage. In the meantime, however, both sides might do well to ponder Lamm's comments on "growth" in his 1976 "State of the State" address to the Colorado State Legislature:

> *Let there be no mistake about it: Colorado cannot stop new population growth and would not want to stop it entirely even if it could. Those of us who were lucky enough to get here early cannot slam the door on others. We cannot keep clean factories that bring new jobs. We cannot constitutionally or morally shut off the supply of talent and creativity that has enriched the state through people born in other areas.*
>
> *We cannot stop growth; but we can guide it; we can plan for it; we can cushion its impact; we can affect its rate and character; and we can protect ourselves against some of its costs. . . . We dare not close our eyes to the problem. We must deal with growth and all of its implications before it engulfs us. This centennial year is the time for a new beginning.*[104]

How the legislature might respond to Colorado's environmental problems, and to Lamm's requests, is uncertain. In the past, as the *Denver Post* noted, western states have "dragged their feet in making the tough decisions on how to protect the environment" and in deciding how land development of any kind should fit into their economies.[105] Colorado has been no exception: more than three years after the Colorado Environmental Commission recommended thirty-three separate ways that state government might improve conservation techniques in the region, "some progress" has been made on twenty-one, while seven have been ignored entirely.[106] Most lacking has been and still is a comprehensive, workable land-use bill. While Colorado has a functional law on the books, it is not strong enough to cope with the multitude of environmental problems the state faces in the future. Even given that fact, however, the legislature killed Lamm's major 1975 attempt at revision, House

Bill 1092, and discouraged him from making an attempt at all in 1976. It also failed to act on almost a dozen energy-related bills supported by the administration in 1976. The major casualty was Lamm's energy-facility siting bill, which would have coordinated and extended the state's control over companies planning to build energy facilities in Colorado. Because of such things critics charge that the state has "a legislature that fails utterly to address the substance of land use." Unless this changes, they add, Colorado cannot hope to progress in land matters.[107]

Perhaps, after all, the future of Colorado lies in the hands of its people. If this is so, it looks somewhat hopeful. Not only have Coloradans voted an environmentalist into the state's highest office, but they have been active in other respects as well. The fight for the establishment of the Powderhorn Wilderness is an example: led by a coalition of conservationists, stockmen, lumbermen and miners, it is an action that would have been unthinkable in times past. Elsewhere, mountain communities are adopting the urban "open-space" concept, buying land adjacent to them and barring development on it; residents of ski areas have become militant enough in defense of their local environments that they have forced builders to take more care in maintaining ecological order (the Middle Park Land and Cattle Company of Denver, for example, hired an environmental control company to advise it during condominium construction near Steamboat Springs); and many energy-development companies have followed suit, attempting to make their activities as environmentally painless as possible. Even in tourism Colorado promoters are attempting to sell the idea that "the visitor come and enjoy, but protect the beauty and save it for another year.[108]

We hope it can be done, for we cannot afford to lose our wilderness—not even in the name and cause of civilization. If we do, we lose something of ourselves. We lose, as Arthur Carhart has said, "perspective on how big a man is and how little a man is," because "only in the wilderness can such perspective be gained." To sacrifice the forest is to forfeit the only place in our existence where we might ponder the "thunderous silence of deep canyons and the solitude of high mountains," where we can feel "wonder that cannot be experienced anywhere else."[109] We must, somehow, come to understand that we today are "tenants on the land and the world the short time we live"—and that our primary obligation is to pass it on, just as we received it from our fathers, to those who came after us.[110] It behooves us to be careful with our heritage. Roderick Nash has written that "today's choices will in large part determine tomorrow's experiences."[111] The same was said in 1900 by Gifford Pinchot and Henry Teller. And just as what they said and did molded our future, so will what we say and do shape ours and that of our children.

Notes

Preface

1. Hildegarde Hawthorne and Esther B. Mills, *Enos Mills of the Rockies,* 58, 72.
2. Hamlin Garland, *Companions on the Trail*, 285, 287.
3. *Denver Post*, January 19, 1975.
4. Luella Shaw, *True History of Some of the Pioneers of Colorado*, 257.
5. *Ibid.*
6. *Ibid.*, iii.
7. *Ibid.*, 261.
8. Garland, *Companions on the Trail,* 289.
9. *Ibid.*
10. *Ibid.*

Chapter I

1. Roderick Nash, *The American Environment: Readings in the History of Conservation*, ix.
2. *Ibid.*, x.
3. William Thayer, *Marvels of the New West*, 640.
4. Roderick Nash, *Wilderness and the American Mind*, 149.
5. Elmo Richardson, *The Politics of Conservation: Crusades and Controversies, 1897–1913*, 9.
6. Frank Smith, *The Politics of Conservation*, 69.
7. Richardson, *The Politics of Conservation*, 28.
8. E. Louise Peffer, *The Closing of the Public Domain*, 93.
9. American National Livestock Association, *Proceedings, 1906*, 19.
10. Richardson, *The Politics of Conservation*, 1.
11. Smith, *The Politics of Conservation*, 70.
12. *Denver Republican*, June 19, 1907.
13. *Portland Oregonian*, April 4, 1897.
14. *Yampa Leader*, January 30, 1904.
15. Smith, *The Politics of Conservation*, 68.
16. Roy M. Robbins, *Our Landed Heritage: The Public Domain, 1776–1936,* 350.

17. *Rocky Mountain News*, February 22, 1907.
18. *Denver Republican*, July 30, 1901.
19. *Colorado Springs Gazette*, February 18, 1973.
20. *Denver Post*, January 21, 1973.
21. *Rocky Mountain News*, May 5, 1972.
22. *Denver Post*, March 18, 1972.
23. *Ibid.*, September 24, 1973.
24. *Ibid.*, April 8, 1973.
25. *Ibid.*, September 6, 1973.
26. *Ibid.*, April 8, 1973.
27. *Ibid.*, March 18, 1973.
28. *Ibid.*, May 6, 1973. The diverse groups have endorsed the creation of the proposed 40,400-acre Powderhorn Primitive Area on the Gunnison-Hinsdale county line twenty miles south of the Blue Mesa Reservoir.

Chapter II

1. *Rocky Mountain News*, March 5, 1891.
2. U.S., *Statutes at Large*, Vol. XXVII, 1103.
3. The best accounts of environmental damage inflicted during the course of the westward movement are contained in Roy Robbins, *Our Landed Heritage*, 217–98, and Elmo Richardson, *The Politics of Conservation*.
4. Nash, *The American Environment*, 9.
5. Frederick Jackson Turner, *The Frontier in American History*, 1. Essentially, the Turner hypothesis is that American institutions, constitutional forms, and social traits (such as individualism, self-sufficiency, and belief in democracy) had been molded into distinct forms by the levelling process of the westward movement. Acting as a "safety valve" which siphoned off the discontented masses of the East and drew them westward, the unoccupied West furnished emigrants with "free land" and freedom of opportunity and provided the primitive environment—the "melting pot"—that shaped them into a self-reliant, progressive, egalitarian society.
6. *Ibid.*, 220–21.
7. David Potter, *People of Plenty*, 93.
8. J. Leonard Bates, "Fulfilling American Democracy: The Conservation Movement, 1907–1921," *Mississippi Valley Historical Review*, Vol. XLIV (1957), 42.
9. Nash, *The American Environment*, 38.
10. The best account of the conservationists' activities is contained in John Ise, *United States Forest Policy*. Perhaps their most important achievement was the establishment of the nation's first national park—Yellowstone—in 1872.
11. A fuller discussion of the General Revision Act may be found in Robbins, *Our Landed Heritage*, 303–305.
12. Marion Clawson, *Uncle Sam's Acres*, 106.
13. Marion Clawson and Burnell Held, *The Federal Lands: Their Use and Management*, 28.

14. Robert Sterling Yard, *Our Federal Lands*, 109.

15. Stewart Udall, *The Quiet Crisis*, 101.

16. James H. Baker and LeRoy R. Hafen, *History of Colorado*, Vol. II, 766.

17. Colorado State Forest Commissioner, *Second Annual Report, 1886*, 9.

18. Conservationists, in general, were urban professionals clustered in Denver, Colorado Springs, and Pueblo. In Denver, for example, they comprised the city council, the chamber of commerce, the real estate exchange, and the water and gas companies, as well as some twenty-six of the city's leading business firms. In Colorado Springs they formed around railroad builder William Palmer and other businessmen. Many also were intellectuals, educators teaching at virtually every college in the state and, on the public-school level, lobbying through the Colorado State Teachers' Association. Finally, some were large farmers; they endorsed conservation through the state Grange, some ten local granges, and the state board of agriculture. Baker and Hafen, *History of Colorado*, Vol. II, 771.

19. Colorado State Board of Horticulture, *Semi-Annual Report, 1897*, 49.

20. Ellsworth Bethel, "The Conifers or Evergreens of Colorado," *Colorado Magazine*, Vol. II (January, 1925), 1–2.

21. Edgar Ensign, "Forestry in Colorado," 1885. Pamphlet in files of Colorado State Historical Society, Denver.

22. Nash, *The American Environment*, 38.

23. M. Nelson McGeary, *Gifford Pinchot: Forester-Politician*, 82. McGeary writes that "no state was more critical of . . . [conservation] than Colorado."

24. The term *insurgent* was applied to anticonservationists by their opponents. In time it became the most popular term in usage. See, for example, *Denver Republican*, March 19, 1909.

25. Henry Nash Smith, *Virgin Land*, 138.

26. Nash, *Wilderness and the American Mind,* 40.

27. *Denver Republican*, November 24, 1907.

28. Richard Hofstadter, *The Age of Reform*, 23. Although Hofstadter's thesis applies exclusively to the farmer, it is not illogical to assume that other pioneer groups, miners and cattlemen, for example, considered themselves no less important.

29. Smith, *Virgin Land*, 138. Like Richard Hofstadter, Smith deals primarily with the farmer. Again, however, other pioneers considered themselves no less noble, no less important to the advance of civilization, no less a part of the nation's destiny than did the homesteading farmer. Miners, for example, have been characterized as the "cutting edge of the frontier." Writes one historian: "To imagine that settlement and growth [in the West] would not have come without mining would be absurd. . . . but the tempo, direction, influence, and significance were changed by the mining frontier and its camps." Duane A. Smith, *Rocky Mountain Mining Camps: The Urban Frontier*, 243, 248. Because of what they did, cattlemen, too, saw themselves as special. It was the stockman who, "in his search for grass, crossed every divide, rode into every coulee, and swam every stream" and who, no less than the miner or the farmer with his "sacred plow," helped convert the "Garden" into "an area . . . where men might live and prosper." Ernest S. Osgood, *The Day of the Cattleman*, 7–9.

30. Colorado Conservation Commission, *Official Proceedings, March, 1909–April, 1910*, 171.

31. Letter from Governor John F. Shafroth to George S. Canfield, member of the Western Conservation League, April 20, 1910. John F. Shafroth Correspondence, State Archives and Records Service, Denver.

32. Theodore Saloutos, "The Agricultural Problem and Nineteenth-Century Industrialism," *Agricultural History*, Vol. XXII (July, 1948). Saloutos' focus is on the farmer, but other pioneer groups were threatened as much as he.

33. Nash, *The American Environment*, 3–4.

34. Colorado Conservation Commission, *Official Proceedings*, 161.

35. *Denver Republican*, September 27, 1908.

36. In time, discord among cattlemen over the question of conservation was to become a significant issue. In 1891, however, Colorado stockmen were fairly well united in their opposition to the reservation idea.

37. American National Livestock Association, *Proceedings of Eleventh Annual Convention, 1908*, 101.

38. Hofstadter, *Age of Reform*, 23.

39. *Leadville Press*, October 23, 1908.

40. State of Colorado, *Senate Journal, 1907–1908*, 304–305. Between 1876 and 1891 the state legislature did not pass a single conservation law. Its attitude, perhaps expressed best in a later 1907 resolution, was that any action on the part of the federal government tending to usurp "the rights of the state and its citizens to develop and acquire title to public lands and to utilize the resources of the public lands" violated both the spirit and the letter of "the act of Congress creating the state of Colorado."

Chapter III

1. U.S., *Statutes at Large*, Vol. L, 993.

2. Department of Agriculture Forest Service, *Golden Anniversary of the White River National Forest*, 4. Pamphlet in files of United States Forest Service, Denver. Lewis R. Rist, "Historical Sketch of White River National Forest," 1934, 1. Typescript in files of Colorado State Historical Society, Denver.

3. *Glenwood Avalanche*, November 9, 1891.

4. Letter from Dr. Charles D. Enison, Royalton, Vermont, to Governor John L. Routt, July 11, 1891. John L. Routt Correspondence, State Archives and Records Service, Denver.

5. Letter from Governor John L. Routt to Dr. Charles D. Enison, July 23, 1891. John L. Routt Correspondence, State Archives and Records Service, Denver.

6. *Meeker Herald*, September 10, 1891.

7. *Rifle Reveille*, September 24, 1891.

8. *Glenwood Avalanche*, October 23, 1891.

9. *Glenwood Echo*, January 3, 1891.

10. *Glenwood Avalanche*, October 15, 1891.

11. Department of Agriculture Forest Service, *Golden Anniversary of the White River National Forest*, 1.

12. *Crystal River Current*, November 4, 1891.
13. *Meeker Herald*, October 17, 1891.
14. *Rocky Mountain News*, November 11, 1891.
15. *Ibid.*
16. *Ibid.*, November 8, 1891.
17. *Denver Republican*, December 17, 1891.
18. *Aspen Daily Chronicle*, December 17, 1891.
19. *Glenwood Avalanche*, November 9, 1891.
20. *Meeker Herald*, December 24, 1891.
21. U.S., *Statutes at Large*, Vol. XXVII, 1006.
22. U.S., Department of Agriculture Forest Service, *The National Forests of Colorado*, 1. (In the files of United States Forest Service, Denver.)
23. Ralph C. Taylor, "Colorful Colorado," *Pueblo Star-Journal* and *Pueblo Chieftain*, August 27, 1972, 2C.
24. The *Gazette* was owned and published by Clarence P. Dodge, a progressive Republican and friend of national conservation leader Gifford Pinchot.
25. U.S., *Statutes at Large*, Vol. XXVII, 1029.
26. *Rocky Mountain News*, November 16, 1891.
27. U.S., *Statutes at Large*, Vol. XXVII, 1044.
28. U.S., Geological Survey, *Twentieth Annual Report, 1898–1899*, Vol. V, 92.
29. *Denver Republican*, June 17, 1892.
30. *Rocky Mountain News*, June 17, 1892.
31. U.S., *Statutes at Large*, Vol. XXVII, 1053.
32. Robbins, *Our Landed Heritage*, 305.
33. Geological Survey, *Twentieth Annual Report*, Vol. V, 243.

Chapter IV

1. Gifford Pinchot, *Breaking New Ground*, 93.
2. U.S., Department of the Interior, *Annual Report, 1893*, 555.
3. Teller was given the title by his biographer, Elmer Ellis, see Ellis, *Henry Moore Teller, Defender of the West*. A native of Illinois, Teller moved to Colorado in 1861, settling at Central City and practicing law. Elected to the United States Senate in 1876, he served until 1882 before accepting the position of secretary of interior. In 1886 he was re-elected to the Senate as a Republican, a position he still held in 1893. A somber, courtly, outspoken man with steadfast political convictions, Teller became, in time, one of Colorado's most famous statesmen. One historian has written that "among the men whose careers reflect honor and credit upon the state, . . . none has risen to a position of higher distinction or left more indelibly his impress upon the history of the nation than Senator Henry M. Teller." Wilbur F. Stone, *History of Colorado*, Vol. II, 5.
4. A "silver Republican" by definition, Teller finally bolted his party and became a Democrat in 1903. It would be remiss to overlook the possibility that, given the pervasiveness of prosilver sentiment in the state, Teller and other Colorado politicians used the conservation issue as a kind of lever

against the consecutive progold administrations of Harrison and Cleveland (and McKinley and Roosevelt after them). Under any condition, a biographer notes that "among his constituents," Teller was "universally popular." Frank Hall, *History of the State of Colorado*, Vol. IV, 590.

5. U.S., *Congressional Record*, 52 Cong., 2 sess., Vol. XXIV, Pt. 1, 618; 53 Cong., 2 sess., Vol. XXVI, Pts. 5 and 6, 5126. A silverite like Teller, Bell had as much Populist support as any politician in Colorado.

6. In 1893, Colorado's other senator was Henry O. Wolcott of Denver. A regular Republican, he bitterly opposed conservation during Cleveland's tenure. The other representative, Populist Lafayette (Lafe) Pence concentrated mainly on the silver issue; when he took a position at all on conservation, he was against it.

7. In the 1890's the main figures in the anticonservation coalition included William Borah, Fred DuBois, and George Shoup of Idaho; Thomas Carter and Lee Mantle of Montana; John Wilson and George Turner of Washington; William Stewart of Nevada; Francis Warren and Clarence Clark of Wyoming; Reed Smoot of Utah; Jonathan Bourne and Charles Fulton of Oregon; Richard Pettigrew of South Dakota; and Stephen White of California in the Senate, and Frank Mondell of Wyoming; James Needham and James Gillett of California; Marcus Smith of Arizona; William Doolittle of Washington; Binger Hermann of Oregon; John Pickler and Freeman Knowles of South Dakota; Charles Hartman of Montana; and Joseph Rawlins of Utah in the House.

8. Robbins, *Our Landed Heritage*, 308.

9. *Rocky Mountain News*, July 11, 1894.

10. *Castle Rock Record-Journal*, May 11, 1894.

11. U.S., *Congressional Record*, 53 Cong., 1 sess., Vol. XXV, Pt. 2, 2434–35.

12. One of the most significant aspects of the General Revision Act was the fact that it did not provide for the beneficial, controlled use of the reserves by settlers who lived in or near them. Historian Robert K. Winters has written that "these were not managed forests; indeed . . . they were simply closed areas, and in theory, at least, they were locked up." In "all fairness," he concludes, "the locked-up policy made no sense by any reasonable criterion." Robert K. Winters, *Fifty Years of Forestry in the U.S.A.*, 4.

13. U.S., *Congressional Record*, 53 Cong., 3 sess., Vol. XXVII, Pt. 1, 371.

14. Ise, *United States Forest Policy*, 12.

15. *Ibid.*

16. Shafroth, a native Missourian, was to become one of the most powerful men in Colorado political history. A portly, outspoken Denver lawyer, Shafroth considered himself a "progressive," championing such causes as Philippine independence and free silver (like Teller he abandoned the Republican party in 1896 to become a Democrat). After serving five terms in Congress (1894–1904), he was to go on to the governorship of Colorado (1908–1912) and become the most stubbornly anticonservationist chief executive in the state's history. G. Michael McCarthy, "Selective Progressivism and the Conservation Movement," *Journal of the West*, Vol. XV (January, 1976), 62–73.

17. James D. Richardson, *A Compilation of the Messages and Papers of the Presidents, 1789–1897*, Vol. IX, 543.

18. The commission was composed of five easterners: arboriculturist Charles S. Sargent, engineer-hydrographer Henry L. Abbott, William H. Brewer, a Yale botanist, geologist Arthur Hague, and forestry expert Gifford Pinchot. Pinchot was probably America's most important conservationist, both then and in the future. Son of a prominent New York businessman-philanthropist, he developed an interest in forestry early in his life. Upon his graduation from Yale he went to Europe to study forestry techniques in Germany and France. Returning to the United States in 1890, he soon became manager of George W. Vanderbilt's Biltmore estate near Asheville, North Carolina, where he practiced "practical forestry" methods learned in Europe. By 1896, Pinchot was "well established as a forester" in the United States, traveling, lecturing, writing on the subject, and rapidly becoming a rallying point for conservationists throughout the nation. In 1898 he was to become chief of the Division of Forestry in the Department of Agriculture. His philosophy of conservation will be discussed more comprehensively in a later chapter. Martin L. Fausold, *Gifford Pinchot: Bull Moose Progressive*, 10–11.

19. The new reserves included Black Hills in South Dakota, Big Horn and Teton in Wyoming, Flathead and Lewis and Clark in Montana, Washington, Olympic, and Mount Rainier in Washington, Stanislaus and San Jacinto in California, Uintah in Utah, Priest River on the Idaho-Washington border, and Bitterroot on the Idaho-Montana border. *Denver Republican*, February 23, 1897.

20. Pinchot, *Breaking New Ground*, 109.

21. McGeary, *Gifford Pinchot: Forester-Politician*, 40.

22. A third reason, often advanced by historians, was that Cleveland's action was a form of political retaliation against a section of the country which had bitterly opposed his gold policies. In Colorado, however, despite the fact that it was strongly prosilver, virtually no mention was made of political revenge in the wake of the proclamations.

23. *Rocky Mountain News*, May 30, 1897. Contempt for eastern conservationists was by no means confined to Colorado. In California, for example, the *San Francisco Chronicle* criticized the "amiable theorists" who mistakenly "believed that what would be well for one part of the country would be best for all." Robbins, *Our Landed Heritage*, 318. The *Portland Oregonian* decried "sentimentalists" intent only on the preservation of pastoral scenery. Richardson, *The Politics of Conservation*, 2. Virtually to a man, western congressmen agreed with the sarcastic observation of Senator John Wilson of Washington that the "talented and learned scientific gentlemen" had "no knowledge" of what they had done. U.S., *Congressional Record*, 55 Cong., 1 sess., Vol. XXX, Pt. 1, 910–11.

24. *Rocky Mountain News*, May 11, 1897. Near Tacoma a Washington newspaper echoed the same sentiment: "This country," it said, "should be held sacred for and dedicated to . . . those who are willing and anxious to become settlers and lend a helping hand in building up the nation." The *Cheyenne Tribune* argued that forest-reserve boundaries became "impassable barriers" to those who needed timber for survival; for that reason the reservations were a "dangerous and ridiculous farce." From Seattle to Deadwood settlers massed

in protest to the withdrawals. Robbins, *Our Landed Heritage*, 316–19. The dominant thought of the West was appropriately expressed by Senator William Stewart of Nevada, who called any action an "outrage upon the West" when it led to the withdrawal of vital land from settlement and its "dedication to folly." U.S., *Congressional Record*, 55 Cong., 1 sess., Vol. XXX, Pt. 4, 1280.

25. Everett Dick, *The Lure of the Land*, 328. Dick points out that Cleveland simply "failed to communicate." Had the West been "educated" concerning the move, it would not have protested as it did.

26. *Denver Republican*, February 25, 1897. Again the sentiment was widespread, and especially so among affronted congressmen. Frank Mondell of Wyoming called Cleveland's action "as outrageous an act of arbitrary power as a czar or sultan ever conceived." *Ibid.*, February 24, 1897. Representative Frank Cannon of Utah, branding Cleveland's action a political action against the "undesirable states in the West," pointed out that had eastern congressmen been treated in the same fashion, they would have had the "sympathy of the entire country." U.S., *Congressional Record*, 55 Cong., 1 sess., Vol. XXX, Pt. 4, 1281.

27. *Rocky Mountain News*, April 3, 1897.

28. *Denver Republican*, February 25, 1897. Just as the reaction of Colorado insurgents typified that of much of the West, so did that of Colorado's conservationists. In Montana, for example, the *Great Falls Leader* approved of the reserves, provided they did not include valuable farming lands. In California the *San Francisco Argonaut* argued that the reserves constituted the "real and permanent interests of the people," and conservationists like John Muir decried the selfishness of western politicians. In Salt Lake City the *Deseret Weekly* added its feeling that the reserves would be beneficial. Richardson, *The Politics of Conservation*, 2.

29. Pinchot, *Breaking New Ground*, 112. Writes Pinchot: Cleveland's veto was "by far the biggest thing that any President had yet done for forestry."

30. David C. Coyle, *Conservation: An American Story of Conflict and Accomplishment*. Coyle notes that McKinley wished to keep Cleveland's reserves, 37.

31. U.S., *Congressional Record*, 55 Cong., 1 sess., Vol. XXX, Pt. 1, 982.

32. *Ibid.*, 914–16.

33. *Ibid.*, 982–84.

34. *Ibid.*, 985.

35. *Ibid.*, 966.

36. *Rocky Mountain News*, May 12, 1897.

37. *Ibid.*

38. U.S., *Statutes at Large*, Vol. XXX, 34. It became known, thereafter, as the "Act of 1897."

39. Robbins, *Our Landed Heritage*, 324.

40. Colorado State Board of Horticulture, *Semi-Annual Report, 1897*, 48. If the majority *did* approve of Cleveland's withdrawals and yet did not assert itself, an interesting point made by Elmo Richardson may be applicable. "The acquiescence of the majority," he writes, "was basically a matter of self-preservation. In most communities all property and order depended upon the

maintenance and growth of a particular economic interest." Richardson, *The Politics of Conservation*, 4. It may have been that in the Colorado wilderness, where cattle, mining, and lumbering interests were so important, settlers feared to do anything to them that might have precipitated a general economic decline.

41. *Rocky Mountain News*, July 2, 1897.

42. Pinchot, *Breaking New Ground*, 85–86.

43. *Ibid.*, 116.

44. U.S., *Congressional Record*, 54 Cong., 1 sess., Vol. XXVIII, Pt. 1, 2726.

45. *Ibid.*, 51 Cong., 1 sess., Vol. XXI, Pt. 10, 10093.

46. From 1891 to 1901 the General Land Office had exclusive responsibility for both planning and administering federal forest reserves. The problem was, however, that most of its officials were law clerks thoroughly unfamiliar with the West. "Trained as lawyers," according to historian Samuel P. Hays, "they had no large view of the possibilities of forest management, but adhered strictly to narrow interpretations of law and emphasized formal procedures rather than results." The consequence was that the reserves often were ill planned, poorly administered, and shut off to virtually all productive use. Samuel P. Hays, *Conservation and the Gospel of Efficiency*, 37.

47. Department of Agriculture Forest Service, *Golden Anniversary of the White River National Forest*, 4.

48. U.S., *Congressional Record*, 55 Cong., 2 sess., Vol. XXXI, Pt. 4, 3509.

49. Pinchot, *Breaking New Ground*, 161–62.

50. Coyle, *Conservation: An American Story of Conflict and Accomplishment*, 42–43. From the time it was put under the jurisdiction of the Department of the Interior in 1849, the General Land Office perennially suffered from what historian Leonard D. White has called the "suspicion of corruption." In areas such as railroad land-grant adjustment, the adjustment of swamp, school, and internal-improvement grants, Indian allotments, the disposal of western lands (particularly timberlands), and the administration of forest reserves, "the presence of misrepresentation, laxness, and outright fraud was documented year after year." Primarily responsible on the local level were land registers and timber agents (rangers). To some extent they suffered from both the absence of good leadership and the impossibility of patrolling and administering land districts often in excess of twenty thousand square miles; in many cases, however, they were, in fact, corrupt or, at least, inefficient. Leonard D. White, *The Republican Era*, 196–208. At fault was the patronage system: ranger appointments—considered among the most lucrative of patronage positions—were based on politics rather than merit. Consequently, many rangers who patrolled the forest reserves knew nothing either about forestry or western people and their problems. "Some were conscientious public servants," writes Robert K. Winters, "but many were not." Winters, *Fifty Years of Forestry in the U.S.A.*, 6.

51. Len Shoemaker, "The First Forest Ranger," *The Westerners Brand Book, 1951*, 99–100.

52. *Rocky Mountain News*, October 2, 1900.

53. U.S., *Congressional Record*, 53 Cong., 3 sess., Vol. XXVII, Pt. 3, 2751.

54. Colorado Conservation Commission, *Official Proceedings*, 118.

55. A classic example of the apparent hypocrisy of some Colorado politicians came in February, 1899, when a stringent proforestry bill was introduced into the state senate by James P. Maxwell. Its provisions were more restrictive than any conservation bill ever introduced in Colorado, requiring all lumbering concerns to be licensed by the state forest, game, and fish commissioner, and compelling them to report to the commissioner all their operations—the number of men they employed, the amount of capital invested in their ventures, the value of the land cut over, and the extent and value of timber cut. The bill, however, was never reported out of committee. State of Colorado, *Senate Journal, 1899–1900*, 326.

56. Colorado State Forest Commissioner, *Biennial Report, 1889–1890*, 106.

57. State of Colorado, *Senate Journal, 1893–1894*, 372.

58. U.S. Geological Survey, *Twentieth Annual Report*, Vol. V, 143.

59. *Ibid.*, 238.

60. *Ibid.*, 93, 104–107.

61. *Ibid.*, 238.

62. Shirley Allen, *Conserving Natural Resources*, 176.

63. U.S., Congress, Senate, 55 Cong., 2 sess., 1898, Doc. 189, 117.

64. U.S. Geological Survey, *Twentieth Annual Report*, Vol. V, 71, 80, 102, 173.

65. The leasing issue, a major one at the end of the century, will be discussed in a later chapter.

66. *Denver Republican*, March 8, 1901.

67. National Livestock Association, *Proceedings of Second Annual Convention, 1899*, 56–58.

68. Trans-Mississippi Commercial Congress, *Proceedings of the Twelfth Convention, 1901*, 266.

69. *Ibid.*, 87.

70. National Livestock Association, *Proceedings of Second Annual Convention, 1899*, 209. The view was ironic in that his allies were the very men he opposed.

71. D. E. Salmon, *Special Report on the History and Condition of the Sheep Industry in the United States*, 789.

72. National Livestock Association, *Proceedings of Second Annual Convention, 1899*, 207.

73. *Ibid.*, 202–205.

74. Peffer, *The Closing of the Public Domain*, 74.

75. Colorado State Board of Horticulture, *Semi-Annual Report, 1897*, 82.

76. *Ibid., 1899*, 51.

77. *Rocky Mountain News*, February 16, 1898.

78. Colorado State Board of Horticulture, *Semi-Annual Report, 1900*, 121.

79. *Denver Republican*, September 8, 1900.

80. Colorado State Board of Horticulture, *Semi-Annual Report, 1897*, 93.

81. U.S. Geological Survey, *Twentieth Annual Report*, Vol. V, 73.

82. National Academy of Sciences, *Annual Report, 1898*, 47.

83. Department of Agriculture Forest Service, *Golden Anniversary of White River National Forest*, 12.

84. Richardson, *The Politics of Conservation*, 9, 12.

85. *Ibid.*, 12; U.S., *Congressional Record*, 55 Cong., 1 sess., Vol. XXX, Pt. 1, 970.

86. Robbins, *Our Landed Heritage*, 317.

87. Dick, *The Lure of the Land*, 336.

88. Richardson, *The Politics of Conservation*, 8.

89. National Stock Growers, *Proceedings of Annual Convention, 1898*, 89; U.S., *Congressional Record*, 55 Cong., 1 sess., Vol. XXX, Pt. 1, 916.

90. Richardson, *The Politics of Conservation*, 8–9; National Livestock Association, *Proceedings of Fourth Annual Convention, 1901*, 46.

91. Richardson, *The Politics of Conservation*, 12; National Livestock Association, *Proceedings of Second Annual Convention, 1899*, 219; *Proceedings of Fourth Annual Convention, 1901*, 56–58.

92. Richardson, *The Politics of Conservation*, 12; National Livestock Association, *Proceedings of Second Annual Convention*, 203.

93. Colorado State Forest Commissioner, *Second Annual Report, 1886*, 103.

94. *Glenwood Avalanche-Echo*, October 19, 1891.

95. Robbins, *Our Landed Heritage*, 319.

96. U.S., *Congressional Record*, 55 Cong., 1 sess., Vol. XXX, Pt. 1, 912, 918. Like their neighbors in other western states, conspiracy-minded Coloradans were influenced by the nature of their times: in a decade dominated by the Populist upheaval, nothing came quicker to the pioneer mind than fear of eastern "persecution." If the eastern crusade against silver "proved" conspiracy, it took little imagination to see conservation as further proof. Both struck at the land and its mineral wealth; both appeared disruptive of western economic progress; both seemed to be class oriented—eastern bankers and "gold bugs" versus western farmers, and patrician eastern "nature faddists" (like the wealthy, educated Pinchot) against western farmers, cattlemen, and miners. In a sense anticonservation and antigold sentiment may have been rooted in the same emotion.

97. *Ibid.*

Chapter V

1. Theodore Roosevelt, "Ranch Life in the Far West: In the Cattle Country," *Century Magazine*, Vol. XXXV (February, 1888), 500.

2. *Denver Republican*, October 19, 1901.

3. *Ibid.*, September 15, 1901.

4. John Muir, *Our National Parks*, 1.

5. These men included geologist-philosopher W J McGee, the conservation movement's chief theorist and one of its staunchest advocates of "multiple use;" Francis Newlands, a United States congressman and proponent of federally sponsored land-reclamation projects; Frederick H. Newell, a geologist-hydrographer and the chief architect of the Roosevelt administration's water policy and one of the primary planners of the conservation movement as a whole; George Woodruff, legal advisor for Roosevelt's conservation programs; Overton W. Price; and George Maxwell, a strong proponent of federal irrigation programs. An example of the kind of thing the West disliked was the fact that three of them—McGee, Newell, and Woodruff (and

Pinchot)—were from Pennsylvania. Hays, *Conservation and the Gospel of Efficiency*, 102, 11, 7, 44, 31, 26.

6. W J McGee, "The Conservation of Natural Resources," Mississippi Valley Historical Association *Proceedings*, Vol. III (1909–1910), 371.

7. Bates, "Fulfilling American Democracy," *Mississippi Valley Historical Review*, Vol. XLIV (1957), 38.

8. Hays, *Conservation and the Gospel of Efficiency*, 2.

9. Norman Wengert, *Natural Resources and the Political Struggle,* 21.

10. Theodore Roosevelt Conservation Congress, *Proceedings, 1958*, 2–3.

11. Pinchot, *Breaking New Ground*, 259.

12. Nicholas Roosevelt, *Conservation: Now or Never*, 62. Roosevelt points out the irony that Pinchot was disliked by eastern "preservationists" because of his utilitarianism and by westerners because of his lack of it. *Ibid.*, 64.

13. Udall, *The Quiet Crisis*, 102, 106–108.

14. William R. Thayer, *Theodore Roosevelt, An Intimate Biography*, 193–94.

15. Bates, "Fulfilling American Democracy," *Mississippi Valley Historical Review*, Vol. XLIV (1957), 47.

16. Michael Frome, *Whose Woods These Are*, 35.

17. Udall, *The Quiet Crisis*, 134.

18. Harold J. Barnett and Chandler Morse, *Scarcity and Growth: The Economics of Natural Resources Availability*, 72.

19. *Ibid.*, 35–36.

20. Roosevelt, "Ranch Life in the Far West," *Century Magazine*, Vol. XXXV (February, 1888), 500.

21. Roderick Nash, "The American Cult of the Primitive," *American Quarterly*, Vol. XVIII (1966), p. 534.

22. Theodore Roosevelt Conservation Congress, *Proceedings*, 1.

23. Paul R. Cutright, *Theodore Roosevelt the Naturalist*, 170.

24. *Denver Republican*, September 29, 1901.

25. *Ibid.*, December 4, 1901.

26. *Glenwood Avalanche-Echo*, December 14, 1905.

27. *Denver Post*, July 11, 1908.

28. *Denver Republican*, June 9, 1908.

29. Bernhard Fernow, *History of Forestry*, 393–94.

30. *Denver Times*, December 30, 1908.

31. U.S., *Congressional Record*, 60 Cong., 2 sess., Vol. XXXXIII, Pt. 4, 3226.

32. Owen Wister, *Roosevelt: The Story of a Friendship*, 175.

33. Arthur Carhart, *Timber in Your Life*, 66–67.

34. *Denver Republican*, May 10, 1907.

35. Pinchot, *Breaking New Ground*, 104.

36. *Elk Mountain Pilot*, March 26, 1908.

37. Richardson, *The Politics of Conservation*, 25.

38. *Denver Post*, December 16, 1908.

39. *Denver Republican*, October 7, 1908.

40. *Leadville Press*, October 23, 1908.

41. *Gunnison News-Champion*, October 16, 1908.

42. Roosevelt, *Conservation: Now or Never*, 64.
43. *Denver Republican*, February 26, 1907.
44. *Ibid.*, October 20, 1908.
45. *Ibid.*, December 29, 1908.
46. Addison C. Thomas, *Roosevelt Among the People*, 203, 207.
47. *Yampa Leader*, January 4, 1908.
48. *Montrose Enterprise*, March 10, 1904.
49. *Steamboat Pilot*, October 21, 1908; *Glenwood Avalanche-Echo*, January 9, 1908; *Denver Republican*, December 16, 1908.
50. Trans-Mississippi Commercial Congress, *Proceedings, 1908*, 112.
51. *Creede Candle*, October 24, 1908. For a capsule evaluation of Pinchot's impact on Colorado see G. Michael McCarthy, "The Pharisee Spirit: Gifford Pinchot in Colorado," *Pennsylvania Magazine of History and Biography*, Vol. XCVII, No. 3 (July, 1973), 362–78.
52. Nash, *The American Environment*, xi. The "misunderstanding" was significant. If, in fact, conservation planners are termed *progressives*, that is, men in the forefront of the urban reform movement during the first decade or so of the twentieth century, it is important to note that some of Colorado's most implacable insurgents were involved in the same movement. In the Congress, Henry Teller, Thomas Patterson, Robert Bonynge, John Shafroth, Franklin Brooks, Herschel Hogg, and, later, Edward Taylor, supported virtually every piece of progressive legislation proposed during the decade. G. Michael McCarthy, "Colorado's Progressives and Conservation," *Mid-America*, Vol. LVII (October, 1975), 213–26.
53. Hays, *Conservation and the Gospel of Efficiency*. A case in point was the stance taken by the Colorado, New Mexico, and Wyoming Lumber Dealers Association which met in Denver in January, 1898. Pledging support to conservation, it denounced the practice of unrestricted timber cutting and called on the government to "insist upon a more strict enforcement of the laws relating to the protection and preservation of the timber on the public domain." *Rocky Mountain News*, January 26, 1898.
54. Theodore Roosevelt, *Autobiography*, 261–66.
55. *Denver Republican*, August 25, 1907.
56. U.S., *Congressional Record*, 60 Cong., 1 sess., Vol. XXXXII, Pt. 6, 5726, 5863.

Chapter VI

1. Hays, *Conservation and the Gospel of Efficiency*, 49–53.
2. Hubert H. Bancroft, *Works*, Vol. XXI, *History of Nevada, Colorado, and Wyoming, 1540–1888*, 545.
3. Such was a common condition among cattlemen in most western states. In almost no areas were stockmen completely united either in favor of or in opposition to leasing. In Arizona, for example, while some argued that leasing was not the answer to range problems, another was prompted to comment that "the cattlemen of Arizona seem to be as thoroughly united in support of range control as our friends from Colorado are divided." Peffer, *The Closing*

of the Public Domain, 29; National Livestock Association, *Proceedings of Eleventh Annual Convention*, 11.

4. Hays, *Conservation and the Gospel of Efficiency*, 264.

5. National Livestock Association, *Proceedings of Thirteenth Annual Convention, 1910*, 89.

6. Baker and Hafen, *History of Colorado*, Vol. II, 683.

7. National Livestock Association, *Proceedings of Eleventh Annual Convention, 1908*, 92–93.

8. *Rocky Mountain News*, February 13, 1900.

9. *Middle Park Times*, February 23, 1900.

10. National Livestock Association, *Proceedings of Eleventh Annual Convention, 1908*, 104.

11. *Ibid.*, 102.

12. National Stock Growers Association, *Proceedings, 1898*, 208–209.

13. *Ibid.*, 82.

14. *Rocky Mountain News*, January 16, 1900.

15. National Livestock Association, *Proceedings of Third Annual Convention, 1900*, 153.

16. *Ibid.*, 276.

17. *Ibid.*, 303.

18. *Ibid.*, 276.

19. *Rocky Mountain News*, February 13, 1900.

20. Taylor, a native of Illinois who moved to Colorado from Kansas in 1881, had lived in the frontier environment of Leadville and Aspen before settling in Glenwood in 1887. Both as a state legislator and United States congressman (1908–1920), he was one of the state's most stubborn anticonservationists. One biographer notes that every vote Taylor cast was "what he believed to be a reflection of the composite wish of Colorado. . . . [and] with the possible exception of Senator Teller, his record of efficient legislation for the welfare of the West" had "never been approached" by any other Colorado congressman. Colorado State Historical Society, *History of Colorado*, Vol. V, 639.

21. *Rocky Mountain News*, February 18, 1900.

22. *Ibid.*

23. *Ibid.*

24. *Ibid.*, February 15, 1900.

25. *Ibid.*

26. *Ibid.*, March 31, 1900.

27. *Ibid.*, April 8, 1900.

28. It must be emphasized that antileasing sentiment was not isolated, but was widespread throughout the state. Present at the meeting and voting for the antileasing resolutions were the Arapaho, Chaffee, Delta, Eagle, Elbert, Garfield, Kit Carson, La Plata, Logan, Larimer, Mesa, Otero, Pitkin, Pueblo, Rio Blanco, San Miguel, Weld, Douglas, Kiowa, Montrose, and Morgan county commissioners as well as delegates from livestock associations which included the North Fork Valley Association, Delta County Stockgrowers, Edwards Stockgrowers Association, McCoy Stockgrowers Association, Fremont County Stockgrowers, Roaring Fork and Eagle River Stockgrowers,

Grand River Stockgrowers, Grand County Stockgrowers, Gunnison County Stockgrowers, Southern Colorado Stockgrowers Association, Rio Blanco County Stockgrowers, Craig Livestock Association, Routt County Stockgrowers, Axial Basin Stockgrowers Association, Saguache County Stockgrowers, and others. *Ibid.*

29. *Rocky Mountain News*, April 8, 1900.

30. *Ibid.*

31. *Ibid.*

32. *Ibid.*, April 10, 1900.

33. *Ibid.*, April 11, 1900.

34. *Ibid.* Irish was one of the West's leading conservationists. Despite the fact that his opinions about resource use were "unscientific and often superficial"—a fact that might have antagonized Colorado cattlemen who stood against him—he was a close friend of Gifford Pinchot. Richardson, *The Politics of Conservation*, 13.

35. *Denver Republican*, September 19, 1900. For Republicans to have run counter to the policies of their national party was not as strange as it might have seemed. Already placed at a distinct disadvantage by William McKinley's stand on the gold standard and conservation, local Republican candidates had little choice but to oppose them both if they hoped to win their campaigns. As for the Democrats, as important as conservation might have been, it was not as important as silver, consequently most of their efforts were expended to undermine the gold standard.

36. *Denver Republican*, September 19, 1900.

37. The new organization was composed exclusively of stockmen from states west of the Mississippi River.

38. *Denver Republican*, March 8, 1901.

39. Roosevelt, "Ranch Life in the Far West," *Century Magazine*, Vol. XXXV (February, 1888), 505.

40. Hays, *Conservation and the Gospel of Efficiency*, 54.

41. Phillip O. Foss, *Politics and Grass*, 43.

42. *Denver Republican*, January 22, 1907.

43. *Ibid.*, February 7, 1907.

44. Foss, *Politics and Grass*, 41.

45. Peffer, *The Closing of the Public Domain*, 75.

46. *Denver Republican*, March 6, 1902.

47. *Gunnison News-Champion*, February 21, 1902.

48. *Routt County Courier*, February 15, 1902.

49. *Glenwood Avalanche-Echo*, March 6, 1902.

50. Member cattlemen changed the name of their organization from the Western Range Stock Growers Association to the Colorado Cattle and Horse Growers Association at their annual meeting in 1901.

51. *Glenwood Avalanche-Echo*, March 6, 1902.

52. *Saguache Crescent*, March 13, 1902.

53. *Glenwood Avalanche-Echo*, April 10, 1902.

54. *Denver Republican*, April 17, 1902.

55. *Ibid.*
56. *Carbondale Item*, May 3, 1902.
57. *Denver Republican*, May 8, 1902.
58. Winters, *Fifty Years of Forestry in the U.S.A.*, 118.
59. National Livestock Association, *Proceedings of Sixth Annual Convention, 1903*, 133.
60. Hays, *Conservation and the Gospel of Efficiency*, 58; Ise, *United States Forest Policy*, 173.
61. Ise, *United States Forest Policy*, 193–94.
62. Richardson, *The Politics of Conservation*, 11.
63. Robbins, *Our Landed Heritage*, 339.
64. Ise, *United States Forest Policy*, 173.
65. National Livestock Association, *Proceedings of Fourth Annual Convention, 1901*, 145.
66. U.S., *Congressional Record*, 57 Cong., 1 sess., Vol. XXXV, Pt. 6, 6204.
67. *Ibid.*, 6522–23. Their fight against the transfer was their last one as congressmen. Both Shafroth and Bell were defeated five months later in congressional elections.
68. Pinchot, *Breaking New Ground*, 198; *Denver Republican*, June 3, 1902. Pinchot illustrates how typical Colorado's division was. During the transfer debate, while one Texas congressman, supposedly speaking for his constituency, supported the shift, another opposed it on the grounds that many reserves contained not "a stick of timber on them" and needed no protection. Similarly, while a California congressman supported the bill, a New Mexico congressman attacked it, charging—like the Texan—that no protection was needed for reserves containing "thousands of acres that would never grow a tree." Pinchot, *Breaking New Ground*, 198–99.
69. Georgianna Kettle and Roy Truman, "A Brief Historical Sketch of San Isabel National Forest," 1935. Typescript in files of Colorado State Historical Society, Denver.
70. *Saguache Crescent*, May 1, 1902.
71. *Salida Mail*, April 8, 1904. In the spring of 1904 the government restored some of the reserve lands to entry. One newspaper, claiming victory in the fight against reservations, announced that the government had "evidently decided to go a little slower hereafter in making forest reserves." *Saguache Crescent*, May 4, 1904.
72. National Livestock Association, *Proceedings of Sixth Annual Convention, 1903*, 271. The issue continued to polarize other westerners. In 1903 the Arizonans were joined by such diverse elements as Wyoming Representative Frank Mondell, one of the area's leading insurgents, and the Idaho Wool Growers Association which sought fairer treatment under Pinchot than it received under the Interior Department. On the other side stood men like South Dakota Senator Albert Kittridge, representing mining interests in the Black Hills. *Denver Republican*, November 13, 1903; Ise, *United States Forest Policy*, 157; Hays, *Conservation and the Gospel of Efficiency*, 43.
73. *Denver Republican*, February 27, 1903.

74. U.S., *Congressional Record*, 57 Cong., 1 sess., Vol. XXXV, Pt. 6, 6202.

75. *Denver Republican*, September 27, 1903.

76. Letter from W. E. Weston to William A. Richards, Commissioner of the General Land Office, December 29, 1903. Letter in files of United States Forest Service, Denver.

77. *Denver Republican*, July 5, 1903.

78. *Lake City Times*, October 15, 1902.

79. U.S., *Congressional Record,* 58 Cong., 2 sess., Vol. XXXVIII, Pt. 6, 5679.

80. Robbins, *Our Landed Heritage*, 343.

81. Hays, *Conservation and the Gospel of Efficiency*, 62.

82. *Gunnison News-Champion*, January 22, 1904. The objective seemed to be the same elsewhere in the West, where the commission was treated more rudely than in Colorado. In Wyoming, for example, a crowd of state officials, editors, lawyers, businessmen, and stockmen met with the committee to denounce every aspect of conservation and unanimously oppose any changes in existing land laws. After a bitter personal clash with Governor Fenimore Chatterton (who Pinchot called a "yellow dog"), the committee assumed that anticonservation feeling in the West was genuinely powerful. In the course of their travels, however, they found few states as against conservation as was Wyoming; in most areas, such as Colorado, they found that "spokesmen of economic and political interests were generally vague or divided" on the major conservation subjects of the day. Richardson, *The Politics of Conservation*, 21–22.

83. Ammons, North Carolina-born but raised in Colorado, had spent most of his life on farms and ranches along the foothills of the Rockies in Jefferson, Arapaho, and Douglas counties. Tall, gaunt, and balding at forty-four years of age, Ammons was the unrivaled leader of insurgent Colorado stockmen both in 1904 and throughout the entire conservation era. A rancher-politician who had served in the Colorado House as a Populist, he was to become in 1912 the state's governor, inaugurating perhaps the most relentless anticonservation administration in the state's history. G. Michael McCarthy, "Elias Ammons and the Conservation Impulse" (Master's thesis, University of Denver, 1964), 4–25..

84. *Proceedings of a Conference Between Special Land Commission Appointed by President Roosevelt and Prominent Stockmen of the West*, 280, 292.

85. *Ibid.*, 258–59, 334.

86. *Ibid.*, 336.

87. *Denver Republican*, January 13, 1904.

88. *Ibid.*, March 15, 1904.

89. Baker and Hafen, *History of Colorado*, Vol. I, 684.

90. *Proceedings of Land Commission Conference*, 299–301.

91. *Ibid.*, 301–302.

92. *Ibid.*, 304.

93. *Glenwood Avalanche-Echo*, August 11, 1904.

94. *Lake City Times*, August 11, 1904.

95. As in 1902, the Democrats' state platform did not mention conservation.

The Republican state platform, while omitting any mention of federal conservation, called for state laws to "prevent the profligate waste of timber." *Denver Republican*, September 15 and 22, 1904.

96. *Ibid.*, October 3, 1904.

97. Conservation attitudes aside, all three men may have benefitted in 1902 from a resurgence of Republican power in the state which had nothing to do with the environment. One analysis of the year's political trends cites the decline of the silver issue—which neutralized both Democrats and Silver Republicans—an upswing in economic prosperity, and the liberal dispensement of patronage by the McKinley administration as reasons why the Republican party "recaptured" the state. Steven J. Kneeshaw and John M. Linngren, "Republican Comeback, 1902," *Colorado Magazine*, Vol. XXXXVIII (Winter, 1971), 15–29.

98. *Denver Republican*, March 21, 1904.

99. *Gunnison News-Champion*, March 28, 1904.

100. U.S., *Congressional Record*, 58 Cong., 2 sess., Vol. XXXVIII, Pt. 6, 5560–63.

101. *Ibid.*

102. *Ibid.*

103. *Steamboat Pilot*, August 31, 1904.

104. George Mowry, *The Era of Theodore Roosevelt*, 176.

105. J. Richard Snyder, "The Election of 1904: An Attempt at Reform," *Colorado Magazine*, Vol. XXXXV (Winter, 1968), 16–26.

106. Robert E. Smith, "Colorado's Progressive Senators and Representatives," *Colorado Magazine*, Vol. XLV (Winter, 1968), 33, 41.

107. *Denver Republican*, April 15, 1905. Essentially, Colorado had twelve "forest-reserve" counties in 1904: Rio Blanco, Garfield, Park, Teller, Douglas, El Paso, Chaffee, Custer, Saguache, Fremont, Delta, and Mesa. All twelve had gone for William Jennings Bryan over William McKinley in 1896, and all but one (El Paso) had supported him against McKinley in 1900. Yet in 1904 all of the reserve counties except Custer (which went for Parker by twenty-five votes) fell to Roosevelt. In several instances the president's victory margin was thin (as in Park County, where he won by only sixteen votes, and Chaffee, where he won by ten), but in other instances it was substantial (in El Paso he swamped Parker by over forty-three hundred votes, and beat him by over twelve hundred in Mesa). Edgar E. Robinson, *The Presidential Vote, 1896–1932*, 150–54.

108. National Livestock Association, *Proceedings of Ninth Annual Convention, 1906*, 19.

Chapter VII

1. Mowry, *The Era of Theodore Roosevelt*, 197.
2. Pinchot, *Breaking New Ground*, 258.
3. *Denver Republican*, October 25, 1903.
4. Richardson, *The Politics of Conservation*, 25.
5. Peffer, *The Closing of the Public Domain*, 64–65.

6. National Livestock Association, *Proceedings of Eighth Annual Convention, 1905*, 40, 92; Richardson, *The Politics of Conservation*, 32; McGeary, *Gifford Pinchot*, 84.

7. Richardson, *The Politics of Conservation*, 40; Ise, *United States Forest Policy*, 195.

8. Pinchot, *Breaking New Ground*, 225; Richardson, *The Politics of Conservation*, 43; Ise, *United States Forest Policy*, 195.

9. U.S., Department of Interior, *Annual Report, 1894*, 94.

10. Colorado State Board of Horticulture, *Annual Report, 1903*, 64.

11. *The Colorado State Forestry Association: Its Origin, Work, and Purpose*, pamphlet in Western History Department, Denver Public Library.

12. *Rocky Mountain News*, January 12, 1905.

13. U.S., Congress, House, *Annual Reports of the Department of the Interior and the General Land Office*, 59 Cong., 1 sess., 1906, Doc. 5, 499–500.

14. *Lake City Phonograph*, March 21, 1903.

15. Colorado State Board of Horticulture, *Annual Report, 1903*, 64.

16. Colorado, *Session Laws, 14th Session*, 541.

17. *Gunnison News-Champion*, February 26, 1904.

18. *Ibid.*, March 4, 1904.

19. *Ibid.* The new reserve straddled the so-called Gunnison Gold Belt, an area of extensive mineral wealth, much of it still untapped. Tin Cup, for example, bolstered by the Jimmy Mack and Gold Cup mines, was a bustling boomtown of two thousand people. Forest-reserve regulations, if enforced, most certainly threatened prospecting activity in the region. Muriel S. Wolle, *Stampede to Timberline*, 191–217, 185.

20. *Ibid.*

21. *Montrose Enterprise*, March 10, 1904.

22. *Gunnison News-Champion*, January 30, 1904.

23. *Ibid.*, February 26, 1904.

24. *Ibid.*, June 10, 1905. Anticonservationists routinely—and often with reason—charged railroads with lobbying for reserves. Under the land-lieu provision of the act of 1897, railroads were able to purchase large forest tracts in advance of reserve proclamations, then exchange them for similarly large tracts outside reserve areas when such proclamations were made. Their interest was less in conservation than in amassing land for monopolistic purposes. Typical of the problem was the situation in New Mexico. Meldon J. Preusser, "Hugo Seaberg and His Land Scrip Enterprise," *New Mexico Historical Review*, Vol. XLV (1970), 5–22.

25. *Gunnison News-Champion*, June 10, 1905.

26. *Delta Independent*, June 17, 1905.

27. U.S., Congress, House, *Annual Reports of the Department of the Interior and the General Land Office*, 1906, Doc. 5, 499–500.

28. Colorado State Board of Horticulture, *Annual Report, 1902*, 116, 120.

29. Only three years prior to the creation of the reserve—in 1902—Leadville had been the scene of one of the more violent mining strikes in western history. Merrill Hough, "Leadville and the Western Federation of Miners," *Colorado Magazine*, Vol. XLIX (Winter, 1972), 19–35.

30. *Summit County Journal*, June 17, 1905.

31. *Gilpin Observer*, June 8, 1905.

32. Their fears, apparently, were ill founded. Despite the presence of the reserve, Lake County continued to lead the state in the production of gold, silver, zinc, and copper. In the decade 1898–1907, Lake's output of gold amounted to $15 million and its output of silver to $30 million. Eugene Parsons, *A Guidebook to Colorado*, 185.

33. *Leadville Herald-Democrat*, November 28, 1905.

34. U.S., Congress, House, *Annual Reports of the Department of the Interior and the General Land Office*, 1906, *Doc. 5*, 499–500.

35. Around 1907, local reservationists, who drew a direct correlation between themselves and the followers of John Muir in California, began a campaign to create a national park out of the Longs Peak region in the southeast part of the reserve. In later years their efforts led to the creation of Rocky Mountain National Park.

36. *Fort Collins Courier*, May 24, 1905.

37. U.S., Congress, House, 56 Cong., 1 sess., 1900, *Doc. 643*, 7.

38. W. J. Morrill, "Birth of Roosevelt National Forest," *Colorado Magazine*, Vol. XX (January, 1943), 178–79.

39. Colorado State Board of Horticulture, *Annual Report, 1902*, 209.

40. Morrill, "Birth of the Roosevelt National Forest," *Colorado Magazine*, Vol. XX (January, 1943), 179.

41. *Ibid.*, 181.

42. *Fort Collins Express*, May 31, 1905.

43. *Fort Collins Courier*, May 3, 1905.

44. U.S., Congress, House, *Annual Reports of the Department of the Interior and the General Land Office*, 1906, *Doc. 5*, 499–500.

45. *San Juan Prospector*, July 22, 1905.

46. Wolle, *Stampede to Timberline*, 314, 362, 334.

47. U.S., Congress, House, *Annual Reports of the Department of the Interior and the General Land Office*, 1906, *Doc. 5*, 499–500.

48. Garland, the "son of the Middle Border" who had spent much of his life participating in the westward movement, wrote often of the desolation of western land and the destruction of pioneers who tried to tame it. In his autobiography, published in 1925, he wrote wistfully of the "taking up" and destruction of America's woods and "flowery savannahs," suggesting that by the end of the nineteenth century "the day of reckoning had come" if the nation were to salvage any of its landed heritage. The national-park scheme may have been his contribution to conservation. Hamlin Garland, *A Son of the Middle Border*, 439.

49. *Denver Republican*, August 18, 1905.

50. *Yampa Leader*, August 26, 1905.

51. *Ibid.*, September 30, 1905.

52. *Routt County Courier*, October 5, 1905.

53. *Ibid.*

54. *Yampa Leader*, October 21, 1905.

55. *Red Cliff Blade*, October 30, 1905.

56. *Yampa Leader*, October 21, 1905.
57. *Denver Republican*, November 17, 1905.
58. U.S., Congress, House, *Annual Reports of the Department of the Interior and the General Land Office*, 1906, *Doc. 5*, 499–500.
59. U.S., Congress, House, 56 Cong., 1 sess., 1900, *Doc. 643*, 4.
60. Wolle, *Stampede to Timberline*, 286.
61. *Denver Republican*, June 19, 1905.
62. *Canon City Leader*, June 22, 1905.
63. U.S., Congress, House, *Annual Reports of the Department of the Interior and the General Land Office*, 1906, *Doc. 5*, 499–500.
64. U.S., Congress, House, *Doc. 643*, 5.
65. *Durango Herald*, June 26, 1905.
66. *Saguache Crescent*, September 24, 1905.
67. *Lake City Phonograph*, July 29, 1905.
68. *Creede Candle*, June 15, 1905.
69. *Saguache Crescent*, June 22, 1905.
70. U.S., Congress, House, *Annual Reports of the Department of the Interior and the General Land Office*, 1906, *Doc. 5*, 499–500.
71. "History of the Region of the Montezuma National Forest and Vicinity," 1. Typescript in files of United States Forest Service, Denver.
72. Ira S. Freeman, *A History of Montezuma County, Colorado*, 212; "Land Conditions in the Montezuma National Forest," 1. Typescript in files of United States Forest Service, Denver.
73. Wolle, *Stampede to Timberline*, 370, 398.
74. *Ibid.*, 386–88.
75. *Durango Herald*, June 26, 1905.
76. U.S., Congress, House, *Annual Reports of the Department of the Interior and the General Land Office*, 1906, *Doc. 5*, 499–500.
77. U.S., Congress, House, *Doc. 643*, 9.
78. *Ibid., Annual Reports of the Department of the Interior and the General Land Office*, 1906, *Doc. 5*, 499–500.
79. Leonard C. Shoemaker, "History of the Holy Cross National Forest," 1. Typescript in files of Colorado State Historical Society, Denver.
80. *Lake City Phonograph*, September 2, 1905.
81. *Denver Republican*, August 29, 1905.
82. Baker and Hafen, *History of Colorado*, II, 762.
83. *Denver Republican*, June 26, 1905.

Chapter VIII

1. Opposition to the grazing tax was prevalent everywhere in the West, not just in Colorado. Hays, *Conservation and the Gospel of Efficiency*, 59–65.
2. The tax was designed, in part, to do precisely that. Conservationists believed that a grazing tax, if prohibitive enough, would reduce the number of cattlemen on the range by driving off marginal operators who could not afford to pay it. They may not have intended to deliver the forest ranges into

the hands of large cattlemen, but such was the logical consequence of their action. See Pinchot, *Breaking New Ground*, 269.

3. *Glenwood Avalanche-Echo*, October 12, 1905.
4. *Yampa Leader*, December 23, 1905.
5. American Forest Congress, *Proceedings,* 228–29.
6. Bernard Frank, *Our National Forests*, 47.
7. *Denver Record-Stockman*, November 17, 1905.
8. *Denver Republican*, December 19, 1905.
9. *Glenwood Avalanche-Echo*, November 24, 1905.
10. *Routt County Courier*, October 19, 1905.
11. *Meeker Herald*, October 14, 1905.
12. *Sugar City Gazette*, December 13, 1905.
13. *Delta Independent*, November 10, 1905.
14. *Glenwood Avalanche-Echo*, October 12, 1905.
15. *Ibid.*, November 2, 1905.
16. *Ibid.*
17. *Meeker Herald*, September 30, 1905.
18. *Glenwood Avalanche-Echo*, October 19, 1905.
19. *Montrose Enterprise*, October 20, 1905.
20. *Glenwood Avalanche-Echo*, October 5, 1905.
21. *Ibid.*, October 12, 1905.
22. *Ibid.*, December 7, 1905.
23. *Ibid.* In 1920, a few years before his death, Ammons looked back on his ranching days on Plum Creek and said, ironically, that "I had more pleasure, perhaps more excitement, more entertainment in the days I used to run cattle in the mountains than I have had ever since." Colorado Stockgrowers Association, *Annual Convention*, 41. Typescript in Colorado State Historical Society Library, Denver.
24. Shoemaker, "History of the Holy Cross National Forest," 57. Typescript in files of Colorado State Historical Society, Denver.
25. *Glenwood Avalanche-Echo*, December 7, 1905.
26. *Ibid.*
27. *Ibid.*
28. *Ibid.*
29. *Ibid.*, December 21, 1905.
30. *Ibid.*
31. *Montrose Enterprise*, December 19, 1905.
32. *Grand Junction Daily Sentinel*, December 19, 1905.
33. *Denver Republican*, December 6, 1905.
34. *Glenwood Avalanche-Echo*, December 14, 1905.
35. *Gunnison News-Champion*, July 21, 1905.
36. *Denver Republican*, January 3, 1907.
37. *Steamboat Pilot*, January 3, 1906.
38. *Glenwood Post*, January 1, 1906.
39. *Saguache Crescent*, January 25, 1907.
40. *Glenwood Avalanche-Echo*, January 11, 1906.

41. *Ibid.*
42. *Denver Republican*, January 24, 1906.
43. *Denver Record-Stockman*, January 12, 1906.
44. *Denver Republican*, January 30, 1906. In later years one Forest Service official, Will C. Barnes, reminiscing on the frequent Denver meetings between government officials and cattlemen, recalled that "Denver was a kind of battleground. . . . We used to come up here . . . and have some lively old rows. Sometimes we thought we won out and sometimes we didn't. But we always find pretty good friends here, in spite of the fact that some of us in the Forest Service in years gone by have had our heads taken off and hung on the fence" by the cattlemen. Colorado Stockgrowers Association, *Annual Convention, 1920*, 26.
45. *Rocky Mountain News*, January 30, 1906.
46. *Denver Republican*, January 31, 1906.
47. *Delta Independent*, February 2, 1906.
48. *Walsenburg World*, February 6, 1906.
49. *Yampa Leader*, February 10, 1906.
50. *Glenwood Avalanche-Echo*, February 8, 1906.
51. *Gunnison News-Champion*, March 20, 1906.
52. *Grand Junction News*, January 30, 1906.
53. *Denver Republican*, January 31, 1906.
54. *Ibid.*, February 3, 1906.
55. Surprisingly, perhaps, the insurgents did not even protest the creation of two new reserves during that time. On January 25, Roosevelt proclaimed the La Sal Forest Reserve (158,462 acres)west of the Uncompahgre on the Utah border, and on February 24 he created the Fruita Forest Reserve (7,680 acres) near Grand Junction. Probably they were not resisted because, first, they were small, and second, they lay in territory dominated by proconservation stockmen.
56. *Denver Record-Stockman*, October 17, 1905.
57. *Denver Republican*, March 29, 1906.
58. *Routt County Courier*, April 5, 1906.
59. *Denver Republican*, January 30, 1906.
60. Peffer, *The Closing of the Public Domain*, 70.
61. U.S., Department of Interior, *Annual Report*, 1530.
62. Ironically, Colorado conservationists had sought coal-land withdrawals as early as 1893. In that year they attempted to pass a law in the state legislature withdrawing both state and federal coal lands from entry, arguing that if such action were *not* taken, numerous Colorado counties would one day be damaged. They failed, however; and even after Roosevelt took his action, the state legislature still refused to pass a law to protect state coal lands. Colorado, *House Journal, 1907–1908*, 561.
63. Stone, *History of Colorado*, I, 449–54. Those counties included Jefferson, Boulder, Weld, Las Animas, Delta, El Paso, Huerfano, Garfield, Montezuma, Rio Blanco, Fremont, Routt, La Plata, Mesa, and Archuleta.
64. Along with that area—which included Routt, Rio Blanco, and Garfield counties—the withdrawals stood to damage three other areas in particular: La

Plata and Archuleta counties were literally covered with the San Juan Reserve, much of Montezuma County was already incorporated into the Montezuma Reserve, and a large area of Delta and Mesa counties was blanketed by the Battlement Reserve. Referring to the situation, an Aspen citizen suggested that a hypnotist put all people in central Colorado to sleep for "a couple of hundred years," then awaken them in time to "assist in developing" their country. *Aspen Times*, August 10, 1906.

65. *Yampa Leader*, September 8, 1906.
66. *Steamboat Pilot*, August 8, 1906.
67. *Denver Republican*, December 7, 1906.
68. *Steamboat Pilot*, August 8, 1906.
69. *Denver Times*, May 24, 1907.
70. Edward N. Wentworth, "Sheep Wars of the Nineties in Northwest Colorado," *The Westerners Brand Book, 1946* (Denver, 1946), 126.
71. James Blackhall, "Survey of the Hayden National Forest," 7. Typescript in files of United States Forest Service, Denver.
72. *Denver Republican*, October 28, 1907.
73. Ann Bassett Willis, "Queen Ann of Brown's Park," *Colorado Magazine*, Vol. XXX (January, 1953), 70.
74. *Ibid.*, 72.
75. *Routt County Courier*, May 24, 1906.
76. *Steamboat Pilot*, March 7, 1906.
77. *Denver Republican*, February 15, 1907.
78. *Glenwood Post*, February 17, 1906.
79. *Ibid.*, February 3, 1906.
80. Richardson, *The Politics of Conservation*, 28–30; U.S., Department of Agriculture Forest Service, *Forest Reserves in Idaho*, Bulletin 67, unpaged.
81. *Glenwood Avalanche-Echo*, February 28, 1907.
82. *Ibid.*, February 7, 1907.
83. *Gunnison News-Champion*, February 15, 1907.
84. *Yampa Leader*, February 23, 1907; *Denver Record-Stockman*, June 10, 1907.
85. *Meeker Herald*, February 16, 1907.
86. *Glenwood Avalanche-Echo*, June 12, 1907.
87. U.S., Department of Agriculture Forest Service, *Golden Anniversary of White River National Forest*, 3.
88. Herbert N. Wheeler, "Memoirs," 43. Typescript in Conservation Library, Denver Public Library, Denver.
89. *Ibid.*, 52.
90. *Denver Republican*, September 20, 1906.
91. Richardson, *The Politics of Conservation*, 28, 30.
92. *Steamboat Pilot*, March 7, 1906.
93. Shoemaker, "History of Holy Cross National Forest," 44. Typescript in files of Colorado State Historical Society, Denver.
94. *Denver Republican*, May 10, 1907.
95. Len Shoemaker, *Roaring Fork Valley*, 228.
96. *Glenwood Post*, March 10, 1906.

97. U.S., *Congressional Record*, 59 Cong., 2 sess., Vol. XXXXI, Pt. 4, 3539.
98. Shoemaker, *Roaring Fork Valley*, 228.
99. *Eagle County Blade*, May 1, 1907.
100. *Denver Republican*, March 21, 1907. Such sentiment was typical of cattlemen throughout the West. In Arizona, according to Elmo Richardson, one rancher summed up local feeling thus: "Looks like every time one of the government scouts finds a tree in the West he wires Pinchot and Pinchot gallops into Teddy's office and says: 'Oh, Teddy, we've found a tree in the What-the-Hell mountains; let's create a new forest.'" Richardson, *The Politics of Conservation*, 28.
101. *Eagle County Blade*, May 1, 1907.
102. Report from W. W. Hooper to Henry Michelson, Supervisor of South Platte Forest Reserve, October 12, 1902. Report in files of United States Forest Service, Denver.
103. "New Mexico Forest Reserves," *Forestry Quarterly* (1907), 11–19.
104. Shoemaker, "The First Forest Ranger," *The Westerners Brand Book*, 95.
105. Wheeler, "Memoirs," 55. Typescript in Conservation Library, Denver Public Library. Mark Woodruff, district supervisor of the Pike, called such accusations "bitter and unfounded." According to Woodruff, the protest leader was the Canterbury Milling and Mining Company, which recently had been caught "cutting and selling timber" illegally on its claims. *Denver Republican*, June 4, 1907.
106. Parsons, *A Guidebook to Colorado*, 320–22.
107. Wolle, *Stampede to Timberline*, 453–54.
108. *Gunnison News-Champion*, June 7, 1907.
109. Wheeler, "Memoirs," 26–28. Typescript in Conservation Library, Denver Public Library. Such feeling was not isolated on the Gunnison, or even in the state. In Arizona, for example, rangers were nicknamed "Teddy's Pets" and were uniformly condemned by insurgent cattlemen. In Williams it had been suggested years earlier that federal "tree agents" be hanged from the trees they had come to protect, and the feeling apparently remained constant through the years. Richardson, *The Politics of Conservation*, 10, 28.
110. Shoemaker, "The First Forest Ranger," *The Westerners Brand Book*, 116.
111. Alice S. Cook, "Kreutzer Mountain," 3. Typescript in files of United States Forest Service, Denver.
112. *Gunnison News-Champion*, February 8, 1907; January 4, 1907.
113. Freeman, *A History of Montezuma County, Colorado*, 220.
114. "History of the Montezuma Personnel," 74. Typescript in files of United States Forest Service, Denver.
115. Carhart, *Timber in Your Life*, 78.
116. Wheeler, "Memoirs," 72. Typescript in Conservation Library, Denver Public Library.
117. "Survey of Montezuma National Forest," 17–18. Typescript in files of United States Forest Service, Denver.

118. Letter from F. S. Clark to Philander C. Knox, July 30, 1907. Letter in files of United States Forest Service, Denver.

119. Letter from Theodore Roosevelt to Philander C. Knox, August 15, 1907. Letter in files of United States Forest Service, Denver.

120. "Survey of Montezuma National Forest," 2–3, 10–11. Typescript in files of United States Forest Service, Denver.

121. *Rico News*, June 8, 1907.

122. *San Juan Prospector*, January 26, 1907. Opposition might have been increased when Roosevelt created the Ouray Forest Reserve to the northwest of the San Juan on February 2, 1907, and the Las Animas Forest Reserve to the southwest on March 1.

123. Arthur W. Monroe, *San Juan Silver*, 220.

124. Shoemaker, "The First Forest Ranger," *The Westerners Brand Book*, 103.

125. *Ibid.*, 105.

126. *Delta Independent*, March 9, 1906.

127. *Glenwood Post*, March 3, 1906.

128. Shoemaker, "The First Forest Ranger," *The Westerners Brand Book*, 103.

129. *Rocky Mountain News*, February 22, 1907.

130. *Denver Republican*, January 25, 1907.

131. *Telluride Journal*, March 7, 1907.

132. *Eagle Valley Enterprise*, February 15, 1907.

133. *Montrose Enterprise*, March 15, 1907.

134. *Denver Republican*, January 22, 1907.

135. *Denver Times*, January 23, 1907.

136. *Denver Republican*, January 23, 1907.

137. *Glenwood Avalanche-Echo*, January 24, 1907.

138. *Gunnison News-Champion*, February 8, 1907.

139. U.S., *Congressional Record*, 59 Cong., 2 sess., Vol. XXXXI, Pt. 4, 3535.

140. *Ibid.*

141. *Steamboat Sentinel*, March 4, 1906; May 2, 1906.

142. *Glenwood Post*, March 17, 1906.

143. *Delta Independent*, February 2, 1906.

144. *Montrose Press*, April 17, 1907.

145. *Ibid.*, January 18, 1907. In some cases "working in harmony" created excesses. On the Holy Cross Reserve, for example, one ranger actually "took sides" with cattlemen "against the interests of the Forest Service" in almost all cases. And on the San Juan another ranger took an eight-hundred-dollar bribe to put a Silverton cattleman's herd on the reserve indefinitely. Wheeler, "Memoirs," 40–41. Typescript in Conservation Library, Denver Public Library.

146. *Denver Republican*, March 7, 1906; March 11, 1906.

147. *Montrose Enterprise*, April 3, 1906; *Glenwood Post*, March 3, 1906; *Denver Republican*, March 11, 1906. This episode offered a revealing look at proconservation cattlemen and their motives. They sought the reserve not for

conservation purposes, but because other stockmen were running their cattle on grazing land just outside the Uncompahgre and Battlement for free. A reserve on that ground would have halted the practice. At the same time, sheepmen from Utah were encroaching on local nonreserve grazing lands; a reservation covering their range would have effectively eliminated them from it. *Montrose Enterprise*, April 3, 1906.

148. *Delta Independent*, March 9, 1906.

149. *Denver Republican*, April 1, 1907.

150. *Glenwood Post*, March 10, 1907; March 17, 1907.

151. *Yampa Leader*, March 9, 1907. Interesting views of Roosevelt's popularity in two other typical states are offered by George S. Hunter, "The Bull Moose Movement in Arizona," *Arizona and the West*, Vol. X (Winter, 1968), 343–62; and Robert W. Larsen, "Ballinger Versus Rough Rider George Curry: The Other Feud," *New Mexico Historical Review*, Vol. XLIII (October, 1968), 271–90.

152. *Gunnison News-Champion*, February 1, 1907.

153. *Denver Republican*, January 24, 1907.

154. *Routt County Courier*, March 14, 1907.

155. *Denver Republican*, December 5, 1906.

156. *Red Cliff Blade*, November 22, 1905.

157. *Routt County Courier*, February 1, 1906.

Chapter IX

1. Ise, *United States Forest Policy*, 159, 199–200. House insurgents were led by two men—Frank Mondell of Wyoming and Herschel Hogg of Colorado. Both, for example, had been instrumental in securing the passage of the Forest Homestead Act of 1906, which opened up much reserve land to farming. In the process Hogg singled out Pinchot for attack, calling him a "theorist" who thought "more of a piece of sagebrush or a tree" than he did of "an American citizen out there." U.S., *Congressional Record*, 59 Cong., 1 sess., Vol. XXXX, Pt. 6, 5394–95.

2. Ise, *United States Forest Policy*, 160.

3. Mowry, *The Era of Theodore Roosevelt*, 212.

4. Richardson, *The Politics of Conservation*, 1, 32.

5. Steven A. Fazio, "Marcus Aurelius Smith: Arizona Delegate and Senator," *Arizona and the West*, Vol. XII (1970), 51–52.

6. Pinchot, *Breaking New Ground*, 299–300.

7. Richardson, *The Politics of Conservation*, 31–32; Ise, *United States Forest Policy*, 194; Pinchot, *Breaking New Ground*, 301; McGeary, *Gifford Pinchot*, 79; R. G. Cook, "Senator Heyburn's War Against the Forest Service," *Idaho Yesterdays*, Vol. XIV (Winter, 1970–71), 5–12.

8. Richardson, *The Politics of Conservation*, 33.

9. *Glenwood Avalanche-Echo*, February 28, 1907.

10. *Denver Republican*, February 20, 1907.

11. U.S., *Congressional Record*, 59 Cong., 2 sess., Vol. XXXXI, Pt. 4, 3534–35.

12. *Ibid.*
13. *Ibid.*, 3538.
14. Peffer, *The Closing of the Public Domain*, 91.
15. U.S., *Congressional Record*, 59 Cong., 2 sess., Vol. XXXXI, Pt. 4, 3534.
16. Ise, *United States Forest Policy*, 159–60.
17. U.S., *Statutes at Large*, Vol. L, 1271.
18. U.S., *Congressional Record*, 59 Cong., 2 sess., Vol. XXXXI, Pt. 4, 3532, 3720, 3723.
19. Ise, *United States Forest Policy*, 198–99.
20. Dick, *Lure of the Land*, 337.
21. McGeary, *Gifford Pinchot*, 79.
22. Roosevelt, *Autobiography*, 404.
23. Robbins, *Our Landed Heritage*, 350.
24. Letter from J. A. Eddy to Governor Henry Buchtel, May 29, 1907, Henry Buchtel Correspondence, State Archives and Records Service, Denver.
25. *Steamboat Pilot*, June 5, 1907.
26. *Denver Field and Farm*, March 7, 1907.
27. *Denver Record-Stockman*, March 15, 1907.
28. Colorado, *Senate Journal, 1907–1908*, 304–305. One historian adds that Colorado Democrats, in control of the legislature, "felt sure that no real concessions would be made" by the government "until their party was in power." Richardson, *The Politics of Conservation*, 34.
29. Colorado, *Senate Journal, 1907–1908*, 662–63.
30. Colorado, *House Journal, 1907–1908*, 1202. Richardson adds that because the gathering promised to be anti-Roosevelt, "only one state in the predominantly Republican region could act as host without political embarrassment: Colorado." Richardson, *The Politics of Conservation*, 34.
31. *Official Call For a Public Lands Convention*, April 21, 1907, Henry Buchtel Correspondence, State Archives and Records Service, Denver.
32. Letters from Governors Joseph K. Toole, Albert Mead, Bryant Brooks, George Chamberlain, J. H. Kibbee, James Gillett, and Frank Gooding to Henry Buchtel, Henry Buchtel Correspondence, State Archives and Records Service, Denver.
33. *Montrose Press*, June 14, 1907.
34. *Address of the Programme Committee Outlining the Object of the Meeting*, April 27, 1907, Henry Buchtel Correspondence, State Archives and Records Service, Denver.
35. Quoted in Robbins, *Our Landed Heritage*, 352.
36. Everett Dick claims that Buchtel "led" the "opponents of the President's conservation policies" in Colorado. Such was not the case, however. Before the convention Buchtel had been an outspoken proponent of forest conservation in Colorado, and after it, as one of his last official actions, he created a powerful state conservation commission to carry out such work. Shortly before the convention a Snoma, South Dakota, farmer congratulated Buchtel on his proconservation work and for "keeping politics" out of the meeting. Dick, *Lure of the Land*, 337; Letter from P. P. Valling to Henry Buchtel, June 10, 1907, Henry Buchtel Correspondence, State Archives and Records Service, Denver.

37. Robbins, *Our Landed Heritage*, 352. It would have been difficult for Buchtel to have avoided putting insurgents in positions of power. The rules stipulated that the committee be composed of one senator and one representative from each western state; inasmuch as most western congressmen were anticonservation, it was virtually impossible to keep them off the committee. Colorado was a case in point. Of its five congressmen, all were insurgents.
38. *Denver Republican*, May 29, 1907.
39. *Denver Post*, June 2, 1907.
40. *Rocky Mountain News*, May 31, 1907.
41. Richardson, *The Politics of Conservation*, 36.
42. *Rocky Mountain News*, June 12, 1907.
43. *Gunnison News-Champion*, June 14, 1907.
44. *Glenwood Avalanche-Echo*, June 6, 1907.
45. *Eagle County Blade*, June 6, 1907.
46. *Boulder Camera*, June 19, 1907. Roosevelt also employed more subtle methods of winning converts. On June 13 he restored 244,000 acres of land to entry from the Fruita, La Sal, and Uncompahgre reserves, 35,300 acres from the Pike, 69,680 from the Las Animas, and 24,950 from the troubled Holy Cross. *Denver Republican*, June 14, 1907.
47. Undated list of delegates found in Henry Buchtel Correspondence, State Archives and Records Service, Denver.
48. *Denver Republican*, June 12, 1907.
49. *Ibid.*, June 18, 1907.
50. *Ibid.*, June 2, 1907; June 8, 1907.
51. *Routt County Courier*, June 6, 1907.
52. *Glenwood Avalanche-Echo*, May 21, 1907; *Montrose Press*, June 14, 1907.
53. *Denver Republican*, June 15, 1907.
54. *Routt County Courier*, June 6, 1907.
55. *Aspen Democrat*, June 19, 1907.
56. *Denver Republican*, June 4, 1907.
57. Richardson, *The Politics of Conservation*, 37. He adds that "apart from Colorado's predominantly Democratic representatives [though according to Buchtel's list, most were Republicans] no uniform political complexion could be ascribed to the delegations of any state."
58. *Denver Republican*, June 18, 1907.
59. *Ibid.*, June 19, 1907. Some historians contend that conservationists were not allowed to speak at all until the end of the meeting. They were represented, however, from the first (though obviously not in large numbers).
60. McGeary, *Gifford Pinchot*, 119.
61. Richardson, *The Politics of Conservation*, 38; *Denver Republican*, June 19, 1907.
62. *Ibid.*
63. Robbins, *Our Landed Heritage*, 351.
64. *Basalt Journal*, June 19, 1907.
65. *Rocky Mountain News*, June 19, 1907.
66. *Denver Post*, June 19, 1907.

67. *Rocky Mountain News*, June 19, 1907.
68. *Denver Republican*, June 20, 1907; *Denver Post*, June 20, 1907.
69. *Denver Republican*, June 20, 1907.
70. *Ibid.*
71. Irving Hale, "The Glories of Colorado," *Sons of Colorado*, Vol. I (March, 1907), 34–36.
72. *Gunnison News-Champion*, June 21, 1907.
73. *Saguache Crescent*, June 20, 1907.
74. *Denver Republican*, June 23, 1907.
75. Richardson, *The Politics of Conservation*, 38.
76. *Pueblo Chieftain*, June 28, 1907.
77. *Denver Republican*, June 21, 1907.
78. *Basalt Journal*, June 29, 1907.
79. *Pueblo Chieftain*, June 28, 1907.
80. *Denver Republican*, June 21, 1907.
81. *Steamboat Pilot*, June 26, 1907.
82. Richardson, *The Politics of Conservation*, 38.
83. *Ibid.*, 39.
84. Robbins, *Our Landed Heritage*, 353.
85. Richardson, *The Politics of Conservation*, 39.
86. *Denver Field and Farm*, June 27, 1907.
87. *Basalt Journal*, June 29, 1907.
88. *Meeker Herald*, June 29, 1907.
89. *Denver Post*, June 21, 1907.
90. *Pueblo Chieftain*, June 28, 1907.
91. *Colorado Springs Gazette*, June 22, 1907.
92. *Denver Republican*, June 22, 1907.
93. Dick, *Lure of the Land*, 337–38.
94. *Paonia Booster*, June 14, 1907.
95. "The Way of the Land Transgressor," *Review of Reviews*, Vol. XXXV (September, 1907), 379–80.
96. In the final analysis it appears as though administration forces did, in fact, attempt to pack the convention just as the insurgents did. The public, however, seemed largely unaware of the fact, despite the attempts of the insurgent press to publicize it. Most significantly, administration efforts were not successful; had they been, and had they been as overt and as clumsy as the anticonservationists', the outcome of the convention might have been altered. Instead of a "backlash" developing against the insurgents, it might have developed against the Roosevelt forces. Peffer, *The Closing of the Public Domain*, 101.
97. *Ibid.*
98. Richardson, *The Politics of Conservation*, 39. A widely disputed point is whether or not the convention forced Roosevelt to take any action to mollify the insurgent West. Richardson points out that federal officials attached no particular importance to the outcome of the meeting and took no immediate steps to redress western grievances. Roy Robbins, however, maintains

that the administration paid "serious attention" to the meeting and its results and moved immediately to improve relations with the West. Samuel Hays says only that the convention "revealed the dilemma into which the administration had plunged" in regard to its land policies. Richardson, *The Politics of Conservation*, 39; Robbins, *Our Landed Heritage*, 354; Hays, *Conservation and the Gospel of Efficiency*, 64.

99. *Boulder Camera*, June 19, 1907.

Chapter X

1. Pinchot, *Breaking New Ground*, 252.

2. *Colorado Springs Gazette*, April 1, 1908. Elmo Richardson points out that while editorials in small-town newspapers usually were "more outspoken and more pungent" than those in the large cities, they still "represented the viewpoint of a minority"—a fact that was easy to forget. Richardson, *The Politics of Conservation*, 4.

3. U.S., *Congressional Record*, 59 Cong., 2 sess., Vol. XXXXI, Pt. 4, 3532.

4. Agnes W. Spring, "Theodore Roosevelt in Colorado," *Colorado Magazine*, Vol. XXXV (October, 1958), 254.

5. *Denver Republican*, June 21, 1907.

6. McGeary, *Gifford Pinchot*, 80; Richardson, *The Politics of Conservation*, 38.

7. "The Way of the Land Transgressor," *Review of Reviews*, Vol. XXXV (September, 1907), 380.

8. Pinchot, *Breaking New Ground*, 323.

9. Wengert, *Natural Resources and the Political Struggle*, 17–18; Pinchot, *Breaking New Ground*, 324.

10. Letter from J. B. Killian to Governor John F. Shafroth, February 2, 1909, John F. Shafroth Correspondence, State Archives and Records Service, Denver.

11. *Report of the Committee on Forestry of the Denver Chamber of Commerce and Board of Trade*, January 27, 1909, John F. Shafroth Correspondence, State Archives and Records Service, Denver.

12. *Steamboat Pilot*, March 3, 1906.

13. John Muir, "The Wild Parks and Forest Reservations of the West," *Atlantic Monthly*, Vol. LXXXI (January, 1898), 21–22.

14. Wengert, *Natural Resources and the Political Struggle*, 21.

15. U.S., *Congressional Record*, 59 Cong., 1 sess., Vol. XXXX, Pt. 8, 7355–56.

16. Hays, *Conservation and the Gospel of Efficiency*, 2–3, 271–75.

17. *Ibid.*, 269–75.

18. Samuel Trask Dana, *Forest and Range Policy*, 158.

19. Letter from Theodore Roosevelt to Philander C. Knox, August 15, 1907, Letter in files of United States Forest Service, Denver.

20. Wheeler, "Memoirs," 41. Typescript in Conservation Library, Denver Public Library.

21. Letter from Herbert N. Wheeler to D. S. Nordwall, District Forester,

December 4, 1962. Letter in files of Conservation Library, Denver Public Library.

22. Hays, *Conservation and the Gospel of Efficiency,* 1–2.

23. Nash, *The American Environment*, xiii.

24. *Denver Post*, September 23, 1973.

25. *Ibid.*, January 14, 1973.

26. *Ibid.*, January 25, 1975; *Colorado Conservation Commission Proceedings*, 147.

27. *Denver Post*, January 26, 1975.

28. *Ibid.*

29. *Rocky Mountain News*, November 20, 1974. In the late fall of 1974, Colorado state-health officials found both strontium 90 and cesium 137 in natural gas and water produced by Project Rio Blanco. Both radioactive substances have been linked with bone cancer, leukemia, and genetic defects.

30. *Ibid.*, April 30, 1972.

31. *Ibid.*, September 3, 1973.

32. *Ibid.*, October 24, 1974.

33. *Grand Junction Daily Sentinel*, January 14, 1972, and May 31, 1972; *Denver Post*, January 28, 1972, November 5–6, 1973, December 15, 1974. Proconservation groups include the Colorado Open Space Council, Rocky Mountain Center On Environment, Environmental Action of Colorado, and such national groups as the Sierra Club and the Audubon Society. Their primary targets include the Colony Development Corporation (Atlantic Richfield Company, the Oil Shale Corporation, Shell Oil Company, and the Ashland Oil Company), the Union Oil Company, Occidental Oil Company, and Superior Oil Company. Until recently (when it was discontinued due to cost overruns), Colorado's major project was the Colony Development Project on Parachute Creek near Grand Junction. It has been estimated that the Piceance Creek Basin—the location of the Colony Project—is capable of producing 160 billion barrels of high-quality shale oil.

34. *Denver Post*, January 10, 1975.

35. *Ibid.*, December 2, 1973. The *Post* editorialized that developers must make sure that "the problems of growth are handled with maximum attention to making this development not only economically attractive but something that Colorado can regard as a social asset."

36. *Ibid.*; *Rocky Mountain News*, December 26, 1974.

37. *Rocky Mountain News*, September 3, 1973. The position of the *News* is interesting in that it was Colorado's premier anticonservation newspaper at the turn of the century. Now, as then, it argues for the environmental independence of the state—only now it argues from a proconservation standpoint.

38. *Denver Post*, February 11, 1973.

39. *Colorado Springs Gazette*, January 21, 1973.

40. *Denver Post*, December 14, 1973.

41. *Ibid.*, December 31, 1974. Strangely, coal men complain that the biggest impediment they face in developing western coal lands is the government

itself—its red tape, court injunctions, and lack of any clear-cut energy policy. "We can handle the environmental matters," says one developer, but "we are being hamstrung left and right and center" by the federal government. *Ibid.*, February 9, 1975.

42. *Ibid.*, January 2, 1975.

43. *Ibid.* The opposite view was taken by a Denver resident who held that coal-development companies are not damaging the environment. "We do not need more federal cooks in our kitchen to tell us how to make the soup," he said. "Kill the bill and all America . . . will come off much better." *Ibid.*, December 18, 1974.

44. *Ibid.*, March 11, 1973, September 23, 1973.

45. *Ibid.*, March 11, 1973. Colorado is by no means the only state with mining problems, no more than it was the only state with environmental problems during the first conservation era. In Montana, for example, developers are calling for the construction of forty-two coal-burning power plants in Powder River, Rosebud, and Big Horn counties (and Campbell County, Wyoming); while the complex would produce more than 400 million kilowatts of electricity in a year (more than any nation in the world except the Soviet Union), it would require 210 million tons of coal annually and would produce more air pollution than New York City and Los Angeles combined. In Butte, mining is physically undermining the very foundations of the city. *Ibid.*, March 11, 1973, September 5, 1973.

46. *Ibid.*, September 6, 1973, May 6, 1973, February 11, 1973. Whether neoconservationists realize it or not, their predecessors a century ago were using identical language in worrying about "economic deterioration" and the declining "quality of life."

47. *Durango Herald*, June 5, 1972.

48. *Alamosa Valley Courier*, June 16, 1972.

49. *Denver Post*, February 11, 1975.

50. *Ibid.*, December 5, 1974.

51. *Ibid.*

52. *Ibid.*, November 15, 1972.

53. *Ibid.*, December 11, 1974.

54. *Ibid.*, December 19, 1974.

55. *Ibid.*, November 6, 1973. At least one other major western ski resort has been under similar attack by conservationists. The late Chet Huntley's Big Sky Recreational Development in Montana (part of which is a ski area), has been accused of being harmful to the local ecology.

56. *Ibid.*, December 15, 1974, January 13, 1975.

57. *Rocky Mountain News*, January 19, 1975. An angry Vail citizen has challenged the figure of forty thousand, maintaining that, at most, no more than twenty-four thousand people would be in the area at any one time. *Denver Post,* January 13, 1975.

58. *Denver Post*, December 15, 1974.

59. *Ibid.*, February 19, 1976, March 24, 1976.

60. *Ibid.*, March 14, 1976.

61. A prime example is Crested Butte, where former Secretary of the Army Howard ("Bo") Callaway was accused of using his influence to secure Forest Service approval for a massive ski-resort project in the region. Although he was absolved of wrongdoing in later Senate Interior Subcommittee hearings, Callaway nevertheless alienated those Crested Butte citizens who were opposed to such extensive commercial growth. *Ibid.*, March 14, 1976, March 16, 1976, March 20, 1976, April 4, 1976, May 23, 1976.

62. *Ibid.*, May 6, 1973, October 23, 1974.

63. *Grand Junction Daily Sentinel*, February 11, 1972; *Denver Post*, September 6, 1973.

64. "Saving The Slopes," *Time*, Vol. CI, No. 2 (January 10, 1972), 62.

65. *Grand Junction Daily Sentinel*, February 11, 1972. As it has turned out, the anti-Olympics coalition failed to win a clear-cut victory: the proposed Beaver Creek project is located precisely on what would have been the Olympics' site.

66. *Boulder Daily Times-Call*, January 15, 1972.

67. *Rocky Mountain News*, May 4, 1972, May 7, 1972. Similar action has taken place throughout the West. In New Mexico, where a subdivider's sign near Albuquerque reads "Tomorrow For Sale, 36 Miles, Then Turn Left," the conservationists' slogans are "Undevelop!" and "Texans Go Home." In Oregon the James G. Blaine Society attempts to discourage outsiders from moving to the state by publicizing (only half-jokingly) its high rain and crime rates and its occasional "quicksand alerts." On the subject of overpopulation, ex-Governor Tom McCall says that its "cost is proving too much to pay, and we want none of it in Oregon." Oregon, along with Washington and California (where the subdivision rate has reached one hundred thousand plots a year) has embarked on large-scale land regulation in an attempt to keep its population down. "The Great Wild Californicated West," *Time*, Vol. CI, No. 34 (August 21, 1972), 15; *Denver Post*, September 8, 1973.

68. *Time,* August 21, 1972, 15.

69. *Aspen Times*, April 6, 1972. Club 20 recently hired former Governor John Vanderhoof to lead it. His views are clearly prodevelopment. It was Vanderhoof who supposedly said in October, 1974, that strip mining could not damage the Western Slope's Piceance Basin: "As my wife says, what difference does it make if they move that God-forsaken earth around? It couldn't look any worse." Vanderhoof denied having made the statement. *New York Times*, October 24, 1974.

70. The legislature's action was not at all unlike action taken by Colorado legislatures during the first conservation era. For a critical look at the 1876–1908 time period, see G. Michael McCarthy, "Retreat From Responsibility: The Colorado Legislature in the Conservation Era, 1876–1908," *Rocky Mountain Social Science Journal*, Vol. X (April, 1973), 27–36.

71. *Rocky Mountain News*, April 4, 1974.

72. *Ibid.*; *Denver Post*, January 12, 1975.

73. *Denver Post*, May 6, 1973.

74. *Ibid.*, April 8, 1973.

75. An excellent analysis of the wilderness movement may be found in the late Donald Baldwin's *The Quiet Revolution, The Grassroots of the Wilderness Preservation Movement.*

76. *Denver Post*, November 6, 1973.

77. The areas include the La Garita Wilderness (62,880 acres in the Gunnison and Rio Grande national forests), the Sangre de Cristo Mountains, the Twin Sisters, Greenhorn, and Spanish Peaks areas between Salida and the New Mexico border, Blanco Creek Divide southwest of Wolf Creek Pass, Cannibal Plateau and Red Cloud Peak near Lake City, Hermosa Creek in the La Plata Mountains north of Durango, the proposed Powderhorn Primitive Area south of Blue Mesa Reservoir, the Weber-Menefee Wilds near Mancos, and Grape Creek south of Canon City.

78. *Denver Post*, March 4, 1972, March 11, 1973.

79. *Gunnison Courier*, February 21, 1972.

80. *Denver Post*, November 11, 1973.

81. *Ibid.*, January 14, 1973, March 11, 1973.

82. *Ibid.*, December 8, 1974, December 16, 1974. In only a slightly different context, the Forest Service is coming under increasing criticism in the mid-1970's for its sometimes questionable timber-management procedures. Its plans, for example, to increase logging on Wyoming's Medicine Bow National Forest by 33 per cent annually over the next decade and to bulldoze eight hundred miles of new logging roads into Colorado's Routt National Forest greatly alarm conservationists more interested in forest preservation than in timber harvesting. At issue, primarily, is the controversial practice of clear-cutting. Referring to resultant waste in a Montana national forest, one disgruntled native commented that "there's enough wasted on forty acres to keep everyone in Bigfork going for a year." *Denver Post*, November 25, 1973, November 12, 1974, November 17, 1974, January 5, 1975.

83. Other areas coveted by conservation groups include North Sand Hills, near Walden; Red Bluff, near Glenwood Springs; Lookout Rim, Cold Spring, and Diamond Mountain Breaks, on the periphery of Dinosaur National Monument.

84. *Denver Post*, December 14, 1975.

85. *Ibid.*, February 11, 1973, March 18, 1973.

86. *Gunnison Courier*, February 21, 1972.

87. *Denver Post*, November 9, 1973.

88. *Ibid.*, May 5, 1975, December 2, 1975, March 1, 1976, March 16, 1976, March 24, 1976, March 25, 1976.

89. *Ibid.*, December 2, 1975, December 10, 1975, March 1, 1976, March 7, 1976, April 8, 1976, June 18, 1976, June 19, 1976.

90. *Ibid.*, March 26, 1976, May 17, 1976; *Rocky Mountain News*, June 22, 1976.

91. The argument is just as critical in other parts of the West. One example is in Idaho, where the United States Forest Service proposes to classify much of the Idaho Primitive Area and the adjoining Salmon River Breaks Primitive Area as wilderness. At the same time, regional foresters have recommended the addition of over 1,500,000 acres of national-forest land to existing wilderness areas. Some Idaho citizens, fearful that such actions will destroy prop-

erty values and discourage business, have come to regard the service as a "bureaucratic monster, with them as its prey." In Wyoming, conservationists currently are urging the addition of some 860,000 acres of timberland to already-established wilderness areas. Calling for additions to the North Absaroka Wilderness and Washakie Wilderness, they also hope to segregate large chunks of land in the Big Horn, Bridger, Cache, Medicine Bow, Shoshone, and Targhee national forests. In almost all cases they face opposition from developers. *Ibid.*, October 14, 1973, October 15, 1973, November 4, 1973, November 25, 1973.

92. "Lamm: A Compass In His Head," *Time*, Vol. CIV, No. 21 (November 18, 1974), 12, 18; *Denver Post*, January 5, 1975. One major reason for Lamm's victory was the nature of the people who supported him. For the most part they were immigrants (as is Lamm himself) from the east, midwest, and southwest, mostly young, professional, and middle to upper-middle class. With regard to such people, it has been widely said that they were and are more concerned about Colorado's natural beauty and its environment than are Colorado natives. In their overriding concern about the "growth ethic" and its increasing impact on Colorado, they turned to Lamm (who already had established himself by spearheading the anti-Olympic drive, opposing nuclear blasting on the Western Slope, and initiating land-use legislation in the Colorado legislature). At the same time they also helped elect Gary Hart to the United States Senate; Hart, too, pledged to work for conservation of the state's energy resources.

93. *Denver Post*, May 3, 1975, October 12, 1975, January 7, 1976.

94. *Ibid.*, January 26, 1974, January 31, 1975; *Pueblo Star Journal-Chieftain*, December 22, 1974.

95. *Denver Post*, December 19, 1974, January 26, 1975, February 8, 1975. Matters of primary regional concern, as outlined by Lamm, Governor Ed Herschler of Wyoming, and Governor Thomas Judge of Montana, include federal coal-leasing policy, federal impact-assistance funds, energy conservation, federal preemption of state laws, interbasin diversion of water, and strip-mining legislation.

96. *Ibid.*, August 3, 1975, March 11, 1976. The governors of Utah and Arizona have been less enthusiastic than Lamm about the success of the office. They maintain that Colorado has got the lion's share of its benefits.

97. *Ibid.*, October 17, 1975, October 23, 1975, October 31, 1975, December 3, 1975.

98. *Ibid.*, December 9, 1975.

99. *Ibid.*, April 1, 1975, July 15, 1975, December 4, 1975.

100. *Ibid.*, August 18, 1975.

101. *Ibid.*, April 10, 1975, May 28, 1975, December 3, 1975.

102. *Ibid.*, November 22, 1975; *Rocky Mountain News*, March 22, 1976.

103. *Rocky Mountain News*, March 22, 1976.

104. *Denver Post*, January 7, 1976.

105. *Ibid.*, January 28, 1975.

106. *Pueblo Chieftain*, November 30, 1974.

107. *Denver Post*, March 31, 1975, March 22, 1976, March 31, 1976, May 16, 1976.

Bibliography

A. Manuscripts

Miscellaneous files, Conservation Library, Denver Public Library, Denver, Colorado.

State Archives and Records Service. Records of the Office of the Governor.
John L. Routt, Correspondence, 1891–93.
Henry Buchtel, Correspondence, 1907–1909.
John F. Shafroth, Correspondence, 1909–13.

United States Forest Service Collection, Denver, Colorado.

B. Government Publications

1. Federal

Congressional Record, 1890–1908.

Report of the National Academy of Sciences, 1898. Washington, Government Printing Office, 1898.

Richardson, James D., comp. *A Compilation of the Messages and Papers of the Presidents, 1789–1897.* Washington, Government Printing Office, 1898.

U.S., Congress, House, 55 Cong., 2 sess., House *Doc. 189.*

U.S., Congress, House, 56 Cong., 1 sess., House *Doc. 643.*

U.S., Congress, House, 59 Cong., 2 sess., House *Doc. 406.*

U.S., Congress, House, 57 Cong., 1 sess., House *Report 968.*

U.S., Department of Agriculture, Forest Service, *Address Delivered at the Golden Anniversary of the White River National Forest,* October 11, 1941. Miscellaneous pamphlet. Washington, Government Printing Office, 1941.

———. *Forest Reserves in Idaho.* Bulletin No. 67, 1905. Washington, Government Printing Office, 1905.

———. *The National Forests of Colorado.* Miscellaneous publication No. 18, 1928. Washington, Government Printing Office, 1928.

U.S., Geological Survey. *20th Annual Report, 1898–1899.* 7 vols. Washington, Government Printing Office, 1900.

U.S., Department of the Interior, *Annual Reports*, 1893–1907.

U.S., Statutes at Large. Washington, Government Printing Office, 1891–1907. Vols. XXVII, XXX, XXXIV.

2. State

Colorado State Conservation Commission, *Official Proceedings, March, 1909–April, 1910.* Denver, Smith-Brooks Printing Company, 1910.

House Journal of the State of Colorado, 1907–1908. Denver, Smith-Brooks Printing Company, 1909.

Reports of the Colorado State Board of Horticulture, 1897–1903. Denver, Smith-Brooks Printing Company, 1897–1903.

Reports of the Colorado State Forest Commissioner, 1886–1890. Denver, Collier and Cleaveland Lithographing Company, 1886–90.

Senate Journal of the State of Colorado, 1893–1908. Denver, Gazette Printing Company and Smith-Brooks Printing Company, 1893–1909.

Session Laws of Colorado, 1903. Denver, Smith-Brooks Printing Company, 1903.

C. Newspapers

Aspen Daily Chronicle
Aspen Democrat
Aspen Times
Alamosa Valley Courier (Alamosa)
Basalt Journal
Boulder Camera
Boulder Daily Times-Call
Canon City Leader
Carbondale Item
Castle Rock Record-Journal
Cheyenne (Wyoming) *Tribune*
Colorado Springs Gazette
Creede Candle
Crystal River Current (Aspen)
Delta Independent
Denver Field and Farm
Denver Post
Denver Record-Stockman
Denver Republican
Denver Times

Deseret Weekly (Salt Lake City, Utah)
Durango Herald
Eagle County Blade (Eagle)
Eagle Valley Enterprise (Eagle)
Elk Mountain Pilot (Crested Butte)
Ft. Collins Courier
Ft. Collins Express
Gilpin Observer (Central City)
Glenwood Avalanche-Echo
Glenwood Post
Grand Junction Daily Sentinel
Grand Junction News
Great Falls (Montana) *Leader*
Gunnison Courier
Gunnison News-Champion
Lake City Phonograph
Lake City Times
Leadville Herald-Democrat
Leadville Press
Meeker Herald
Middle Park Times (McCoy)
Montrose Enterprise
Montrose Press
New York Times
Paonia Booster
Portland (Oregon) *Oregonian*
Pueblo Chieftain
Pueblo Star-Journal
Red Cliff Blade
Rico News
Rifle Reveille
Rifle Telegram
Rocky Mountain News (Denver)
Routt County Courier (Craig)
Saguache Crescent
Salida Mail
San Francisco (California) *Argonaut*
San Francisco (California) *Chronicle*
San Juan Prospector (Del Norte)
Steamboat Pilot (Steamboat Springs)
Steamboat Sentinel (Steamboat Springs)
Sugar City Gazette

Summit County Journal (Breckenridge)
Telluride Journal
Walsenburg World
Yampa Leader

D. Books

Allen, Shirley. *Conserving Natural Resources.* New York, McGraw-Hill Book Company, 1955.

American Forest Congress, *Proceedings, 1905.* Washington, American Forest Congress, 1905.

American National Livestock Association, *Proceedings of First Annual Meeting, 1906.* Denver, Smith-Brooks Printing Company, 1906.

———. *Proceedings of Eleventh Annual Convention, 1908.* Denver, Smith-Brooks Printing Company, 1908.

Baker, James, and LeRoy Hafen. *History of Colorado.* 5 vols. Denver, Linderman and Company, 1927.

Baldwin, Donald. *The Quiet Crisis: The Grassroots of the Wilderness Preservation Movement.* Boulder, Pruett Press, 1973.

Bancroft, Hubert H. *Works: History of Colorado, Nevada, and Wyoming.* 39 vols. San Francisco, The History Company, Publishers, 1890.

Barnett, Harold, and Chandler Morse. *Scarcity and Growth: The Economics of Natural Resource Availability.* Baltimore, Johns Hopkins Press, 1963.

Carhart, Arthur. *Timber in Your Life.* Philadelphia, J. B. Lippincott, 1955.

Clawson, Marion. *Uncle Sam's Acres.* New York, Dodd, Mead and Company, 1951.

Clawson, Marion, and Burnell Held. *The Federal Lands: Their Use and Management.* Baltimore, Johns Hopkins Press, 1957.

Colorado State Forestry Association. *The Colorado State Forestry Association: Its Origin, Work, and Purposes.* Denver, Colorado State Forestry Association, 1905.

Colorado State Historical Society. *History of Colorado.* 5 vols. Denver, Linderman and Company, 1927.

Coyle, David C. *Conservation: An American Story of Conflict and Accomplishment.* Brunswick, N. J., Rutgers University Press, 1957.

Cutright, Paul R. *Theodore Roosevelt the Naturalist.* New York, Harper and Brothers, 1956.

Dana, Samuel Trask. *Forest and Range Policy.* New York, McGraw-Hill Book Company, 1956.

Dick, Everett. *The Lure of the Land.* Lincoln, University of Nebraska Press, 1970.

Ellis, Elmer. *Henry M. Teller, Defender of the West.* Caldwell, Idaho, Claxton Press, 1941.

Ensign, Edgar. *Forestry in Colorado.* Denver, Colorado State Historical Society Library, 1885.

Fausold, Martin L. *Gifford Pinchot: Bull Moose Progressive.* Syracuse, Syracuse University Press, 1961.

Fernow, Bernhard. *History of Forestry.* Toronto, University of Toronto Press, 1907.

Foss, Phillip O. *Politics and Grass.* Seattle, University of Washington Press, 1960.

Frank, Bernard. *Our National Forests.* Norman, University of Oklahoma Press, 1955.

Freeman, Ira S. *A History of Montezuma County, Colorado.* Boulder, Johnson Publishing Company, 1958.

Frome, Michael. *Whose Woods These Are.* Garden City, Doubleday and Company, 1962.

Garland, Hamlin. *Companions on the Trail.* New York, The Macmillan Company, 1931.

———. *Son of the Middle Border.* New York, The Macmillan Company, 1925.

Hall, Frank. *History of the State of Colorado.* 4 vols. Chicago, S. J. Clarke Publishing Company, 1895.

Hawthorne, Hildegarde, and Esther B. Mills. *Enos Mills of the Rockies.* Boston, Houghton Mifflin Company, 1935.

Hays, Samuel. *Conservation and the Gospel of Efficiency.* Cambridge, Harvard University Press, 1959.

Hofstadter, Richard. *The Age of Reform.* New York, Alfred A. Knopf, 1955.

Ise, John. *United States Forest Policy.* New Haven, Yale University Press, 1920.

McGeary, M. Nelson. *Gifford Pinchot: Forester-Politician.* Princeton, Princeton University Press, 1960.

Monroe, Arthur W. *San Juan Silver.* Private printing, 1940.

Mowry, George. *The Era of Theodore Roosevelt.* New York, Harper and Brothers, 1958.

Muir, John. *Our National Parks.* Boston, Houghton Mifflin Company, 1909.

Nash, Roderick. *The American Environment: Readings in the History of Conservation.* Reading, Massachusetts, Addison-Wesley Publishing Company, 1968.

———. *Wilderness and the American Mind.* New Haven, Yale University Press, 1967.

National Livestock Association, *Proceedings of Annual Conventions, 1899–1906.* Denver, Smith-Brooks Printing Company, 1899–1906.

National Stock Growers Association, *Proceedings of Annual Convention, 1898.* Denver, News Job Printing Company, 1898.

Osgood, Ernest S. *Day of the Cattleman.* Chicago, University of Chicago Press, 1957.

Parsons, Eugene. *A Guidebook to Colorado.* Boston, Little, Brown and Company, 1911.

Peffer, E. Louise. *The Closing of the Public Domain.* Stanford, Stanford University Press, 1951.

Pinchot, Gifford. *Breaking New Ground.* New York, Harcourt, Brace and Company, 1947.

Potter, David. *People of Plenty.* Chicago, University of Chicago Press, 1954.

Proceedings of Conference Between Special Land Commission Appointed By President Roosevelt and Prominent Stockmen of the West, 1904. Denver, Smith-Brooks Printing Company, 1905.

Richardson, Elmo R. *The Politics of Conservation: Crusades and Controversies, 1897–1913.* Berkeley, University of California Press, 1962.

Robbins, Roy M. *Our Landed Heritage: The Public Domain, 1776–1936.* New York, Peter Smith, 1950.

Robinson, Edgar E. *The Presidential Vote, 1896–1932.* Stanford, Stanford University Press, 1934.

Roosevelt, Nicholas. *Conservation: Now Or Never.* New York, Dodd, Mead and Company, 1970.

Roosevelt, Theodore. *Autobiography.* New York, Charles Scribner's Sons, 1927.

Salmon, D. E. *Special Report on the History and Condition of the Sheep Industry in the United States.* Washington, Government Printing Office, 1892.

Shaw, Luella. *True History of Some of the Pioneers of Colorado.* Hotchkiss, Colorado, Coburn, Patterson, and Shaw, Publishers, 1909.

Shoemaker, Len. *Roaring Fork Valley.* Denver, Sage Books, 1958.

———. "The First Forest Ranger." In *The Westerners Brand Book,* 1951. Denver, Artcraft Press, 1952.

Smith, Duane. *Rocky Mountain Mining Camps: The Urban Frontier.* Bloomington, Indiana University Press, 1967.

Smith, Frank. *The Politics of Conservation.* New York, Pantheon Press, 1966.

Smith, Henry Nash. *Virgin Land.* New York, Alfred A. Knopf, 1950.

Stone, Wilbur F. *History of Colorado.* 4 vols. Chicago, S. J. Clarke Publishing Company, 1918.

Thayer, William. *Marvels of the New West.* Norwich, Connecticut, The Henry Bill Publishing Company, 1891.

———. *Theodore Roosevelt: An Intimate Biography.* New York, Houghton-Mifflin Company, 1919.

Theodore Roosevelt Conservation Congress, *Proceedings, 1958.* Denver, private printing, 1958.

Thomas, Addison. *Roosevelt Among the People.* Chicago, L. W. Walter Company, 1910.

Trans-Mississippi Commercial Congress. *Proceedings of the Twelfth Convention, 1901.* Cripple Creek, Colorado, Press of the *Morning Times-Citizen,* 1901.

———. *Proceedings, 1908.* San Francisco, Calkins Publishing House, 1908.

Turner, Frederick Jackson. *The Frontier in American History.* New York, Henry Holt, 1920.

Udall, Stuart. *The Quiet Crisis.* New York, Holt, Rinehart, Winston, 1963.

Wengert, Norman. *Natural Resources and the Political Struggle.* New York, Doubleday and Company, 1955.

Wentworth, Edward N. "Sheep Wars of the Nineties in Northwest Colorado." In *The Westerners Brand Book, 1946.* Denver, Artcraft Press, 1947.

White, Leonard D. *The Republican Era.* New York, The Macmillan Company, 1958.

Winters, Robert K, ed. *Fifty Years of Forestry in the U.S.A.* Washington, Society of American Foresters, 1950.

Wister, Owen. *Roosevelt: The Story of a Friendship.* New York, The Macmillan Company, 1930.

Wolle, Muriel. *Stampede to Timberline.* Chicago, Swallow Press, 1969.

Yard, Robert Sterling. *Our Federal Lands.* New York, Charles Scribner's Sons, 1928.

E. Periodicals

Bates, J. Leonard. "Fulfilling American Democracy: The Conservation Movement, 1907–1921," *Mississippi Valley Historical Review,* Vol. XLIV (1957), 29–57.

Bethel, Ellsworth. "The Conifers or Evergreens of Colorado," *Colorado Magazine,* Vol. II (January, 1925), 1–3.

Cook, R. G. "Senator Heyburn's War Against the Forest Service," *Idaho Yesterdays*, Vol. XIV (Winter, 1970–71), 5–12.

Fazio, Steven A. "Marcus Aurelius Smith: Arizona Delegate and Senator," *Arizona and the West*, Vol. XII (1970), 50–60.

Hale, Irving. "The Glories of Colorado," *Sons of Colorado*, Vol. I (March, 1907), 34–36.

Hough, Merrill. "Leadville and the Western Federation of Miners," *Colorado Magazine*, Vol. XLIX (Winter, 1972), 19–34.

Hunter, George S. "The Bull Moose Movement in Arizona," *Arizona and the West*, Vol. X (Winter, 1968), 343–62.

Kneeshaw, Steven J., and John M. Linngren, "Republican Comeback, 1902," *Colorado Magazine*, Vol. XXXXV (Winter, 1971), 15–29.

"Lamm: A Compass in His Head," *Time*, Vol. CIV, No. 21 (November 18, 1974), 12, 18.

Larsen, Robert W. "Ballinger Versus Rough Rider George Curry: the Other Feud," *New Mexico Historical Review*, Vol. XLIII (October, 1968), 271–90.

McCarthy, G. Michael. "Retreat from Responsibility: The Colorado Legislature in the Conservation Era, 1876–1908," *Rocky Mountain Social Science Journal*, Vol. X (April, 1973), 27–36.

———. "The Pharisee Spirit: Gifford Pinchot in Colorado," *Pennsylvania Magazine of History and Biography*, Vol. XCVII, No. 3 (July, 1973), 362–78.

———. "Colorado's Progressives and Conservation," *Mid-America*, Vol. LVII (October, 1975), 213–26.

———. "Selective Progressivism and the Conservation Movement," *Journal of the West*, Vol. XV (January, 1976), 62–73.

McGee, W J "The Conservation of Natural Resources," Mississippi Valley Historical Association, *Proceedings*, Vol. III (1909–1910), 365–79.

Morrill, W. J. "Birth of Roosevelt National Forest," *Colorado Magazine*, Vol. XX (January, 1943), 178–81.

Muir, John. "The Wild Parks and Forest Reservations of the West," *Atlantic Monthly*, Vol. LXXXI (January, 1898), 21–31.

Nash, Roderick. "The American Cult of the Primitive," *American Quarterly*, Vol. XVIII (1966), 517–37.

"New Mexico Forest Reserves," *Forestry Quarterly* (Spring, 1907), 11–19.

Preusser, Meldon J. "Hugo Seaberg and His Land Scrip Enterprise," *New Mexico Historical Review*, Vol. XLV (1970), 75–90.

Roosevelt, Theodore. "Ranch Life in the Far West: In the Cattle Country," *Century Magazine*, Vol. XXXV (February, 1888), 495–510.

Saloutos, Theodore. "The Agricultural Problem and Nineteenth-Century Industrialism," *Agricultural History*, Vol. XXII (July, 1948), 156–74.
"Saving the Slopes," *Time*, Vol. CI, No. 2 (January 10, 1972), 62.
Smith, Robert. "Colorado's Progressive Senators and Representatives," *Colorado Magazine*, Vol. XLV (Winter, 1968), 27–41.
Snyder, J. Richard. "The Election of 1904: An Attempt at Reform," *Colorado Magazine*, Vol. XXXXV (Winter, 1968), 16–26.
Spring, Agnes W. "Theodore Roosevelt in Colorado," *Colorado Magazine*, Vol. XXXV (October, 1958), 241–55.
"The Great and Wild Californicated West," *Time*, Vol. CI, No. 34 (August 21, 1972), 15.
"The Way of the Land Transgressor," *Review of Reviews*, Vol. XXXV (September, 1907), 37–80.
Willis, Ann Bassett. "Queen Ann of Brown's Park," *Colorado Magazine*, Vol. XXX (August, 1953), 70–75.

F. Miscellaneous Unpublished Materials

"Annual Convention of the Colorado Stockgrowers Association, 1920." Typescript. Colorado State Historical Society Library, Denver.
Kettle, Georgiana, and Roy Truman. "A Brief Historical Sketch of San Isabel National Forest." Typescript. Colorado State Historical Society.
McCarthy, G. Michael. "Elias Ammons and the Conservation Impulse." Master's thesis, University of Denver, 1962.
Rist, Lewis R. "Historical Sketch of the White River National Forest." Typescript. Colorado State Historical Society, Denver.
Shoemaker, Leonard C. "History of the Holy Cross National Forest." Typescript. Colorado State Historical Society, Denver.

Index